M000106818

In Praise of
Mixed Religion

The Syncretism Solution
in a Multifaith World

WILLIAM H. HARRISON

McGill-Queen's University Press
Montreal & Kingston • London • Ithaca

© McGill-Queen's University Press 2014
    ISBN 978-0-7735-4358-4 (cloth)
    ISBN 978-0-7735-9202-5 (ePDF)
    ISBN 978-0-7735-9203-2 (ePUB)

Legal deposit second quarter 2014
Bibliothèque nationale du Québec

Printed in Canada on acid-free paper that is 100% ancient forest
free (100% post-consumer recycled), processed chlorine free.

This book has been published with the help of funds received from
the University of British Columbia.

McGill-Queen's University Press acknowledges the support of the
Canada Council for the Arts for our publishing program. We also
acknowledge the financial support of the Government of Canada
through the Canada Book Fund for our publishing activities.

Library and Archives Canada Cataloguing in Publication

Harrison, William H., 1965–, author
    In praise of mixed religion : the syncretism solution in a multifaith
world / William H. Harrison.

Includes bibliographical references and index.
Issued in print and electronic formats.
ISBN 978-0-7735-4358-4 (bound). – ISBN 978-0-7735-9202-5 (ePDF). –
ISBN 978-0-7735-9203-2 (ePUB)

    1. Syncretism (Religion). 2. Religions – Relations. 3. Religion.
I. Title.

BL410.H37 2014   201'.5   C2014-900691-8
                                        C2014-900692-6

This book was typeset by True to Type in 10.5/13.5 Sabon

To Keith Gilbert and Richard and Charles Harrison

Contents

Why I Wrote This Book   ix

1 Syncretism Happens   3

2 What Is Religion?   34

3 Soft Boundaries   74

4 When Syncretism Is a Good Thing   91

5 ... And When It's Not So Good   130

6 When It Should Have Happened, But Didn't   150

7 The Problem of Labels: What Is It Now?   160

8 Critical Openness   174

9 The Last Taboo: Education about Religion   206

10 An Intellectual Transformation   227

Notes   237

Index   255

Why I Wrote This Book

This is a "forest" book. I like to distinguish between forest books and tree books. There's an old line – I'm sure you've heard it – that goes, "They can't see the forest for the trees." The line is a warning about the danger of getting so caught up in details that overall patterns get lost. As it happens, books about details are really very important because we need to know a lot of basic information in order to think about the big picture. This, however, is a big-picture book. The information that it contains is meant to help in the construction of overall patterns of relationships, rather than be an especially thorough description of one particular incident, text, or way of thinking.

This book is about religions. In fact, it offers a theory of religions, which is a technical way of saying that I make some fairly broad generalizations about what religions are and how they work, supported by evidence garnered from the study of a variety of religious traditions. Histories of religions are a big part of our discussion, of course, but history often remains in our minds as a collection of discrete bits. This book goes beyond giving the kind of data that helps us to compare religions. I will raise two of the biggest questions in the field: "What is religion?" and "How do, and how should, different religions relate to each other?"

My suggestion that religions should relate to each other in a particular way is part of why I emphasize that this is a theory about religions. Instead of just saying that religions do certain things, I add that religions ought to do something quite specific: they ought to engage in syncretism, which is the blending of religions, the effort to incorporate wisdom from one religious context into another. I think that religions should commit to learning from one another. This book proposes an "advocacy" model of syncretism.

Most people have some sort of theory of religions; functioning without one in any society, let alone one as complex and mixed as the twenty-first century West, is next to impossible. A theory of religions provides the mental file into which we deposit Judaism, Christianity, Islam, and perhaps various other movements, including anything from African traditional belief systems to Zoroastrianism, with many stops in between. We understand these religions in particular ways; in addition, we make judgements about their truth and helpfulness, and about the ways that we should react to them. Unfortunately, the evidence that most of us are able to gather tends to be rather limited. Religions are large and complex; moreover, they tend to extend back into history – sometimes, rather a long way. Consequently, though very nearly everybody has a theory about religion, a book like this is meant to be a journey into religious history, towards a different sort of vision of what religions are and how they function.

This book is unusual because it is a hybrid of sorts. It is aimed at the general reader. I avoid jargon where possible, and explain it when I need to use it. In that sense, the book is a popularization. However, I am not simply trying to make available material that is already generally known within the academy. Some of that will happen; most of the evidence that I rely upon is common knowledge among scholars, because this book is not about original research into a defined area of religious history. In addition, I will supply details that most scholars will already have at their fingertips, because some readers will need some background on the origins of Buddhism if they are going to understand the encounter between Buddhism and Taoism in China. Nonetheless, the way that I assemble the evidence is not widely accepted. It may even be somewhat controversial. I am placing before the general reader a theory about the nature and development of religion, combined with an assertion about values, that is – dare I say it? – new. I'm going to come out and say that syncretism is a good thing and we need more of it. This is my advocacy approach to blending religions.

Intentionally, and for several reasons, I have chosen to argue an academic point in accessible language that can be read by any capable reader. The primary reason is that this is what I do: I interpret the complexities of religion to non-specialists. Religion is a large part of everyone's life. Religion is not the same as, for example, high-energy physics. Undoubtedly, our daily lives are affected by all of the things studied by people in that area of the university and industrial world. However, few people in their daily lives and work have a sense of being deeply involved in the intimacies of high-energy physics. We may occasionally read about the search for the Higgs boson in the newspaper, but only a select few people can claim to be associated with research about it in any significant way. By contrast, very few people can claim to be uninvolved in religion. Many of us intentionally pursue religious goals and understand religion as central to our lives. When religious issues arise in the newspaper, everyone has an opinion and a sense of being part of the debate. Religion belongs to ordinary people.

To my mind, this means that people who do not have university degrees in religion or theology should be involved in discussions of theories of religions. Everyone – you, me, your children and mine, your neighbours and mine – must make decisions about religion. Everybody in the modern West needs to decide how to respond to Christmas, for example, and that means having some consideration for those to whom Christmas is irrelevant or even offensive. We see this as schools get caught up in debates about the suitability of decorations, concerts, and, most of all, language. What are we to call that winter holiday season? Likewise, the West has had to consider decisions about mosques (New York has been in the midst of a great battle over the placement of one of these) and minarets (Switzerland has been roiled by a battle over these), and the availability of kosher and halal foods. As a consequence, we all need some basic principles of religious theory to ground our choices. In fact, most people have some such principles, although they may not have been carefully formulated and examined. Even the decision not to go to a temple, synagogue, or church is evidence that some understanding of religion is at work – especially in the cases of people who were raised to attend, as it were, religiously.

I write about religion partly because people are avidly interested and emotionally involved in the topic. When I tell people that I teach and write in this field, I encounter a nearly unbelievable amount of excitement. The words are barely out of my mouth when my conversation partner unleashes. I hear stories and face questions of all kinds. People tell me about their experiences being raised in Islam, Christianity, or Judaism, or their recent encounters with Baha'i or Buddhism. I hear suggestions about how the religions of the world can bring peace to all humanity. I hear complaints about how the religions of the world are at the root of all war and violence. People want me to comment on the latest debate about the *niqab* or clergy wrongdoing. Issues of sexuality emerge. The complicated and very nearly irresolvable challenges of biomedical ethics enter the conversations. All of the world's issues come up; nothing is out of bounds. The fascination with religion is intense because it is so immediate and all-encompassing.

Because people who do not specialize in the study of religion have an important stake and a real interest in the discussion, they ought to be as involved as specialists in formulating and testing theories about religion. Neither being religiously active nor being religiously uncommitted stops people from thinking about a theory of religions. In an important sense, theory is what scholars call "a second-order activity": religions do what they do and then theorists try to understand what has been done. However, in an equally important sense, theory is a first-order activity: we reflect on religions precisely because what religions do matters quite intensely to us and has an impact on our daily lives. Our theoretical conclusions have a way of becoming part of our practice; indeed, they become part of our identity.

Although scholars try to recognize the influence that our own preferences and judgements have on our research and try to control for these things, people in the academy are not simply impartial; academics also have basic commitments that play a role in their processes of understanding. I bring to this discussion firm beliefs that: (1) love is greater than hatred; (2) knowledge is better than ignorance; (3) every person can and does know some things that are true; and (4) we can all benefit from shared wisdom. Each one of these assertions is debatable, but these are my fundamental and existential (indeed, religious) commitments; they come with me into this investigation. They are, in fact, some of the primary conditions that make possible my theoretical assertions.

There is an issue that is more important than whether we have commitments that we would call religious. This issue is the personal, existential nature of the questions that are raised in this book. I ask you and the whole world to take them seriously. I want to know whether we are prepared to take to heart the questions that are raised by this discussion of religion. Can we honestly and fairly ask, "Is my religion like this? Does my personal religion, the one that I live, reflect the theory that is being proposed?" If so, then will we allow the challenges that syncretism brings to filter into our daily relations with other people? These are questions for everyone, which is the most basic reason that I ask non-specialists to be involved in formulating theory.

These questions are important to me. I wrote this book because of them. The origins of this book are in two specific experiences. The first came from listening to a group of Christians (this is part of my heritage and my primary area of study) talk about sexuality. A common refrain went like this: "People keep arguing on the basis of evidence that comes from non-Christians. We need evidence that comes from within Christianity. Otherwise, we will look and act just like everybody else." In fact, there is a whole account of what being Christian means that is based upon this kind of call to separation and purity. A sizable number of Christians try to live in a realm defined by their own viewpoints.

My initial reaction to this experience was to announce that any such isolationist approach is impossible and unhelpful. I followed that up with some of the assertions that I have previously stated, about other people knowing things that are true and the benefits of shared wisdom. As it happens, these are values that I learned from within my own tradition of Anglican Christianity, which has a too-often-ignored commitment to learning from the rest of the world.

However, when I came to write my next book (this is my second), I began to realize that I had not fully imbibed my own advice. I can be remarkably good at giving answers; I am not always so good at living by them. I sat down to write about Christianity and politics; these are two of my long-time enthusiasms and, indeed, the need for an adequate politics was what eventually caused me to raise religious questions. I determined that the two kinds of activity must be related, and have spent over a decade thinking about their relationship, primarily in the context of my work on Richard Hooker, a sixteenth-century English theologian and political theorist.

However, as I began my writing project, I soon found myself derailed. I realized that I was asking the wrong kind of question. I was making the same mistake as those people who wanted to hear from Christians and only Christians when decision-making time arrived. I came to the conclusion that there is not really a book to be written about Christianity and politics – at least not one that fails to discuss other religions at the same time. The need to incorporate many religions may seem obvious in today's multi-religious world – especially because most of the current big questions involve Islam. However, as I thought about religion and politics, I realized that this has always been true. There never was a purely Christian view of politics or form of political life. Indeed, there never has been a pure Christianity.

The result of my rethinking the whole project is this book. The book about politics never did get written, though it may in the future. Instead, I have dedicated my time to reflecting upon the complex nature of religion, the boundaries among particular religions, and the mutual relationships among religions. Politics will be discussed, of course, as will economics, education, and the days of the week – all of which are relevant to religion, just as religion is relevant to them. Buddhism, Hinduism, Sikhism, Judaism, Islam, Christianity, First Nations' religions, and numerous other religions will be touched on. Some of the religions discussed will likely fit into the "I never thought of that as a religion before" category, because a significant part of this book is a rethinking of the definition of religion as such.

This book, then, is an effort to name the problem, to focus our attention on the ways in which we oversimplify the discussion of religion. We have a habit – and, yes, I fall into it too – of seeing clarity and simplicity where there is really only messy complexity. The discussion about syncretism is a way of pointing to this complexity. A word should be said here about the term "syncretism." It is a common term in religious theory and in linguistics, anthropology, and some other academic disciplines; "syncretism" is a shorthand way of saying that a viewpoint or element can arise in one system and become an integral part of another. However, the word is rarely used in ordinary conversation. When it arises, the term is usually pejorative, an insulting announcement that someone has fallen away from religious purity. It declares that the speaker is religiously faithful while the religion or person described is fatally compromised. Syncretism is commonly seen as a threat, and use of this term sets up a dynamic of rejection. This dynamic is a symptom of the precise kind of blindness that this book criticizes. Religion – indeed, the world – is always more complicated than we might initially imagine. Part of what makes this book different from conventional discussions of religious theory is that I encourage common usage of language that has previously been limited to academia or the dangerous fringe.

I hope that this book will help us to think more deeply about the nature of religion and its role in society, perhaps even to see religion where we have not previously noticed its presence. I want to make the conversation about religion a little bit richer, more profound, and, most importantly, more honest.

A few words about the order and structure of this book may help the reader understand where we are going. The first chapter, "Syncretism Happens," demonstrates that religious syncretism is a universal process, even in religions that oppose it. "What Is Religion?" tackles the complex issue of defining religion, arguing that it affects more aspects of our lives than we tend to realize. "Soft Boundaries" contends that religious identities are prone to change under influences from outside because religious boundaries are permeable and often indistinct. The next three chapters focus upon historical examples of syncretism and resistance, respectively showing how syncretism can be beneficial ("When Syncretism Is a Good Thing") or destructive ("... And When It's Not So Good"), and how the failure to mix religions can undermine the most powerful institutions ("When It Should Have Happened, But Didn't"). "The Problem of Labels" draws attention to the limitations of names in a world where every religion is a mixture and every person's religion is a personal mixture. Because syncretism is both universal and potentially very beneficial, we need to ensure that our attitude toward it is helpful; "Critical Openness" discusses some of the relevant issues. Attitudes do not grow by themselves; they require cultivation, which is why "The Last Taboo" addresses the challenge of education about religions. Finally, "An Intellectual Transformation" calls the world to rethink its approach to religious syncretism, advocating mixing religions as valuable progress in a multifaith world.

Before closing, I should say something about my use of the word "I." I use it with some regularity in this book, which goes against both my habit and general academic convention. Academia frowns on writing in the first person for excellent reasons. An argument should be able to stand on its own. If authors are perennially inserting themselves into debates, as use of the word "I" tends to do, then discussions that ought to be about ideas too easily become personal; disagreement with a particular argument starts to look like an attack on a person. Whenever this happens, the search for understanding suffers.

However, I have chosen to take this risk and depart from convention in this book, for reasons that I think are valid and important. As we have already seen, the matters that will be discussed on these pages are delicate, existential, and personal. The tone of academic detachment tends to sound rather stiff and high-handed; it can give a feeling of being lectured from a kind of safe and independent perch, high above the mess of human complexities. I have written this book precisely because I am not safely outside the complicated phenomenon of syncretism. Instead, it affects me, both as surely and as profoundly as it affects you or anyone else. I share the blind spots that I notice in the larger world and I seek the subtlety of mind necessary to find them in myself just as I hope that you will. Thus, while I certainly believe that this book's argument can stand on its own and could be presented in a wholly academic style, I think that the truth is best served by a more personal tone. I sincerely hope that this will not prove too offensive to academic colleagues who value the give-and-take of intellectual conversation.

One last word: I owe a special vote of thanks to my editor, Mark Abley, and all of the people at McGill-Queen's University Press, without whom this book would not be in your hands. Of course, I also owe thanks to my wife, Rita, and my sons, Richard and Charles, who show remarkable tolerance for the hours that I spend in libraries and facing my computer, researching, and writing.

William H. Harrison

IN PRAISE OF MIXED RELIGION

I

Syncretism Happens

In 2008, a *National Geographic* reporter, Marguerite Del Giudice, visited Iran, one of the most strictly and clearly defined Muslim countries in the world today, looking for signs of ancient Persian identity. To her astonishment, she found a culture that is Islamic indeed, but still shows signs of Zoroastrianism in the midst of a society run largely by Shia Muslim religious thinkers (*ulama*).

Giudice observed the New Year's festival, called "Nowruz" (also spelt "Naurûz" or "No Ruz"). She described it as "a thirteen-day extravaganza during which everything shuts down and the people eat a lot, dance, recite poetry, and build fires that they jump back and forth over. It's a thanksgiving of sorts, celebrated around the spring equinox."[1] Nowruz is of ancient origin; its beginnings are shrouded with the mists of time, so that we can only speculate about how it started. One theory is that Nowruz predates even Zoroaster (who lived sometime around 1700–1500 BCE),[2] and was a New Year's Day celebration among the "Old Avestan" people. Zoroaster took over and transformed this festival, making it into an annual prefiguration of the end times, the "New Day" of eternal life when evil is destroyed and good triumphs. Nowruz became the last and highest of seven Zoroastrian feasts, dedicated to the final creation, which is fire.[3] Sacred fires have always been the main symbols at traditional Zoroastrian shrines, and fire is central to Zoroastrian religion.

Some Muslims have tried to strip Nowruz of its Zoroastrian meanings.[4] However, as Giudice notes, the Iranian people are well aware that their New Year's celebration is not Islamic in origin or intention. It began with another religion and has been fitted into Islam. Nowruz is not the only survival, though it may be the most obvious; Zoroastrian ideas have burrowed deep into Islamic ways of thought and action. As it happens, Giudice is not alone in her experience: at the end of the twentieth century, Paul Kriwaczek, a journalist and historian, visited Iran and found traces of Zoroastrianism everywhere. Moreover, he discovered that Iranians are still quite proud of the ancient religion that exists as an undercurrent beneath and behind their Islam.[5] Kriwaczek landed in a city named after Mithra (a servant to Ahura-Mazda, who is God in Zoroastrian terms), where he saw Zoroastrian symbols in every aspect of Iranian life, including in mosques. He discovered that people still fear the evil spirits that walk after dark – the *Divs*, known to ancient Persians as *Daevas*. In addition, Kriwaczek discovered evidence of Zoroastrian theology in the words of strict Shia Muslims, noting especially Shia use of language about the battle between good and evil that will be resolved at the return of the Hidden Imam ("Twelver" Shia Muslims believe that the Twelfth Imam, who vanished in 874 CE, will return one day to lead true Muslims).

Scholars concur with Giudice and Kriwaczek. "The pre-Islamic customs and usages, as well as the national holidays which were found to be amenable to Islam, were retained. Indeed, the borrowings were legion and would require a separate volume,"[6] says one scholar, while another notes that Islamic thinking about rulership and the caliphate are deeply rooted in Persian notions of kingship.[7] Zoroastrian astronomy, ethics, cosmology and eschatology played a significant part in Iranian life, in both conversation and syncretism with Islam, until Zoroastrianism was suppressed by Shia Muslims in 1694. Even then, elements of the old religion were revived by the Qajar and Pahlavi rulers, most especially Shah Reza Pahlavi.[8] In short, we have long-standing evidence of the presence of syncretism in Iran, at least some of which has survived Islamic purification efforts, including the 1979 revolution.

In Japan, the Buddhas (enlightened ones) and *bodhisattvas* (ones who are on the way to becoming Buddhas, or have rejected Buddha status in order to aid seekers of enlightenment) of Mahayana Buddhism were, for many centuries, united with the *kami* (gods or, more precisely, spirits) of ancient Japanese religion, now known as Shinto. The teachings of Gautama Buddha did not depend upon spirit or divine figures, though he believed in their existence. However, as Buddhism took on a life of its own and grew beyond its original Indian boundaries, the notion that divine or semi-divine figures can help one on the right way became a significant part of Buddhist teaching. When Buddhism reached Japan (from China), Japan already had a strong, though unorganized, religious heritage. This focused upon local gods, who inhabited particular areas (a mountain, for instance) and were served at local shrines; the religion now known as Shinto is sometimes called "the religion of shrines."[9] People would pray to the gods for various forms of assistance; often particular kami specialized in particular things – for example, one was likely to turn to Hachiman (the deified spirit of Emperor Ojin, who lived in the third and early fourth centuries CE) for assistance in warfare, although he was not the only kami who attended to wars.[10]

When Buddhism came to Japan in the sixth century, Buddhism and the traditional religion competed, but within a century they became functionally one. They fitted together as one system supporting imperial order. Under a doctrine that came to be known as *honji sujaku* ("universal forms of deities and their local traces"), the Japanese kami were incorporated into a Buddhist system, as emanations of universal, Buddhist divinities.[11] The result was that Japan developed a thoroughly integrated Buddhist/Shinto religious structure. Although the emperors depended upon Shinto beliefs for their legitimacy – the emperor was understood as being a direct descendant of Amaterasu, the sun-kami – Buddhism was established as the official state religion, with imperial patronage, by the middle of the seventh century. The Emperor Shomu (ruled 724–729 CE) was ordained as a Buddhist monk and built a massive Buddhist temple.[12]

The result of this powerfully syncretistic process was that Japanese society functioned on two tracks: Buddhist temples contained Shinto shrines, and Shinto shrines were understood as being means of access to Buddhas and bodhisattvas. The two religions never quite lost their distinct identities, though Buddhism clearly dominated and Shinto was also extensively influenced by Confucian, Taoist, and yin-yang traditions from China.[13] However, Japanese people lived in a world that was defined by both Buddhism and Shinto, and could turn to either in times of need. We can see this in the context of war, where the options for the devout, or merely desperate, samurai were manifold:

> Of all the *kami* the ones more likely than others to be addressed by samurai were the 'gods of war.' Hachiman is often referred to as *the* god of war, but even though his name was frequently invoked there were others. The list included three Buddhist deities ... ; three Shinto *kami* from ancient mythology; and historical or semi-historical personages who had been deified, such as Hachiman, his mother Empress Jingu, Takeuchi Sukune, and, very surprisingly, Prince Shotoku, Nara Buddhism's greatest spokesman. If there was any confusion over the gods' identities, rituals might simply be offered to 'the 98,000 gods of war.'[14]

Undoubtedly, various people had their own preferences. Buddhist monks, from various sects and with a variety of attitudes toward Shinto, certainly maintained a firm grip on their privileges. The standing of Shinto declined as a result of integration, so that by the seventeenth century (under the Shogunate) even Shinto priests and their families had to register at Buddhist temples and be buried by Buddhist priests.[15] This situation lasted until the nineteenth century and the Meiji Restoration, when (in 1868) *shinbutsu bunri* – the separation of Shinto from Buddhism – became imperial policy. Buddhists were ousted from shared shrines and State Shinto became the official religion of Japan;[16] thus ended twelve centuries of highly successful syncretism in Japan.

As Indigenous people in North America rediscover their heritage, torn from them by years of colonial domination, they are starting to integrate traditional ideas and practices with Christianity. Theologians such as Vine Deloria, whose book, *God Is Red: A Native View of Religion,* has been tremendously influential, have transformed Indigenous Christianity. It is moving away from the system that predominated from the eighteenth to the twentieth century, according to which Indigenous people were to be remade in the form of Christian Europeans. Residential schools were created by governments and administered by churches as one means toward this end. Where native tongues were allowed to continue, the Bible and some liturgical resources were translated into native languages. Elsewhere, worship happened in European languages. Indigenous people were formed in European denominational differences, so that they became Catholics, Anglicans, Methodists, Presbyterians, etc.; whatever sort of Christianity showed up in their area became the religion of the local Indigenous peoples, though they had none of the history that led to the creation of these identities.

In this process of Europeanization, major elements of Indigenous religion, such as sweet grass ceremonies, sweat lodges, totem poles, and potlatches, were suppressed. These changes caused Indigenous people to lose their intimate relationship with the Creator and the land that had been central to their religion. The wisdom that had sustained them for generations was dismissed, even made illegal.

Today, this is changing. Christian denominations are becoming aware – though very slowly – that Indigenous people have religious insights to share. I have attended services in two major Canadian religious denominations where sweet grass ceremonies have been a formative part of the worship experience. Sweat lodges are returning: the Dr. Jessie Saulteaux Resource Centre, a training centre for Indigenous ministers for a variety of Canadian denominations, has a sweat lodge. Totem poles are returning to Indigenous communities, and are finding their way into the religious mainstream. Vancouver School of Theology (VST), a seminary affiliated with the Anglican Church of Canada and the United Church of Canada, and used by many other denominations, now has a totem pole in its yard. That pole is called "All My Relations," signifying the intimate connection to all aspects of creation that Indigenous Christians feel. A totem pole is an expression of identity; it is a public display of the history of the people in the dwelling by which the pole stands. Moreover, a totem pole tells the story of where those people stand in relation to the whole of the cosmos; in an important sense, the meaning of the people can be read from the totem. "All My Relations" has representations of Raven holding the moon, Salmon, Frog, Bear, Chief, and Eagle. It is designed to link past, present, and future, while placing humanity in a family with various non-human creatures.[17]

While teaching at VST, I have occasionally assigned students to write about the totem pole and what it says to Christians – a most informative exercise that causes people to think differently, especially about the church and salvation. When a salmon becomes a relation, the church community grows. The fish ceases to be merely an instance of "natural resources" meant to be exploited, as it is in Enlightenment thought. Instead, the salmon becomes a participant in every aspect of our lives. This causes a reconsideration of the nature of salvation, of who and what is saved and how. Interestingly, the shift redefines Christianity in a way that is closer to part of its ancient Greek heritage: Irenaeus of Lyons thought of salvation as something that God does for the whole cosmos and for all of history, though he certainly did not incorporate what we think of as the "natural world" in the same degree or same way.

The use of the totem pole in seminary work, however, is a reminder of something more than just the views of a particular ethnic grouping: the totem pole points to the theological influence that Indigenous thought is starting to have on Christianity as a whole. Partly as a result of Indigenous tutelage, Christians are becoming more aware of the risks inherent in the Enlightenment doctrine of dominance. Christians are questioning the basic assertion that Europeans could "discover" North America and claim ownership, using any means handy to obtain and retain control. Christians are also shifting to a notion that people are stewards of the Earth, rather than its masters. Indigenous people, including Indigenous thinkers, have been active in effecting these changes, and have been a visible symbol of the necessity to make them. Some Christian denominations have created unique structures for Indigenous people so that they may experiment with melding traditional and Christian ways, and so that the conversation between Indigenous views and European-derived views can be sustained. This is a syncretistic venture that is in its infancy but promises to be tremendously fruitful.

THE ADVOCACY APPROACH TO SYNCRETISM

"Syncretism" is often a dirty word in religious conversation. It describes the process of mixing and matching bits from more than one religion, which is anathema to the many people who tend to get defensive about syncretism. There is a label for the whole branch of religious scholarship that treats syncretism as morally undesirable: "subjective." Presumably, this label is used because the people who regard syncretism as an evil are attached to particular religions and have a particular commitment to opposing any blending. Therefore, they regard syncretism as disturbing an assumed purity. The other standard way of viewing syncretism is called "objective." It means treating syncretism as morally neutral, a natural part of the history of religions.[18] This tends to be the scholarly approach.

I want to say something different from either of these viewpoints. In this book, I am going to argue that syncretism is not merely neutral or generally bad. Instead, syncretism is a good thing, a healthy process. Since we probably need a label to match those attached to other schools of thought, and since I encourage religions to engage in syncretism, we can call this view "advocacy." To my eye, syncretism is a very important process, by which humans learn from one another. It is not always and inevitably good; sometimes, it is rooted in violence and oppression, so that evil beliefs triumph, at least temporarily, over good. Sometimes, syncretism means taking the wrong track, moving from a position that helps to attain valuable goals to one that fosters destruction. On the whole, however, syncretism is a means by which religions grow in wisdom and understanding, and this is a thing to be desired greatly.

Syncretism is a helpful description for the process whereby religions grow, both in understanding and in numbers. Like plants and animals, religions can display "hybrid vigour" (*heterosis* is the technical label). There is a kind of strength that comes from the melding of viewpoints. Christianity has grown and developed by incorporating insights and rituals from traditions as diverse as Judaism (obviously), Greek and Roman thought, Manichaeism (officially rejected, but not quite escaped), and European folk religions. Indeed, Christianity's greatest theological failures have come from entering new cultural contexts without engaging in syncretism. The encounter with Indigenous Peoples in North America is a prime example.

Other religions do it, too. We will see plenty of cases of syncretism from a whole variety of religions: Judaism, Islam, Buddhism, and others. Indeed, all religions have a syncretistic history, as far as I can tell. We cannot investigate examples from every religion; that would be an impossible task. Nonetheless, I will try to demonstrate the universality of the syncretistic process and explain some of the reasons that it happens.

Syncretism, I suggest, is both normal and necessary, a part of all religious life; in the long run, religions cannot survive without it. We are all syncretists, by necessity and as a product of the way that humanity has always worked. I intend to argue that syncretism is also a good thing. The most successful religions, and the ones most genuinely faithful to their core principles, tend to be ones that are good at engaging with other religions and learning from them. Failure to do so leads rapidly to irrelevance. It can also lead to unfaithfulness because religions are always oriented toward life in the present, as well as the future. Life has a tendency to require new resources in order to answer new questions. Syncretism is a tremendously important and helpful way to acquire those resources. Thus, syncretism can bring a kind of hybrid vigour to religions that might otherwise become too narrow in their mindset or too disconnected from the world in which they exist. This is true for all religions. The failure of some religions, such as Communism (yes, it is a religion, and I will tell you why), can be traced directly to a refusal to listen to other traditions. Closed-mindedness commonly kills people and always kills systems. Consequently, it is a good thing that religions pick up elements from other religions: otherwise they might easily become one-sided or stale. So, people branch out, incorporating bits of ancient or contemporary wisdom from different sources.

I know many people with different religious commitments who do t'ai chi, which originated in Taoism. Tai chi is a superb exercise programme, and I recommend it to anyone who needs to develop a more meditative approach to life, along with physical flexibility, balance and mobility. Yoga, with roots in Hinduism, Jainism, and Buddhism, helps many others – again, with different religious commitments – to do the same sorts of things. Christians are among the people who have taken up these Asian and Indian disciplines, because Christianity lacks a parallel, though Christians still have the needs that t'ai chi and yoga meet. Christianity has a meditative tradition, but it does not involve the same bodily development. People who claim to have no religion at all often find these disciplines helpful, because they have the same needs but no traditions upon which to draw. In obvious ways like this, and in many less evident forms, people adopt solutions to life challenges from many religious traditions.

Moreover, religious traditions from the past continue to be present in our cultures, even when we think that we have shed them completely. People who know nothing of Celtic, Greek, Roman, or Norse religions still use names and ideas from them. The old gods and old stories still survive, and they enrich our lives on a constant basis. The evidence is all around us. Have you ever tossed a coin into a wishing well or a fountain? You may not realize it, but in the process you are living out an ancient Celtic and Germanic religious ritual.[19] The Celts and Germans tended to dedicate springs, bogs, lakes, and other watery places to gods. Offerings would be dropped into these places as a means of ensuring the co-operation (or, at least, the quiescence) of the god of the place. This was, for instance, a common procedure after a successful battle, when the victor would give some of the booty to the god by dropping it into a bog or lake. People could also implore the assistance of a particular god, who might specialize in certain kinds of blessings, by dropping an offering of money or a votive image into the water. Your gift, dropped into the water and accompanied by a wish, carries on this same tradition of linking an offering with a request for a blessing – and that is the root of the notion that people can make wishes by placing gifts in water. The religious origin of this practice may be more obvious if you think about the disadvantages of putting money in water, compared with dropping a coin in a collection box. Not only does the fountain and/or pool need construction and up-keep, both of which are far more involved and expensive than having a box, but removing the money requires draining the water and send-ing in workers to collect all the coins off the bottom. We respond to the notion of tossing a gift into water and uttering a prayer, which is what a wish really is, because our society's ancestors have done it for many centuries. Hard-headed modernity has not stripped us of all our ancient religious practices; we may claim unbelief but our actions betray us.

To bring the point really close to home, think about the days of the week: Sunday (Sun's Day, with traditional solar religious associations – Sunna, the sun, is a god in Germanic religion); Monday (Moon's Day, with traditional lunar religious associations – the moon is a god in some Germanic religions); Tuesday (Tiw's Day, after a god in Norse and German religions); Wednesday (Woden's Day, after the highest of all gods in the Germanic pantheon); Thursday (Thor's Day, after the Germanic god of thunder); Friday (Frigg's Day, after Woden's wife, supreme goddess in the Germanic pantheon); Saturday (Saturn's Day, after Saturn, one of the earliest and most powerful Roman gods). Some months of the year show the same influences: January is named for Janus, the Roman god of beginnings and endings; February is named for Februus, probably an Etruscan god, and Februalia, the Roman version of Februus; March celebrates Mars, the Roman god of war; May is named for Maia Maiestas, the Roman version of a Greek goddess; and June remembers Juno, the wife of Jupiter in the Roman pantheon and protector of Rome. What about the planets and constellations? Many of the names that we have for these things are based on the ancient religious stories of Greece and Rome. Of course, the still remarkably common practice of following one's horoscope is a direct inheritance from ancient religion – astrology can be traced back to the ancient Babylonians – and one that continues to use the names of Greek gods.

The great holidays of the Christian year, still celebrated by many who claim no real Christian association, are essentially syncretistic. Christmas is on 25 December, situated shortly after the winter solstice and around the end of Saturnalia (the Roman feast time dedicated to Saturn), in a purposeful effort to integrate pieces of other religions that also celebrated this time. Conveniently, this enabled an incorporation of the Northern European celebration of Yule. The lit trees, feasting, drinking, carousing, and preoccupation with giving and receiving, reveal that all of these festivals are still tied together. The birth of Jesus is celebrated in an uneasy linkage with orgiastic rites of many kinds. And this can be a good thing. I enjoy the pleasures of good food, parties, and lights, too, (although I sometimes wonder about the astounding use of electricity involved, as well as the degree to which the holiday seems to be dominated by junk that will soon hit the landfill – but that is part of my whole critique of consumerist religion). Easter, with its attachment to traditional rites of spring and fertility, and Hallowe'en (All Hallows' Eve), with its roots in Samhain (the Celtic festival at the end of summer, when the boundaries between this world and the spirit world are especially permeable) have similar stories and similar benefits.

Art is another aspect of our lives that demonstrates the influence of syncretism. Next time you go to an art gallery, observe the paintings and statuary with an eye to the variety of religions represented in them. You may be surprised. The greatest works of Western art are commonly constructed out of symbolic systems from various religious heritages: the European, Roman, and Greek mythologies are thoroughly mixed with Christian, Jewish, and Muslim elements (and sometimes even aspects of Asian religion). Indeed, God the Father (First Person of the Christian Trinity) appears on the ceiling of the Sistine Chapel in Rome looking much like Jupiter or Zeus from ancient Greek and Roman art – minus the thunderbolts. Religions end up juxtaposed; though the relationship can be uncomfortable, it allows for mutual criticism and strengthening. The same can be said of poetry, literature, and drama; you simply cannot understand any of the realms of what has traditionally been called "English literature" without an awareness of several religious traditions.

As our introductory examples suggest, this kind of syncretism is not limited to societies with explicitly European heritages. Consider a number of examples in a single, fairly recent, edition of *The Economist* magazine (9 January 2010), which is not a particularly religion-oriented publication. A brief article about Saudi Arabia notes that religious authorities there have decided that the decades-long policy of enforcing a ban on the mixing of the sexes (known as *ikhtilat*) is unnecessary. "Saudi jurisprudence has erred, they say, by confusing conservative tribal custom with the rules of *sharia*, thus lumping the innocent mingling of the sexes with the true sin of *khulwa*, meaning an unmarried, unrelated couple's 'seclusion'" in a context where inappropriate behaviour could occur.[20] On the facing page, there appears an article about the polygamous, Zulu marriage of South African president, Jacob Zuma. In the second article, a former editor of a South African newspaper is cited as saying that traditional religion is routinely mixed with Christianity: "Many black South African Christians still also worship their ancestors, he notes. Most weddings mix the traditional with the Christian. Many people practise customary law alongside the Western kind and take traditional as well as Western medicine."[21]

There is an obituary in this issue of *The Economist*, for Abdurrahman Wahid (Gus Dur), a former president of Indonesia, in which the variety of influences on Wahid's thought, which had substantial impact on his country, is recognized: "Mr. Wahid had imbibed the gentle Hindu-flavoured Islam of Java and the café-table cut-and-thrust of Baghdad's student circles, as well as the doctrinaire rote-learning of al-Azhar University in Cairo, and had plumped for free expression every time."[22] The broadness of his reading and musical taste is celebrated, as is his work with Nahdlatul Ulama, "the world's largest Muslim organisation, heavily rural and steeped in animist Javanese tradition, which his grandfather had founded and his father had run."[23] We have Islam mixed with traditional tribal religious/ social custom in Saudi Arabia; Christianity mixed with traditional religion, including ancestor worship, in South Africa; and a rich Hindu/animist/Islamic combination in Indonesia – and all of this shows up on the routine reporting pages of a single issue of an economics-oriented news magazine! We need to face it: mixing-and-matching religion is standard procedure, and even the most puritanical of believers (and non-believers) does it.

THE MEANING OF WORSHIP

Since we have now encountered a (very brief) mention of ancestor worship, this is probably an appropriate moment to introduce a bit of complexity into the word "worship." To the Western ear, it tends automatically to imply Christian services, offered to one God who is understood as almighty. However, it is traditionally a highly flexible word, referring to a surprising variety of relationships. In the old Anglican and Episcopalian wedding services, the groom would say "With my body, I thee worship, and with all my worldly goods, I thee endow," as part of the marriage vows.[24] The word "worship," in this case, is a statement of the legal and personal significance of the bride to the groom; she is truly his wife and he is giving both himself and his goods to her (though, oddly enough, all of the property that was not carefully protected by trust actually ended up in the groom's hands). The effect of the promise, however, is that the possibility of the groom marrying someone else is officially ruled out, as he has nothing left to give in any future service, unless the bride dies before he does. Anyone familiar with the history of male/female relations among people who were married under this form of service (a very large number, around the world) will realize that the promise to worship certainly does not imply that the man would bow down before the woman or place himself under her authority. Indeed, elsewhere in the service, the woman promises to "obey" and "serve" her husband – promises that are not reciprocal; he is not called upon to make similar commitments.

For South Africans to worship their ancestors while being Christians is certainly syncretism. But, it need not be an irresolvable contradiction, just as a Christian groom worshipping his wife with his body is not automatically contradictory. African ancestor worship tends to be a recognition of the legal and social significance of the ancestors – a way of demonstrating that they continue to play an important role in the world.[25] Such a viewpoint can be reconciled with Christianity. Indeed, the African approach is not necessarily very different from the standard Christian belief in the community of saints, according to which Christians of past days are still active today and participate in the church's life. One way of construing the notion of eternal life is that it means being dead is not the end of involvement in the created order. Icons, common in Christian worship in many places, are means of enabling contemporary Christians to be with saints of past days; these saints are, effectively, Christian ancestors, and are so understood in the world of Eastern Christianity (Orthodox and Catholic) where the dead are never very distant.

Because the word "worship" is so flexible, knowing when we are doing it and toward whom (or what) is often rather difficult. We make simple declarations, like "I am a Christian," and then talk and act in ways that are more rooted in modern, individualistic, liberalism than in the ancient religion derived from Jesus Christ. We say things like, "I am a Muslim," and handle our money in ways that are more obviously capitalist than traditionally Islamic. Because these various strands of our lives are exactly that – strands of our lives – we often do not recognize the origins of the theories that guide our actions.

Our ways of understanding life come from many sources. We learn different things from different people, with different heritages, all the time. Of course, if we really tried to identify the exact roots of each and every thing that we do, we could be quite successful, but only because we'd never have a chance to do anything. The more time spent researching, the less time spent acting, but even research is an action (born of Western assumptions about knowledge), so that sooner or later we would be at an absolute standstill, which would be followed, quite rapidly, by death. We are forced to live with some uncertainty about the larger meanings of our actions.

Worship is giving homage: showing respect to the other by allowing the nature of that other, as we understand that nature, to guide our relationship with her/him/it. The roots of the word "worship" are in Old English; in its origins, the word has to do with recognizing the worthiness of another. Worship is a declaration of the worth of the other (or the other's official status, as when we call a mayor "Her Worship" or "His Worship"); it is a statement of respect. It implies a recognition that my life is not lived entirely in relation to myself, my needs and my wishes. Other people are involved and their status must be considered and is worthy of appropriate response.

Everything that we do or say is worship toward someone or something. Since we learn from many sources, our worship ends up being the result of many faith histories; it is intrinsically syncretistic. If modern liberalism helps a Christian evangelical to emphasize personal involvement in religion, then that can be a good thing. It means, however, that the Christian evangelical understands God in the light of liberal thinking, as One who particularly values the autonomy of the individual. Consequently, whenever the evangelical bows to God, that person is also paying homage to modern liberalism. This is true even though the influence may be invisible to the evangelical Christian, who may assume that religious ideas come straight from the Bible. Influences all meld together, so that we cannot distinguish them without serious intellectual exercise, and, sometimes, even dedicated investigation will not enable us to identify separate strands. Our lives and histories are very complicated. Worship is always worship toward another, and that other is continually redefined as we learn more. Because of the complex ways in which we are influenced by different people and streams of thought, we do not remain still in our thinking and we usually cannot enumerate all of the ways our understanding of worship and its objects shift.

Syncretism, therefore, cannot be evaded. It is everywhere. Indeed, I cannot imagine a world of absolutely pure and discrete religions, unless it is a world with one monadic übermind, of the kind beloved of some science fiction writers. In our world, with multiple minds and multiple histories, syncretism is now, and always has been, a universal and necessary part of the structure of our thought.

The reality, then, is that syncretism is a common process and one that touches every religion. It is so truly universal that we often do not recognize its presence. However, syncretism is a good thing and a necessary survival skill, for both individual persons and for whole religions. Throughout this book, we will see numerous examples of the ways in which syncretism happens, and we will investigate some of the ways in which we benefit from it.

SYNCRETISM IS A SOLUTION

This constant presence of syncretism is the reason that this book speaks of "mixed religion"; we all live in mixed religious contexts. Even if we dismiss syncretism in principle, we do not have the option of rejecting it in practice. No amount of historical digging will enable us to reach some sort of pure religion uninfluenced by other traditions.

This is merely an illustration of a historical reality, a statement that syncretism happens and is unavoidable. The fact of syncretism is not necessarily sufficient justification for embracing it. However, the subtitle of this book declares that I regard syncretism as a solution, and you may well wonder about that. Why "solution"? The word "solution" has two relevant meanings that will help in understanding the purpose of this book: (1) "an act or the process by which a solid, liquid, or gaseous substance is homogeneously mixed with a liquid or less commonly a gas or solid that may consist of simple physical mixing of components or may involve chemical change" and (2) "an answer to or means of answering a problem."[26]

The first definition is one that applies, but only metaphorically. Religions involve substances that are solid, liquid, and gaseous – some people would like to suggest that they are all gas – but I am more interested in the mixture of ideas that make up religions. Religions are solutions, in the sense of being mixtures of components , as we see in the fact that Christmas is celebrated at the time of the traditional Yuletide, and its celebration includes an uneasy juxtaposition of Christian and pagan components. Religions also cause fundamental changes in the nature of the things which shape them, as we see in the encounter between Shinto and Buddhism in Japan, or the meeting between Islam and Greek thought in the former territories of Byzantium. Religions are mixtures, and that is a good thing.

Moreover, religions are sets of solutions to problems, and thus the second definition applies more exactly. One, though not the only, basic reason that they become mixtures is precisely because they are

trying to resolve problems. Religions attempt to answer cosmic questions: "Why do we exist? How did we come to be here? Why do bad
things happen?" They also answer mundane questions: "With whom
should we trade? How much profit should I make? Whom should I
marry? Where should we live?" Everyone needs to answer these questions, which is why everybody is religious, though some people refuse
to admit that their belief systems are religions.

In the process of asking and trying to answer these questions, we
become aware of possible ways of responding, and of various responses. Encountering others increases our selection of questions and range
of answers, as well as our choice of methods for answering, and thus
syncretism becomes the solution to particular questions. As religions
meet one another, they become incorporated into one another, helping to resolve each other's challenges. The result is not an amorphous
mass; instead, we have a richly complex world in which systems of
thought and action maintain their own identities while developing –
even metamorphosing – as people encounter one another and work
together on the common projects of understanding and living. Religions become solutions, such that there is not a pure thing called Buddhism, for example, that one can lift and transport to another place
and time. There are only Buddhisms, inspired by the Buddha and traditions of Buddhism as thought, lived, and transmitted by people,
developing all the time, and mixing with other religious answers in
the process. Thus, Buddhisms will almost always have something in
common with other Buddhisms, but the differences may be more
obvious and more significant than the similarities.

In addition, at the centre of many conversations about religion is
one particular problem that has a huge impact on our lives: the challenge of living together in a world where there are many religious
viewpoints, and the challenge to go beyond fighting, then beyond
mere tolerance, to living together in a kind of mutual support. This is
what I call "the challenge of mutuality." We are all in this world together and our thoughts and actions have consequences for other people,
as theirs do for us. We need to find ways to help one another. Syncretism is one part of the solution to this problem, also. When we realize that other people have solutions to our intellectual challenges and
we have solutions to theirs, and, moreover, that all religions, including
our own, are composed of borrowings from others and borrowing is

a perfectly legitimate strategy, then we can work together on facing our common challenges. In that way, syncretism is an important part of the solution to the challenge of living together in a pluralist, multi-religious world.

This book suggests that mutuality, understood as both a willingness to accept wisdom from others and a generosity about sharing wisdom with others, is valuable as a solution to life challenges. We suffer when we reject the answers that others have found solely or primarily because the answers come from other people or other contexts. Internet conversation is remarkable for its refusal of the kind of mutuality that undergirds syncretism; ridiculous insults tend to rule, and disagreements swiftly descend into exchanges of names, such as "fascist" and "communist." This name-calling, of course, is mere illiterate brawling, and represents a missed opportunity: the chance for us to learn and grow together. Mutuality has always been important; however, it may be more significant than ever in our world of fast global communications.

This book, therefore, has several purposes. The first is to investigate the nature of religion and demonstrate that syncretism is a routine and universal process; it occurs whether we will it or not. The second is to discuss the benefits of syncretism and point out some of the disadvantages of failing to be syncretistic. The reality of its occurrence is not sufficient justification for committing ourselves to it, but the advocacy approach encourages exactly this sort of commitment. Therefore, we will investigate some of the reasons that syncretism is truly helpful and some of the contexts in which benefits of syncretism have been realized. The third purpose is to say something about the conditions that tend to enable syncretism to happen, so that we can generate and sustain our own useful syncretisms. By the end of the book, I hope to have convinced you that syncretism happens, and that this is a good thing.

THE COUNTERPOSITION:
PEOPLE REJECTING SYNCRETISM

Before continuing with an exploration of the desirability of syncretism, we need to have a deeper understanding of the opposing positions; we need to meet some of the people who reject the very idea of syncretism and get an idea of the arguments that they make. These are of several types: some people insist that only certain kinds of religion can possibly be syncretistic, and those religions are inferior (as Hendrik Kraemer argues); other people regard syncretism as an unacceptable compromise of a clear, received truth (Christian fundamentalism); and the most vigorous critique is that syncretism is apostasy, a departure from the true religion, and a danger to the community. Proponents of the latter view tend to believe that anyone who engages in syncretism must be shunned or destroyed (as we see in the Sikh treatment of Harjot Oberoi, and in Saudi Wahhabism). Religion is not always gentle and friendly. At the root of all these types of rejection is the problem of group identity and its control: who will define a particular religious identity, and how will the identity be sustained and controlled?

Hendrik Kraemer, a decisively important Christian scholar of world religions, argues for a distinction between "naturalistic" religions, by which he means any religion that does not depend upon a specific revelation claimed as coming from God, and "religions of revelation" (Christianity, Judaism, and, "to a certain degree" Islam), religions of the Book, which claim to be the product of a specific, historical revelation.[27] The difference between the two is that naturalistic religions find "in nature and its cyclic course ... the perennial pattern and source of the interpretation of life and its problems,"[28] while religions of revelation are built around prophetic declarations from the Divine.[29] Kraemer understands religions of revelation as having an absolutely given and unchangeable identity, while the identities of naturalistic religions are more fluid and amenable to influences from outside.

To Kraemer's mind, naturalistic religions are "totalitarian," meaning all-embracing.[30] Kraemer argues that "non-Christian religions ... are all-inclusive systems and theories of life, rooted in a religious basis, and therefore at the same time embrace a system of culture and civilization and a definite structure of society and state."[31] This is rather an overwhelming generalization which is altogether true in some cases and less true in others. It is a helpful reminder that religions cannot be treated as mere systems of metaphysical speculation, isolated from matters of this-worldly (which is what "secular" literally means) concern. However, Kraemer is suggesting something more: naturalist religions are essentially human efforts to ask and answer questions about life in the world.

To Kraemer's mind, this places them in direct opposition to religions of revelation, especially Christianity; he thinks that Christianity is "the religion of revelation" and that the Bible is the record of God's assessment of the problem of existence (sin and guilt) and the divine answer to the challenge.[32] Thus, whatever concrete problems or complexities might emerge in actual Christianity in history, at the centre of Christianity is God's set of claims. Human reflections are largely beside the point. Christianity is purely and simply about doing whatever God wills,[33] which need not make sense to the human mind.[34]

Aside from the complicated issues of how his theory treats Judaism and Islam, the biggest difficulty with Kraemer's argument is that it is fundamentally ahistorical. Many who read this book will find Kraemer's account of Christianity to be exactly what they believe Christianity to be, whether they regard it as the truth or not. However, Kraemer is a Protestant Christian, making a specifically Protestant statement about what Christianity looks like. The Bible did not simply appear from heaven, but took centuries to develop as early Christians decided what they understood their message to be and which books conveyed it best. Kraemer's notion of what Christianity has to say is not exactly what some other Christians, notably Catholics and Orthodox, think – which is why Kraemer criticizes Thomas Aquinas and Catholicism.[35]

Most of all, Kraemer is, quite intentionally, declaring that syncretism is entirely the province of naturalistic religions. Religions of revelation, especially Judaism and Christianity, have God's words to guide them, instead. This is simply a false account of how Christians have come to believe what they believe. The early centuries, in which the Christian Bible was being assembled and Christian positions formulated, were years of vigorous syncretism for Christians. The central assertions of this religion – such as that Christ is God, one person of a Divine Trinity – are products of complex syncretistic thought. The rules of the debates were set by Greek categories; the answers were found and stated with the help of Platonism and Stoicism. This does not make them untrue, but it certainly makes them syncretistic rather than the straightforward product of Divine revelation. The purity that Kraemer imagines is just that: the imagining of a modern Protestant who simply assumes that his Christianity is pure and unsullied while all others are impure failures.

The (more radical) near cousin of Kraemer's kind of thinking is Christian fundamentalism, an important part of the world's story over the last one hundred years. Its roots are in a set of essays, published in the early part of the twentieth century, called *The Fundamentals*. The basic point of these essays is that the Bible, directly and literally inspired by God, is the only valid resource for understanding the issues upon which religion touches. Any intrusion of wisdom from other sources that appears to change or contradict the Bible is simply unacceptable. Any hint of syncretism is ruled out by this simple, indeed simplistic, move. This is a strong version of the resistance that we have seen in Kraemer, where the assertion of an infallible body of knowledge that is not open to question makes syncretism logically inadmissible.

At the heart of the argument is the Bible. Essays contained in *The Fundamentals* argue for a very strong definition of "inspiration," the Christian teaching declaring that God participated in the composition of the Bible. In "The Inspiration of the Word of God: Definition, Extent, and Proof," James M. Gray asserts that whatever fallibility or error might creep into the lives of the biblical authors, "such fallibility or errancy was never under any circumstances communicated to their sacred writings."[36] Thus, the argument begins with an assertion of the perfection of the text, though Gray will add that "the record for whose inspiration we contend is the original record – the autographs or parchments of Moses, David, Daniel, Matthew, Paul, or Peter, as the case may be, and not any particular translation or translations of them whatever."[37] This allows for what was called the lower criticism, an effort to ensure that translation and punctuation and other aspects of the text are as accurate as possible, and based upon the highest-quality manuscripts, so that the text as presented represents the original record as precisely as can be.

However, this severely limits the higher criticism, which is a set of techniques for understanding a text (any text) that does not begin with an assumption that the text must be (or must have been originally) perfect and infallible. Indeed, this sort of examination often begins with a hermeneutic of suspicion, which is a theory of interpretation (that is what "hermeneutic" means) built on the expectation that the text will be imperfect; in this theory all texts are products of specific historical circumstances and agendas, constructed by authors with partial and limited insights, and participating in a variety of the rationalities and irrationalities current when the texts were composed, recorded, and handed down. Since many of the books of the Bible (note that this is not quite a fair title, since different denominations have different collections of material in their Bibles) are composed of material that was first oral and then written, further complexities are introduced by the presence of editors before the writing, in addition to the usual editors afterward. One of the main purposes for which *The Fundamentals* came into being was to reject the hermeneutic of suspicion and all of its assumptions, which are deemed to be "rationalistic."[38] The essays support the view that the Bible is a "divinely inspired, heaven-given book";[39] God created it and God gives it meaning.

At the root of all this is a theory of knowledge that eliminates the human mind from the search for "spiritual truths."[40] These truths are revealed by God to faith – here, understood as the willingness to believe – entirely bypassing human intelligence. Reason merely misleads, so the mind must be subservient to the biblical text – and not just the text, but the Bible as understood by the fundamentalists. Officially, any sort of intuition is also ruled out, yet one can hardly avoid the conclusion that what is really meant by a faith response to the words of the Bible is an intuitive response. Certainly, any sort of concrete evidence is welcome only if it reinforces the conclusions of the authors of *The Fundamentals*. Even traditional demonstrations of the existence of God are derided as being an inadmissible use of the human mind.[41]

The fundamentalists go even further than Kraemer in rooting out any syncretistic possibilities. The human role in writing and formulating the Bible (or Bibles) is utterly unimportant. The spiritual truths that it conveys are passed directly into the human mind by God's agency. There is no human activity of asking and answering questions; instead, there is only God's choice of people whom God fills with divine truth.

As with all non-rational assertions, the fundamentalist position cannot be argued from the inside; one must find its roots in order to criticize it. Fundamentalism has no rational arguments in its favour because it makes no reference to anything that we might recognize as evidence. The contrary arguments are all rational and historical, and fundamentalism dismisses such things with an airy wave of the hand. From outside the system, however, we can recognize that fundamentalism is itself a syncretism; its roots are in a blending of various kinds of Protestantism with (1) romanticism, which leads to the speech about spiritual truths as distinct from rational truths because romanticists base knowledge on feeling and intuitive knowing (as opposed to Enlightenment thinkers' emphasis upon empirical reason and deduction), and (2) empiricism (oddly enough), which leads to the expectation that one can find all the important truths in the Bible, which is treated rather like a modern scientific textbook instead of as a collection of disparate ancient texts. When evidence is brought against the arguments, the fundamentalist can take refuge in assertions about faith. When accused of relying on a kind of non-rational, even irrational, sort of faith, the fundamentalist can argue that the Bible is empirically "true" – even though we know that much of its history and science are flawed. The deepest weakness of the fundamentalist critique is that it is based upon a self-deception: the choice to reject reason means that reason is used in ways that are not understood by fundamentalists themselves.

Fundamentalism, therefore, is a complex syncretism that rejects the possibility of syncretism. This rejection of reason and the syncretistic possibilities that accompany rational thought appears to provide fundamentalists with tight control over their religious identity: it is what is given in the Bible. However, in addition to fostering a misunderstanding of the history and meaning of the Bible, their lack of rational investigation of their own and other faith traditions causes the fundamentalists' control over identity to be nothing more than a mirage, an illusion that is endlessly chased. In fact, the identity floats and shifts, partly because of the ongoing syncretistic process that even fundamentalism – perhaps, especially fundamentalism – cannot escape.

Opposition to syncretism is not limited to Christians. As we have seen, many Muslims are open to learning from other religions. The history of Muslims trading insights with other religions goes back to the very beginning of Islam. However, syncretism is distinctly unpopular in certain parts of Islam. One of the more vigorous sources of opposition is Wahhabism, which is intellectually structured around a rejection of all other influences. The astonishingly thoroughgoing understandings of *tawhid* (the theology of absolute monotheism) and *shirk* (violations of absolute monotheism) presented in the writings of Ibn Abd al-Wahhab (circa 1703–1792 CE) provide the roots of a notion of religious purity that distinguishes, and often divides, Wahhabi Muslims from others in the Islamic community.[42] This purity is enforced by religious authorities in Saudi Arabia, the heart of Wahhabism. Note that this example is something of a shift from the Protestant Christian examples that we have seen: the latter are based upon an authoritative text, with a somewhat amorphous community sustaining an interpretation of the text and disciplining departure from orthodoxy. In the example of Wahhabism, we will see a complex tradition of reflection, with discipline maintained by a more-or-less-clearly defined set of authorities.

Tawhid is the basic theological assertion of Islam: the declaration that Allah is One and indivisible, and only the one, true Allah is to be worshipped. All Muslims share this belief; it is the most important defining characteristic of Islam. However, it can be interpreted in different ways, and the Wahhabi understanding is among the most stringent. To al-Wahhab, true monotheism excludes not only the existence of multiple persons in the one God (as in the Christian Trinity) as all Muslims do, but also ordained clergy; a papacy or other magisterial teaching/law-making body; and any binding interpretations of scripture produced by rabbis, priests, or other authoritative teachers.[43]

To al-Wahhab, tawhid means that Allah has absolute power over all things; everything is at Allah's disposal. Moreover, all of creation must serve and worship Allah and Allah alone. "Thus, anyone who serves or worships anyone or anything else, even the Righteous Ancestors (*Salihin*) or angels, has departed from Islam."[44] Consequently, Allah's characteristics belong only to Allah. They cannot be attributed to any human beings. Only Allah can create, and only Allah truly possesses all things. Only Allah can bless or curse. Therefore, all worship, service and obedience are owed to Allah.[45]

Grasping the significance of this means that we must also consider the concept of shirk, the category of activities that violate monotheism (tawhid). One can very easily fall away from the pure monotheism that al-Wahhab promotes and end up in the associationism that he decries. One must utterly avoid the making of statues or any kind of image, since that might encourage a worshipful attitude toward that which is not Allah. Making an offering to a *jinn* or other power that is not Allah is obviously ruled out. However, less evident examples include turning to any kind of human knowledge, whether traditional or innovative; only the Qur'an and *Hadith* (sayings of the Prophet Muhammad and stories about him, which occur in various collections; Muslims differ on which ones are legitimate) are acceptable sources of authority.

The uniqueness of Wahhabism becomes most evident when one asks the awkward question that we have broached earlier in this book: "What is worship?" Al-Wahhab had exactly the insight that we have discussed: to engage in any activity built upon respect for another way of thinking, to incorporate into one's life an insight from some other system of thought, is to show worship toward other people and even other gods. Al-Wahhab realized that this would mean that "calling on anyone or anything other than God for help, assistance, refuge, or any other thing is strictly, totally, and permanently forbidden because 'this calling signifies worship of the one called upon.'"[46] Similarly, calling upon holy men, saints, or the Companions of Muhammad is associationism, the act of ascribing Allah's characteristics to humans and associating humans with divine power. If one accords respect to something that is other than Allah, then one is performing an act of worship toward that other. Al-Wahhab grasped exactly the point of this book, except that he rejected syncretism rather than celebrating it; he realized that everything is religious, and that allowing any insights from outside his religious sources, any reliance on anyone or anything other than Allah, is syncretism.

The effort to avoid syncretism involves tremendous intellectual contortions and is doomed to failure. The immediate problem for al-Wahhab was that many Muslims did not (and do not) share his understanding of tawhid. Many were in the habit of gathering at the tombs of great Muslims in order to pray, sometimes invoking the assistance of the dead in their prayers. Al-Wahhab destroyed a number of tombs which had become special shrines with canopies and other decorations – and blamed Shias, whom he called by the insulting term "Rejectors" for the syncretistic activity of importing the Christian habit of worshipping at gravesites.[47] Many Shias treat their imams

with great esteem, believing them to be equipped with special authority to speak about the law and its meanings and functioning as the
voice of Muhammad on earth. By Wahhabi standards, these Muslims
commit a great sin, a profound violation of monotheism which Christians also commit: they "take men of religion as lords alongside
God."[48]

These challenges, which are part of a whole Wahhabi commitment to
the purification of Islam, are small in comparison to the great problems
that modernity has brought. Wahhabism has thrived in Saudi Arabia
because of the alliance between Wahhabi leaders and the House of
Sa'ud. This has been a notable asset for Wahhabism, because the Sa'uds
have been content to run a closed kingdom, limiting access from other
countries, Islamic or not. However, the last century has included four
major incursions into Saudi Arabia, all of which have compromised the
purity of Wahhabi tawhid. The first is education; a significant number
of Saudis, including members of the royal family, have obtained education outside the country.[49] Even within Saudi Arabia, education has
been modernized, creating schisms within society; the battle between a
traditional notion of the universe as geocentric (earth-centered) and a
more modern understanding of the universe as heliocentric (sun-cen-
tered) has emerged in the country.[50] The second major incursion is
modern technology, including mass media: King Faysal introduced
radio to Saudi Arabia,[51] which has been followed by the whole range of
modern communications systems, while cars and other contemporary
implements have become indispensable parts of Saudi life. The third
transforming factor is the oil industry, which has brought numerous
people from other parts of the world into Saudi Arabia; efforts to isolate them in separate communities have not prevented Saudis from recognizing the greater freedoms and benefits that foreigners receive.[52]
The fourth source of change is the infiltration of jihadism, the violent
Islamism that we see on our television screens; Saudi authorities have
been unable to prevent the Muslim Brotherhood and other voices of
international jihadism from reaching the country's streets.[53] This last
influence has been particularly important because it has forced Wahhabism to oppose its traditional allies, the ruling House of Sa'ud and its
American allies (upon whom they depended for support when Iraq
invaded Kuwait). Jihadism is a syncretistic force from the perspective of
Wahhabism. Jihadis have a rather different set of priorities, including a

commitment to authority that comes out of the barrel of a gun. The consequence of all these things is that Wahhabis find themselves walking with, talking with, learning from, and giving authority to systems of thought and people from outside a Wahhabi understanding of the Qur'an and the Hadith. Modern structures of bureaucracy, driven by Westernizing impulses and the communications technologies that carry those impulses, order the most Wahhabi nation on earth. The only means of rejecting Western values is to engage in modern, Western-style warfare, using Western weapons, under the influence of jihadism, which is itself a syncretism of Islam and Western notions of revolution.

Al-Wahhab was right about the radical approach needed to maintain the sort of purity that he regarded as necessary for true monotheism, but he was wrong about the possibility of sustaining it. He was also wrong about the desirability of attempting that level of purity, because it demands a kind of isolation and other-worldliness that dooms a community, and, therefore, dooms its worship. Moreover, sustaining that kind of other-worldliness in a community demands a high level of control over the community's religious identity. The most obvious challenge to Wahhabism has been keeping control in the hands of Wahhabi religious authorities while sustaining the intended purity. The joint challenges of relations with the House of Sa'ud, ongoing Westernization, and jihadism have all forced Wahhabis to compromise their principle of tawhid in order to maintain the religious power needed to preserve it. In order to prevent syncretism, Wahhabis have become syncretists.

As is evident in the Wahhabi example, opposition at the level of theory results in opposition at the level of practice; if syncretism is rejected in thought, it will be partly, though not entirely, rejected in practice. As will become evident in later chapters of this book, people are attached to their religious identities. Assertions of syncretism threaten the kind of purity that Kraemer sees in religions based on revelation, and that fundamentalist Christians, Wahhabi Muslims, and many, many others try to defend. The result can easily be a battle over authority, especially when the rights of a community to control its voice and maintain its self-definition collide with the rights of scholars to investigate and reveal the evidence of history.

Such a battle emerged between representatives of the Vancouver Sikh community and Harjot Oberoi, a professor at the University of

British Columbia (UBC) who has made a significant contribution to the discussions in this book.[54] In 1987, members of the British Columbia Sikh community raised part of the money necessary to endow a chair in Sikh studies (the first in North America). However, not long after Oberoi was appointed to the chair, some Sikhs began to object to his work. Efforts to remove him began in earnest in 1994, when he published a book arguing that Sikhism is a syncretism, the product of Hindu, Muslim, and other influences. Several hundred Sikhs began working together to remove Oberoi from the chair because they found him "insulting, heretical, and anti-Sikh." They appealed to the Canadian government and hired a lawyer to work on their behalf. Ultimately, Oberoi resigned from the chair, but continued to teach at UBC as a Professor of Asian Studies.

These Sikhs found the suggestion that their religion is rooted in syncretism threatening because it appeared to strike at the basis of their self-identity. Perceived threats to a group's identity and/or its control over its identity are always a challenge in the syncretism discussion, and we will pursue this question further in this book, but we need to be alerted to this problem at the beginning of the discussion because it is always a consideration. It was particularly important in the Sikh case because of Sikhism's complicated relationship with Indian religious and political identities and the desire that some have for an independent Sikh state.[55] The offended Sikhs believed that assertions about Sikhism that are at variance with how the community understands itself – which is to say, assertions that differ from those expressed by the Khalsa ("pure") Sikh authorities in Akal Takht, Amritsar – are either simply inaccurate or are not really comments about Sikhism. True Sikhism is that which is defined by the Khalsa community; any teaching that falls outside the parameters established by this community is simply not helping the world to understand Sikhism, but is doing something else, instead.

This, of course, is a collision between the mission of a religious community to spread what it believes to be true, on the one hand, and the mission of the university to question everything, vigorously and critically, on the other hand. However, it also helpfully reveals what is hidden beneath all of the discussions that we have seen about interpretation of sacred texts and teachings. At the root, the problem is about the authority of a particular community to control meaning,

whether of a text, of history, or of the communal identity. Commonly, people find the notion of syncretism to be dangerous because it
threatens their self-identities and the structures of their world, which
tend to be built around teachings which can lay some sort of claim to
authoritative status. Oberoi argues that Sikhism only gradually developed a clear identity distinct from Hinduism and Islam, in a process
that culminated in the nineteenth century. This runs counter to the
standard Khalsa sense of particularity rooted in the teachings of Guru
Nanak. Sikhs are concerned that the scholarly world is undermining
their identity and self-presentation.

The Oberoi example has some complexities that make it unusual.
The Sikh community's recent establishment in North America affects
the conversation in several ways. First, it accounts for the community's lack of experience with North American norms. Most North
Americans are aware that funding a university chair ordinarily grants
the funders few rights; providing money for the position does not
usually bring control over either appointments to the chair or their
research activities. There are means by which control can be exerted
over scholarly research, such as funding particular projects by scholars
who have proven amenable to the community's positions. However,
funding a chair is ordinarily understood as a hands-off gift to the university, with donors expected to allow the university to exercise its
judgement freely thereafter.

As some Sikhs have pointed out, the newness of the community
means that there are relatively few Sikh scholars in the North American system.[56] This means that there is not a large body of scholars to
draw from, and therefore chairs are filled by recent PhDs rather than
by scholars of high stature with extensive publication records – an
unusual situation. Nor is there a large body of published literature
against which to measure the accomplishments of these new scholars.
Oberoi and a handful of others are pioneering a field of study (more
accurately, a "sub-specialty," because Sikh studies is a subdivision of
Religious Studies and Asian Studies). This is a very exciting moment
in a discipline, and the scholarship of a few has a large impact. Both
errors and uncomfortable truths can make an extraordinary difference
to the way in which Sikhism is understood.

The important thing to recognize about this whole debate is that
Oberoi and the Vancouver Sikhs are not arguing central theological

questions. This is not a discussion about the nature of the divine or how humans ought to respond to it. Instead, this is a debate about historical questions, about the origins and identity of Sikhism. That does not mean that the question is unimportant, only that it is a question of a different kind. The Sikh community is in the process of establishing an identity in North America. As the bearer of particular insights and hopes, the community wants to be able to share its message. In order to do so, it feels a need to control its self-presentation. If Sikhs want to be known as members of a proud and independent religion with its own insights about God and the world, then having their religion portrayed as a result of a lengthy syncretistic process is unhelpful for them. Sikhism is a "Religion of the Book," the Adi Granth. As we shall see, Oberoi and others have suggested that the Sikh book is itself a syncretism, an assemblage of materials from other sources combined with specifically Sikh writings. Such suggestions make the community feel that its identity is under attack.

Unless syncretism is accepted as a good thing – and few people think this way – then Oberoi's scholarship represents a clear and present danger. The identity of both the community and its holy book, the two sources of authority in Sikhism, appear to be vanishing before Sikh eyes. Control of identity and self-presentation becomes the challenge. The result is that fear and anger become significant motivating forces. If scholarship that bolsters the case for syncretism becomes widely known, then the community's self-understanding risks being obscured or even lost.

THE CHALLENGE OF OPPOSITION

The discoveries that we have made about self-identity and authority help us to see why the problem is wrongly framed by Kraemer. Kraemer argues that people will not engage in syncretism if they belong to a religion of revelation, especially if that religion is Christianity, because people who truly hold to a revelation will not, and can not, compromise their views by accepting insights from elsewhere. This argument finds its strongest expression in Christian fundamentalism, which simply rejects the legitimacy of any authority beyond the Bible and declares that human intelligence is of no value in relation to spiritual matters. Syncretism is simply impossible under these circumstances because syncretism always involves people asking questions and finding that the best answers come from various religious contexts.

As we have seen, Kraemer and the fundamentalists are wrong about the most basic of their assertions, that believing in a revelation from God will prevent – or, at least, can prevent – syncretism from happening. In fact, some of the central beliefs of Christianity to which these people are wholeheartedly committed are products of syncretism. The Bible does not state the doctrine of the Trinity; it was developed over centuries, as people asked and answered questions using all of the intellectual resources at their disposal, whatever the religious provenance. Only contemporary Protestantism, with its Enlightenment rejection of religious authority structures and its unwillingness to embrace history as a process that affects religion, could really make the claim that syncretism does not happen to it – and that is only because this kind of religion is built around ignoring its own intellectual processes. Protestantism has the added advantage that, to Protestants, modern liberal capitalism looks exactly like Protestantism, enabling the pretence that no syncretism has occurred.

In fact, Kraemer has both misstated and misplaced the real debate that governs religious discussions. The relationship between the preservation of insights, on the one hand, and progress, on the other, is truly what Kraemer, Christian fundamentalists, Wahhabi Muslims, and Vancouver Sikhs are concerned with. They want to see the basic insights of their religious traditions preserved. They fear that the beliefs that they hold, positions which they judge to be true, might vanish in a mist of relativism, criticism, and historical thinking. Kraemer also misplaces the problem; it is not located at the boundary between religions of revelation and naturalist religions – if that is even a valid distinction/characterization. Instead, the challenge of syncretism is located wherever ownership of identities and definition of boundaries are at issue. This becomes clear when Christians try to form what Stanley Hauerwas and William Willimon call (approvingly) "the Christian colony,"[57] a form of social organization built around Christians depending upon one another and limiting their interactions with the rest of the world to preaching opportunities. Wahhabi Saudi Arabia, with its efforts to isolate a purist form of Islam, is the same sort of example. The Vancouver Sikhs who attacked Oberoi were attempting the same kind of hard boundaries and firm control in relation to North American forces of modernity.

The real problem, therefore, is the challenge of identity and boundaries. It poses itself as a series of questions that appear in daily life: "Who's in and who's out? What's in and what's out?" Perhaps, most of all the problem is: "Who gets to decide?" These are the questions that emerge any time that we leave our isolation and attempt some sort of mutuality. These are some of the themes of this book. Any discussion of syncretism needs to recognize boundary and identity challenges. Syncretism is a means of progress, but it must preserve existing insights that are helpful or potentially helpful.

However, syncretism theory does not stop with these questions, because embracing and advocating syncretism means overcoming fear. The point of an advocacy approach to syncretism is to seek a new and different kind of mutuality. This approach asks questions like "What can others teach me? What can I learn that will enhance my understanding of the world and enable a richer life for the whole earth and beyond?" Most of all, syncretism involves disposing of the assumption that truth is my individual possession, and pushes the question "What can we know and accomplish together?" The advocacy approach to syncretism assumes that life in the world is a project of mutuality. As a means of progress, syncretism undermines the whole project of establishing ownership and boundaries. Boundaries turn out to be soft and permeable. Religious identity emerges as complex and amorphous. Religious authority, if it is to be faithful to the impulses that bring it into existence, must be both open-minded and willing to engage in critical thought. Syncretism is a good thing and a challenging thing.

2

What Is Religion?

In the modern West, that which is officially called "religion" tends to get sidelined; it is kept on a tight leash, and it can be very difficult to find in public spaces. Yes, there are plenty of churches, temples, mosques, and other places of worship around. Yes, anyone who wants to be President of the United States must give evidence of a deep and abiding Christian commitment, and use strong Christian rhetoric. In the end, however, very few people really want to see religion associated with politics. Billy Graham, the most famous American minister and a man who has hobnobbed with presidents for decades, has expressed regret for mixing the two.[1]

Other Western countries, generally with less-strict rules about the separation of church and state, paradoxically expect even less religious concern on the part of their leadership. Canada's Prime Ministers quietly bury their religious identities when elected – and often before then. The current Prime Minister comes from a fundamentalist Protestant background, about which he says as little as possible. His predecessors for some time have been Catholics who have displayed zero interest in seeing their co-religionists (especially their bishops) call politicians to some kind of public allegiance to the morality of their church.

I am not bemoaning the situation. I understand something of why the West has taken this path and have sympathy for concerned people.

I am not going to demand more religion in the public square. Instead, I am going to argue that it is already there. I think that we have defined religion so that we can pretend we do not have it or that it touches only carefully selected parts of our lives, when religion – of some sort – is truly everywhere. Religion is always present and cannot be banished.

First, though, we should ask why we want religion to be kept carefully penned, perhaps even caged, so that it hardly touches our lives. The primary answer is that it is dangerous. The world has seen too much violence in the name of religion, between Western Christians and Eastern Christians during the Middle Ages; Protestants and Catholics in Ireland and, before that, in Continental Europe, on Britain's shores, and on the high seas; and between Christians, Druze, and Muslims in Lebanon. We see violence also in acts carried out in the name of political Islamism all over the contemporary world; in the ancient Christian-Muslim battles for control of the Mediterranean world; the persecution of Jews by everyone, which has resulted in a militant Israel that deals harshly with Muslim and Christian Arabs; Hindu-Muslim battles in India; Maoist attempts to crush Tibetan Buddhism; and so on. What a dreary history!

At the root of our fears of religious violence is an abiding belief that religions are fundamentally irrational. Enlightenment progress was based upon the conviction that religion is accepted for reasons that cannot be tested by scientific method; if religions have any evidence in their favour, then it is beyond the capacity of science to test. Consequently, religion has no solid claim on the modern mind; the only assertions that can claim intellectual value are those which science clearly supports. Religion (to Enlightenment thinkers) is largely concerned with two things: (1) issues of morality, of right and wrong, which can better be answered by science and technology than by religious doctrine; and (2) questions about life after death, which are both irrelevant and unanswerable. Religion emerges as a simple playtoy or a crutch, an acceptable form of recreation for some people, and a support for the weak – permissible as long as it does not interfere with running the world.

From an early twenty-first-century standpoint, the Enlightenment case is a weak one. We have seen the gifts of science and technology and are not convinced that all of them are blessings. Science tells us something about what is and what might be, and technology tells us what we can do, but neither is sufficient to clarify what we *ought* to do. We have a habit of doing what we can do because we can do it, only finding out later that the "side-effects" or "collateral damage" – in short, the undesirable consequences of our actions – are immense and destructive. Something more is necessary if human life is to continue – something that can give us some sort of moral guidance about the treatment of our land, water, and air, if nothing else. However, we have also discovered that religion is therapeutically necessary; much of late twentieth-century Western religious practice was taken up with the task of repairing people shattered by the technology that was supposed to be making our world into a paradise. Life is faster, more competitive, more individualistic, more sedentary, and more dependent upon intellectual ability; these stresses and others destroy people, in both body and mind. Ultimately, though, we need a reason to live, which is something that science and technology cannot offer.

We are becoming aware that religion is about much more than questions about life after death. Indeed, a significant number of religions treat these issues as secondary or ignore them entirely. Ancient Hebrew religion (pre-first-century CE) is a helpful example. The focus of today's Judaism is firmly on this earthly life because that is the real concern of *Torah*, the ancient Hebrew teaching that we think of as "law." While notions of an afterlife have developed amongst Jews – in rich profusion, as it happens[2] – the prophetic tradition of the *Tanakh* (the Hebrew scriptures) speaks about God's reign of justice on earth. The orientation of early Hebrew religion was not toward salvation after death, because the earliest sense of post-death existence was not defined in moral terms. The very earliest of Hebrew people seem to have regarded death as a return to the ancestors; as Israel developed a sense of national identity, the sense of post-death-being shifted. The idea that people entered a sort of common, faded, shadow existence (*sheol*) after death became the norm.[3] The prophets called people to live according to God's justice, in the right covenant relationship with God so that they might live in peace in the land that they had received from God. God was understood as the saviour of the Hebrew people in this life, rather than in a putative next life. Ancient Hebrew religion was not about an afterlife, and this is reflected in much of contemporary Judaism where the emphasis tends to be on the here-and-now.[4] Enlightenment thinkers were wrong to assume that their partial understanding of a kind of Christianity would serve as an explanation for religions of all sorts.

Religion is really about meaning, the way in which we understand life, the universe, and everything. Some religions involve assertions about the supernatural – God, or a spirit world, or something of that nature – but many are primarily concerned with the most mundane things. Our religions consist of our larger viewpoints, the explanations that define our lives. They are not necessarily irrational. In fact, they tend to engage the best efforts of our minds, because we seek to understand our world and our places in it through religious inquiry. Our religions consist of the fundamental reasons that we have for being. As a result, they constitute the basis for whatever we have in the way of plans for life.

Religion, therefore, is the origin and locus of ultimate value, of ultimate concern.[5] In other words, tell me what you really want, what you care about at the most fundamental level, and I can tell you about your religion. Your most deeply rooted beliefs and inclinations dictate what you care about. Conversely, what you care about affects your most profound commitments. The religions that you live – and the ones that you communicate to other people, though sometimes inadvertently – are the ones that are defined by the deep priorities that direct your life.

This seems counterintuitive to some people. After all, isn't religion about God, the Bible, church, and all that sort of thing? It might be. Indeed, there has been a tendency to think of religion as looking roughly like Christianity, so that Christianity serves as a kind of ideal religion. That suits the Latin history of the word *religio*, from which the term "religion" is derived. Until the sixteenth century, *religio* meant "the careful and even fearful fulfilment of all that man owes to God or the gods."[6] After the triumph of Christianity, *religio* came to refer only to Christianity since it was regarded as the one true religion.

Popular usage has opened up over time, and now anything that approximates Christianity also counts. Islam and Judaism are relatively easy to include because they are commonly treated, along with Christianity, as religions of the Book and of the one God. These three even claim the same root: the religion of Abraham, an ancient Semite.

Hinduism – which is really just a broad name for the various religions of India, a geographic rather than theological identity – gets included. Folk religions, including animism (belief that everything has a soul or spirit), are usually accepted, though they have often been called "pagan" or "heathen" and summarily dismissed. Buddhism? That is one of the places where things get complicated. Buddhism does not have a God in the official sense that Christianity does. Though Buddhists may recognize spiritual beings – call them gods if you wish – the Buddha rejected the idea of a creator. Moreover, the priority of Buddhism is not association with divine Being, but a proper relationship to the cycle of birth, death, and rebirth – whether that is release from the cycle or acceptance of it out of willingness to care for others. Zen Buddhism is less concerned with this cycle, focusing instead on enlightenment as an escape from the alienation and duality of existence; this form of Buddhism has even less need for divine Being than the others. To some minds, therefore, Buddhism is a philosophy rather than a religion.

Thus, religion is not always easy to define, and it may not look like what we usually expect. Indeed, the term "religion" is endlessly debated, partly because it is so loaded. Especially in contexts where formal recognition as a religion brings with it certain privileges, being identified as a religion can be valuable and desirable. In a landmark study of The Church of Scientology, Hugh B. Urban demonstrates that some people will go to tremendous lengths to acquire and maintain recognition as a religion. Scientology was not originally conceived as religious; L. Ron Hubbard presented it in 1950 as a health regime called Dianetics, at a time when Hubbard was rather critical of institutional religion. In 1953, however, he incorporated The Church of Scientology, and since that time, Scientology has fought vigorously to be treated as a religion.[7]

The conversation can also become tangled in precisely the opposite direction. Many people who think that they are not religious actually are very religiously committed. They do not realize that their self- and world-definitions are religious, because standard labels, such as Christian, Jewish, Muslim, Hindu, Buddhist, or Sikh, do not really apply to their situation. Indeed, the strongest denial of religious identity is likely to come from a Marxist-Leninist, since that label is associated with vigorous atheism. However, especially in its state-sponsored Soviet

Russian form, Marxism-Leninism displays all of the characteristics of a religion.

THE FIVE CHARACTERISTICS OF A RELIGION

In my view, a religion needs to have five things in order to count as a religion:

1 Forms of organization
2 An overarching explanation of reality, including an understanding of the place and purpose of humanity in relation to the larger order (or disorder), which defines the meaning of life for practitioners
3 An account of human predicaments and of the means by which they may be resolved
4 An expectation of faith commitment
5 A tendency to define the values of its practitioners

You might think of this as something like a sociological definition of religions; rather than trying to establish some kind of ideal example or model of what a religion ought to be, and then looking around to see what matches it, I am noting the characteristics that seem to define movements that function according to our expectations of what constitutes a religion. These are the things that religions have in common.

1 Forms of Organization

Forms of organization may be loose, disparate, and hard to recognize, or tightly defined, generally consistent, and evident. One scholar ascribes the success of Hinduism in surviving Muslim invasion (during the twelfth and thirteenth centuries CE) to the Hindu ability to spread throughout society, leaving "no identifiable heart at which to strike," in contrast to the Buddhist tendency to concentrate in easily destroyed monasteries and universities.[8] Hinduism is no less a religion (more accurately, a family of religions) than Buddhism for having diffuse structures of authority and organization. Similarly, some forms of Protestant Christianity exist today as house churches and cell groups; they are no less a part of a religion than Catholicism, with its large and clearly identifiable church structure.

Consequently, we cannot easily define what constitutes a form of organization. However, we can identify the goal that such forms are intended to meet, which will help us to recognize them when we see them: forms of organization are means by which a community is structured and ordered, so that the life of the group has some degree of identity and longevity. A form of organization is the difference between a few people meeting occasionally and chatting about religion, on the one hand, and a group having a designated organizer, a stated objective, and some clear rules about how its purpose will be accomplished, on the other hand. Of course, sociologists can speak more precisely about how this transformation takes place, if it does, and about the various types of structure and systems of authority that religions take on. Max Weber famously distinguished traditional (sustained by inherited custom), legal-rational (sustained by legal structures), and charismatic (sustained by the inspirational gifts of a single leader) systems.[9] Contemporary theorists have much more complex, sometimes very different, understandings of forms of organization.

We need not, however, examine these in depth because we are not really interested in the particular options that are available. Instead, we need only to be aware that some structures must be in place for a religion to be something more than one person's opinion, however brilliant and insightful it might be. Your opinion may be your religion, but it won't have any standing as a religion in society unless some variant of it is generally shared, communicated, and supported. Again, I want to stress that forms of organization need not be extensive, complex, and bureaucratic. In today's world, a religion can be formed around a blog or someone's tweets; the religion may not prove to be very long-lasting, but it might be quite significant in some way. Social media can change the world; a religion can be as amorphous as any creature of social media and still count as real. Some organized commonality of viewpoint is necessary, however; otherwise a religion never reaches beyond the level of personal eccentricity to become a religion in the community.

2 An Overarching Explanation of Reality

The central point of a religion is that it explains life, making it intelligible to people. An explanation of reality usually has, at its heart, two things: (1) an account of the whole of the cosmos, however that is understood; and (2) a declaration of the part that each person plays in that whole. These explanations are not permanent; instead, they change and grow. However, a religion must always have some account of the nature and meaning of life. The presence and adequacy of its explanation of life is an important part of what determines how satisfying a religion seems to people. In other words, a religion must serve as a solution to life's questions; if it cannot do so, then it will decline in popularity because the demands that it makes are not balanced by the benefits that it confers. The expectations will be disproportionate to the returns.

A religion is an explanatory framework for life. Religions are contexts within which people talk about the big questions: "Why does the world exist? Why does humanity exist? What is the purpose of it all? What is the meaning of life?" Part of what constitutes a particular religion is that its adherents agree, often in a very general way, on the key answers to these questions.

Religions can be built around particular people. Adherents may share a belief in a charismatic founder whose teachings are understood as revelations about the nature and purpose of the cosmos. Jesus Christ of Christianity, Gautama Buddha of Buddhism, Prophet Muhammad of Islam, and Bahá'u'lláh of Bahá'í are all examples of such teachers. Ongoing reflection about the meaning of their words and actions provides their respective followers with a message about life – a message which is both explanation and guide for the community – while providing the community with news to share with the rest of the world.

Religions can also be constructed around books. A text or a set of inherited stories may function rather like a founder, providing material around which ongoing thought and conversation may be built. The Tanakh of Judaism works in precisely this way; its guides for ethical reasoning (Torah), prophetic stories and sayings (Nevi'im), and writings about many things including ancient Hebrew history (Ketuvim), are at the centre of the ongoing identity/ritual/life/debate that makes up Jewish religion. Hindu religion (or religions) tends to proceed in reflection upon and discussion about a broad range of literature, including such notable collections as the Vedas and Upanishads. The plurality and variety of the stories included, combined with the complex and multiple allegiances involved and the many kinds of ritual practices pursued, suggest that Hinduism is really a family of religions, with multiple, loosely related accounts of the whole, rather than a single religion. In a similar way, liberalism finds its roots in a number of texts, though liberalism's founding documents have identifiable authors, such as Thomas Hobbes, John Locke, and David Hume. Christianity and Islam, of course, have both founders and books; in a more complicated way this is true of Sikhism, also.

Indigenous religions, such as those among African and American tribal groups, commonly depend upon the re-telling and re-enactment of ancestral stories. Consequently, any action that deprives a group of its ability to receive and live its stories is exceedingly destructive to that group's identity. The suppression of Indigenous stories was central to the strategy employed by Europeans in their efforts to eliminate Indigenous identity. Those stories, with their descriptions of the origins of life, places, people, and creatures, situate Indigenous peoples in the world. Life is life-in-the-narrative of the people. When the stories are taken away, so are meaning and possibility. When the stories are mute, so are the people and the world. Life becomes, in the most complete and profound sense, pointless.

None of these approaches rules out the emergence of further charismatic leaders, popular texts, new strains of thought, or new groups of followers, with notions substantially different from what has come before. Religious thought systems can be quite amorphous and are prone to change. Even in their earliest incarnations, they tend to take multiple forms; over time these various forms can move in different directions. People change. Stories change. Texts change, especially as they are received and translated. The result is that religious thought develops and cannot, therefore, be understood as constrained in precise and static systems. Today's Christianity is very different from that prevalent in the medieval era, and is even more radically distinct from that of the first century. Central ideas of Christianity, such as the belief that Jesus Christ is both fully God and fully human, were not defined until the fourth and fifth centuries, after a long period of investigation and controversy. Yet, Christianity is one of the most textually defined religions; its commitment to the written word might be assumed to slow its change.

Development of religions over time is not the only historical variable that we must consider when we seek to identify the beliefs of a particular religion; indeed, it may not even be the greatest. We must realize that no religion is univocal, speaking with only one voice. Instead, every religion of significant size includes the expression of many viewpoints; only tiny, carefully regulated groups may have a single leader who does the thinking for the whole and serves as its lone voice. Thus, one can reasonably point to Islam as a more or less coherent religion, structured around the words of the Prophet Muhammad expressed in the Qur'an and, most especially, the belief that "God is One and Muhammad is His Prophet." This is sufficient information to give us an identifiable religion. However, a closer look at Islam entails an investigation of many variants of Sunni, Shia, and Sufi Islam, some of which imply that the others are not even truly Muslim.

In other words, Islam undoubtedly possesses criteria 2, 3, 4, and 5, as well as 1. It provides an overarching account of reality, a description of the human predicament and of the means by which it can be resolved, an explicit form of faith commitment, and instruction about human values and the meaning of right and wrong. However, in some very important ways, Islam may be said to have several of these, which is why Salafi Muslims (who are strictly orthodox Sunni Muslims) can be quite repressive and even violent toward other Muslims. By Salafi standards, some of the other Muslim traditions of thought are erroneous and, therefore, count as apostasy (abandonment of the faith, which is frowned upon in Islam). Then again, some forms of Sufism have never been acceptable to mainstream Sunnis of any stripe.

Consequently, we must not expect too much clarity about systems of thought, when we try to identify religions. Religions have soft boundaries and may have very fuzzy centres, also. This looseness of identity and definition is, indeed, part of the point of this book. Religions have unity, to be sure, but we must not confuse that unity with rigid structure and uniform thought. Instead, religions tend to be composed of relatively broad, interacting collections of people, all of which have some particular ways of thinking and acting, many of which are the result of specific syncretisms.

3 *Human Predicaments and Their Resolution*

Every explanation of how a person can live a good life is accompanied by some comment on what the basic problem of life is and how that problem can be resolved. A basic aspect of what is sometimes called "the human condition" is our sense that life could be better, deeper, richer, and/or more complete, somehow. Religions help us to think about the shortcomings in life and how they can be remedied. A religion will usually pinpoint a limited set of conditions and define these as undesirable, destructive, or evil. Precisely because it is intended to be a solution, a religion will posit a more or less clear and definite way of overcoming life's basic problem. Those accustomed to Christian language will recognize this as "the way of salvation," but other religions use different language.

Humans tend to have a deep-rooted dissatisfaction with life. As Augustine of Hippo, a significant Christian theologian of the fourth and fifth centuries, notes, "Our heart is restless"; of course, as a Christian, Augustine finishes his comment by suggesting that rest is found in God – as understood by Christians.[10] However, the challenge of heart-restlessness is not known only to Christians; desire for life to be better is commonly recognized as something universally felt. Augustine is not suggesting that this sort of restlessness is a bad thing. Instead, he sees it as an impulse that can lead us toward the right kind of rest, the right kind of life. Thus, Christianity regards human sinfulness, the failure to live in God's way combined with the determination to live in a way that seems good to human appetites, as the fundamental problem with the world; it creates a situation of alienation from God. This can be resolved by placing oneself in God's hands (various means of doing this are recommended by different Christians) and doing God's will.

Shinto suggests that a failure to live in right relationship with ancestors and kami, the powers that belong to different places and things, will have disruptive consequences in our lives. What we call "evil" is the result of a failure to honour those who have influence over our lives. This can be resolved by treating these beings and their locations properly, by caring for the places that the ancestors and kami occupy, worshipping them (in the sense discussed in chapter 1, where worship means recognizing and responding appropriately to the status of the other), and giving them gifts to make restitution for past disrespect and indicate that their authority is now being honoured.

Buddhism is based in a belief that we are caught in a cycle of endless repetition of birth and death (*samsara*) which is characterized by suffering. Samsara and the suffering that comes with it can be escaped by letting go of desire, because desire is what clouds our understanding and makes us unhappy with what is. Desire undermines joy and causes us to see the other, whatever that "other" might be, as a means to our own satisfaction while simultaneously making satisfaction impossible. Therefore, Buddhists engage in a variety of practices to release desire and attain *nirvana*.

Note that what I have said about these examples comes in the form of generalizations. As every person's religion is a syncretism, my descriptions of Christianity, Shinto, and Buddhism – loose though my accounts are – will not hold precisely for every believer in any of these religions. While what I have said is generally defensible, different people join religions for different reasons. A person might, for example, follow Shinto in order to fit in with social expectations, and for that believer Shinto solves the problem of social acceptability and advancement, regardless of what theologians may say.

Moreover, even the most universally held account of life's problem and the nature of its solution will change with historical and social context. Paul Tillich has helpfully described this process within Christianity: "While the norm for the early Greek church was the liberation of the finite man from death and error by the incarnation of immortal life and eternal truth, for the Roman church it was salvation from guilt and disruption by the actual and sacramental sacrifice of the God-man. For modern Protestantism it was the picture of the 'synoptic' Jesus, representing the personal and social ideal of human existence; and for recent Protestantism it has been the prophetic message of the Kingdom of God in the Old and New Testaments."[11]

While the problem that Christians – note that this is always some, not all, Christians – believe that Christ solves continually fits within the general category of human sinfulness and alienation from God, sin and alienation are redefined as they are experienced differently in different cultures. So, while it is true to say that Christianity has an account of life's problem and its solution, one might as easily argue that Christianity has several such accounts. The same is true in all religions of significant size and longevity. The earliest forms of Theravada Buddhism define both the problem (self-orientation, of which desire is the primary symptom) and the solution (renunciation of self and desire) in a rather different way from the Ch'an (Zen) tradition of Buddhism, where the problem is alienation within the self and the solution is to reunify the self. The "Pure Land" form of Mahayana Buddhism is different again, understanding the problem as exile from perfection and the solution as entrance into nirvana – the place of perfection where desire is unnecessary and all self-orientation falls away. A religion, therefore, may have – indeed, is likely to have – more than one account of life's problem and its solution. Most of these solutions, however and whenever they emerge, tend to live on in a tradition. Consequently, all of the options that we have seen in Christianity and Buddhism continue to exist as live options and may even be mixed and mingled or thoroughly integrated. Religions are complex, and this certainly applies to their notions of the problem(s) that humanity faces and the means of resolution.

We have seen only three examples of problem and solution, and these in only the loosest, most general, way. There are many more, and we will encounter some of them throughout this book. We need to remember that this is one place where religions genuinely differ; some people look at a range of behaviours that seem to be held in common among several religions and, therefore, assume that these religions are essentially the same. That conclusion may not follow because people may do the same things for very different reasons. The actions are, therefore, quite different because they are directed toward different ends. The sacrifice of a lamb in a temple is different from the slaughter of a lamb on a farm, even if the way in which the two deaths come about is largely similar.

Recognizing a religion's account of life's problem and its solution is tremendously important. Indeed, this might be the most immediately significant aspect of any religion, as it is lived out on a daily basis. Often only professionals, carefully tucked away in monasteries, temples, universities, and other such thought-oriented institutions, spend real time focusing upon the larger worldview that underlies any particular religion. However, the ordinary faithful build their lives' routines on their sense of what the world's problem is and how it can be resolved. This, commonly, is what people join religions for and what they commit themselves to. Later in this chapter, we will discuss consumerist capitalism as a religion. People commit themselves to this system because they believe that the fundamental problem of their lives is a lack of material wealth; these people dedicate themselves to obtaining the money necessary to increase their quantity of material possessions. These people are not necessarily trained to think about the nature of capitalism or its account of the nature and order of the world. Most consumers are simply convinced that the problems of their lives are a function of not having enough things, or not enough of the right things, so they get as much money as possible and go shopping.

Naming the problem is also quite significant as an impetus toward syncretism. In chapter 1, we saw something of the power of Buddhist-Shinto syncretism in Japan. When Shinto kami are treated as Buddhas and bodhisattvas, both religions have their accounts of life's problem and its solution changed. In traditional Japanese religion, the Emperor was understood as the descendant of Amaterasu, the sun-kami. Worship toward him continued, because the Shinto priority of order and respect was maintained. Society would founder if it failed to honour Amaterasu, in and through his human presence. Yet, the Emperor was also incorporated into Buddhism, and honour toward him became a means by which to reach nirvana (which was differently understood by different sects). Suffering, therefore, could be construed as a consequence of insufficiently respecting the Emperor, both because of his kami status and because of his role in enabling one to attain Buddhahood. In this way, a reorientation of both Shinto and Buddhist accounts of life's problem and its solution result in (and form) a syncretism. We shall see further examples of this process at work, especially in the encounters of Christianity and Buddhism with capitalism, where both capitalism and its partners find that their understandings of life's problem and solution shift.

4 Faith Commitment

In many eyes, the real distinction between religious and non-religious life has to do with religion's call for a faith commitment. We tend to speak of having a particular faith. Sometimes, we speak of having no faith at all. That is because we associate the notion of faith with assumptions about a transcendent God. Buddhism does not ordinarily make reference to an ultimate Creator God, and this can be one of the sticking points in the debate about whether it is a religion. However, the language of faith is usually spoken about in opposition to reason. The standard distinction posits religion as faith-based, while secular life is understood as relying solely upon scientifically affirmed evidence. This is not really a helpful distinction, partly because of confusion about what faith is, and partly because religion and science both work in ways that tend to create holes in the simplistic wall that we try to construct between them.

"Faith" is a fundamental life orientation. It is a decision about the direction of one's life which will order other decisions. The decision of faith is a kind of giving-oneself-away or giving-oneself-over-to. When I place faith in my wife, I am giving myself over to her, trusting her to act in loving wisdom. The same is true, only more so, when I say that I have faith in God, because my religion calls me to absolute trust and a belief that God is worthy of that trust. Faith, therefore, establishes bonds of commitment; we place our trust in people, organizations, or things, all the time. Part of the reason that our religions are complex syncretisms is because we live in complicated webs of faith commitments which place competing demands on us.

"Faith" means a life commitment which depends upon a sort of evidence that does not automatically follow the latest conclusions of academia, because the kind of faith decision that we are discussing is not, and cannot be, made solely on the strength of the daily, conflicting reports of evidence. Instead, faith is the orientation that underlies our reception of the evidence that the world provides. Faith is the life-direction that decides how we will understand and accept everything that we hear. Faith, therefore, is rooted in decisions that are made by the whole person. Involvement of the whole person is unavoidable; I may claim a faith that is at odds with my deepest hopes and fears, but what I do and say will undermine my claim – perhaps only at moments of particular stress, or maybe in my constant day-to-day, routine behaviour. I will make what we tend to call "Freudian slips," in which my real feelings and preoccupations are revealed.

Usually, therefore, at least some of the evidence which grounds our faith decisions will not be material or directly contingent upon the material world, so it cannot easily be tested by scientists. The physical sciences are specifically committed to repeatable experimentation on subjects that are (in principle) measurable. This helpfully limits their field of study and accounts for their tremendous successes. However, I do not know anybody who lives on scientific conclusions alone. Instead, everyone I know has some sort of faith commitment, even if it is nothing more than an unstated but firmly held belief that scientific progress drives technological developments, which, in turn, make life better. The assertion that a more technological life is a better life is firmly in the realm of unverified and unverifiable conclusions because it depends upon a whole set of judgements about what constitutes improvement. To the ancient Roman citizen, every modern person would look like a slave, forced to work unimaginable numbers of days and hours and unable to enjoy a proper social or intellectual life. In short, we all live on some kind of faith.

For a variety of reasons, people need something more than the physical sciences to live fully human lives. The greatest reason is simply that we know there is more to life than the material and measurable stuff of the world. Love, joy, and peace are real, as are hatred, fear, and anger – and none of these can be fully explained by physical stimuli or reactions. Last night, my family and I listened to a reading of "The Gift of the Magi," by O. Henry, in which a poor wife sells her beautiful, long hair to buy a watch chain for her husband, who turns out to have sold his watch to buy combs for her hair. In one sense, they now have two gifts, both of which are entirely useless. However, O. Henry's final words on the issue go like this: "And here I have lamely related to you the uneventful chronicle of two foolish children in a flat who most unwisely sacrificed for each other the greatest treasures of their house. But in a last word to the wise of these days let it be said that of all who give gifts these two were the wisest. Of all who give and receive gifts, such as they are wisest. Everywhere they are wisest. They are the magi."[12] From a practical and material perspective, O. Henry is quite wrong. The gifts have no concrete value to the recipients; if the material is all that is real, then they have no meaning. We know, however, that the author is correct. The gifts have a transcendent value, symbolizing the deep love between two people, which is greater than mere physicality. The non-material is not less real for being non-physical; measurability is not a necessary criterion for existence.

One consequence of the reality of the non-material is that the physical sciences cannot be fully understood on their terms alone; the love of rocks that drives a true geologist is rooted in something more than the simple usefulness of limestone. That particular love is actually a faith response to observed beauty and an assertion that there is an intelligible order to the beauty that has been discovered. That particular love can turn into an active use of the mind to understand only if it comes with a faith assertion that we can understand and do so helpfully. You may find our ability and inclination to do this to be obvious. Of course, we can understand things and make good decisions. There is plenty of counterevidence, however. Just think about the destruction that we have wrought on our earth with the aid of science and technology. I could easily argue that we really do not know much about our world and we misuse a large part of the tiny store of knowledge that we have. We cannot even figure out how to sustain our fisheries – and we have been fishing for thousands of years!

A faith commitment is not opposed to the employment of human intelligence; instead, faith is a necessary prior condition and co-condition for the use of reason. If we do not have both a love of something that drives us to understand it and a belief that we can understand that thing, along with – and this is most important – a trust that understanding that thing is worthwhile, then all of the might of our combined intelligence will still amount to nothing.

We have not yet plumbed the complexities of doing science, however. We need to realize that scientists do not deal in simple and clear facts in the way that people on the street appear to expect. Instead, scientists attempt to find the best explanations for the evidence that they possess. Scientists are like detectives, seeking the most plausible way of understanding the data that they have and continually trying to discover more relevant information. As with all branches of human knowledge, the physical sciences deal in probabilities and revisable conclusions. Even where the evidence is agreed upon, any three scientists can provide at least three possible explanations because there is usually more than one reasonable way of assembling the data.

This gets all the more complicated when we leave the laboratory and its controlled studies. Making use of scientific insights in the larger world is a very complex and uncertain activity, as any climate change scientist (or climate change sceptic) will tell you. The number of variables involved increases dramatically when we try to act on the things that we think we know from our computer models and small-scale experiments. The physical sciences are not a clear and straightforward repository of certainty. Instead, they are a means (though not the only means) by which we can come to a deeper understanding of ourselves and the universe in which we live.

On the other side of the conversation, religions are not ordinarily as unreasonable as some people think. Humans have always demanded evidence for the truth of religions. That is part of why syncretism happens and why people modify religions: people find that their religions no longer match the available data and, therefore, they make the necessary adaptations to their beliefs. For the same reason, some people change religions entirely, or very nearly, because eliminating all the evidence of a prior religion from one's life is an immensely difficult process. In other words, this whole book is about people using their heads in relation to religious questions. There are, undoubtedly, fanatics; they exist in every part of life: sports, religion, politics, physics, chemistry, economics, etc. However, the existence of hard-line believers in supply-side economics – people who will not hear any criticisms or questions directed at their pet theory – does not invalidate the whole field (or even the contributions of supply-side economists, as such).

Religion is similar to other areas of life. Undoubtedly, some people are irrational (sometimes violent) in their approach to religion; this is just as undeniable as the existence of irrational (sometimes violent) sports fanatics. Undeniably, also, people hold to religions for no better reason than simple inheritance ("this is what my parents believed"), or escape from responsibility for thought and decision. However, many people follow particular religions for reasons that make sense – and a more than simply utilitarian and self-centered kind of sense. If such people find errors in their religions, then they commonly leave their religions or modify them in ways that may or may not be obvious to outsiders. The evidence for this approach to religion is contained in thousands of years of complex thought and demonstrated in countless books.

This argument is quite personal for me. I grew up in a fundamentalist Christian context; the history of religious thought (Christian or otherwise) was largely closed to me. At university, I began to find that my original beliefs were untenable. However, I also discovered that Christianity possesses a rich heritage of discussion over the exact questions that exercised me: religion and politics, the nature and conditions of belief, and the possibility of divine involvement in the world. Facing the reality that my religion was not viable, I pursued studies that resulted in my retention of the label "Christian" but remarkably few of the original meanings that I had attached to that label. My religion changed.

I am not alone in making such a shift. Siddhartha Gautama left a life of status, comfort and wealth to pursue an answer that would satisfy his deep questions about the world and the right way to live. The result was the founding of Buddhism, with its commitment to the "Middle Way" – neither pure asceticism nor attachment to material belongings. Ancient Arabs deserted their tribal religions (and wars) for Islam; likely, very few did so in expectation of financial or other immediate benefit, since the Prophet Muhammad's message disrupted existing systems by which such reward might be accomplished. In turn, many Islamic scholars adopted Aristotelian thought as part of their intellectual equipment, because Aristotle helped them to answer questions that otherwise might have remained unsolvable. Citizens in the Roman Empire became Christians when Christianity was socially unacceptable and a bar to political or economic advancement (even dangerous, at times); by their own account, people like Augustine of Hippo did this precisely because the new religion offered more reasonable answers to questions about life, the universe, and everything than other available options had provided. Simultaneously, Christianity itself was changing as it incorporated insights from Greek and Roman thought (notably, but not only, Plato and various Neo-Platonists). We would need to define religion very narrowly indeed in order to see it as entirely irrational, if we accept the evidence of development that is at the centre of religious history.

The issue of rationality gets us to the heart of what some people regard as the distinction between religions and other systems of thought: religions are understood as depending upon a different kind of evidence – a divine revelation known intuitively – distinct from philosophies and scientific theories, with their emphasis upon rational inquiry. However, this is not really the truth about either religion or science. We have seen that religion is more complicated than this dichotomy suggests. Science is also more complicated, being neither a pure search for truth nor a simple process of straightforward, rational deduction.

We can easily overstate the difference between religious knowing and scientific knowing – which is a basic argument of postmodern theory. Scientists are not merely involved in an intellectual exercise driven solely by the need to understand. As a matter of fact, the claim of disinterested philosophical and scientific investigation is often a cover story concealing a variety of interests, motivations, priorities, and historical limitations.

Perhaps the most widely recognized evidence of this is the degree to which issues like profit-making can interfere with scientific activity, as in the realm of drug research. Here, blatant dishonesty sometimes affects results. Sergio Sismondo and Mathieu Doucet have noted a phenomenon that they call "ghost management," in which pharmaceutical companies operate behind the scenes, controlling the output of scientific research.[13] "Companies aim to maximize the number of publications from positive trials, minimize those from negative trials, and ensure that the results of the study are published promptly and in prominent journals."[14] The behaviours involved in ghost management are unsavoury, giving a misleading sense of the value and dangers of medicines.[15] Such activities remind us that the scientific process is not necessarily driven purely by the search for truth. Other motives, such as the need to make profits or obtain research grants can also intervene.

Precisely because of the level of concern displayed by academic journals, administrators and others in positions of authority, I doubt that the sort of outright dishonesty seen in ghost management is really prevalent in the scientific community. The community is taking steps to ensure that research is performed and presented in as open and upright a manner as can reasonably be expected, through mechanisms such as peer review, out of a real commitment to truth.

However, there are even deeper challenges to the notion of a kind of independent scientific objectivity that come from elsewhere. Sciences are culturally embedded. They function in ways that are conditioned by their historical contexts – including, as it happens, their religious contexts. Arguments about origins and evolution of the universe, earth, and humanity and about funding and use of various kinds of research (think of the controversy over stem cell research) are merely the most obvious.

The assumptions at the core of the scientific project, as such, and any scientific project in particular, are complex and often opaque. The result is that the sciences do not always know what they are over-looking. Feminists argue that the sciences have traditionally mishandled, in very important ways, issues related to women.[16] Women have been excluded from the sciences for a long time – and their ways of knowing have been rejected with them. Women have been inadequately studied, and, when they have been the object of study, often misunderstood. The medical diagnosis of hysteria, no longer regarded as a disease, may be the most famous example of scientific misunderstanding of women.

A decisive blow against the simplistic assumption of scientific rationality came with Thomas Kuhn's book, *The Structure of Scientific Revolutions*.[17] Kuhn coined the term "paradigm shift" to describe the changes in theoretical stance that the scientific community undergoes. According to Kuhn, scientists ordinarily function with a standard model of how things work, which Kuhn calls "normal science." As scientists work on filling out and proving that standard model, anomalies emerge and accumulate, eventually causing a crisis out of which a new normal science will develop. The interesting part is what happens in the crisis: while some scientists will be persuaded of the need to think and work differently, others will stick with the old model until they die. For a variety of reasons, some rational, some less so, a full paradigm shift depends upon the retirement or death of a generation of scientists. "Conversions will occur a few at a time until, after the last hold-outs have died, the whole profession will again be practicing under a single, but now a different, paradigm."[18]

Steven Johnson provides a beautifully detailed example of this process in *The Ghost Map*, an account of the work done by John Snow (a physician) and Henry Whitehead (an Anglican clergyman) in tracking down the means by which cholera is transmitted.[19] The commonly accepted paradigm was miasmatism: the belief that cholera travelled by air, in the dreadful smells that dominated parts of nineteenth-century cities, especially London, and notably Soho, the part of London where Snow and Whitehead lived. In 1854, a massive outbreak of cholera gripped Golden Square, in Soho. Snow and Whitehead, working independently as curious researchers and then together as members of a Vestry Committee, were able to prove conclusively – through careful, door-to-door, interviews and then by excavation of a cesspool – that the epidemic could be traced to a common water-source, the Broad Street pump. The Committee released its report, with decisive evidence for Snow's theory that cholera is waterborne. A few weeks later, the public Board of Health released its report, utterly dismissing that idea, while reaffirming miasmatism. It took more than a decade, and another cholera outbreak, for the waterborne theory to be generally accepted. The great champion of miasmatism, Edwin Chadwick, died in 1890 still firmly convinced that diseases were the result of bad air.

The ideal of a kind of independent reason, purified of all external connection, has proven to be misguided at best. As we have seen, it conceals both the love that drives the very best researchers and thinkers, and the profit motive that sustains both good and evil in today`s scientific world. Sometimes, it hides much worse things; the notion of a kind of pure reason can be deliberately dishonest – a tool to sustain the dominant position of men, or white people, or particular economic and political arrangements. Sometimes, it merely pretends to be a kind of pure and simple rationality which is not really evident in the lives of human beings.

Moreover, ostensibly non-religious investigations often proceed intuitively rather than by a process of clear, step-by-step, logical deduction. Commonly, inquiry is driven by hunches and imagination , the kind of "thinking around corners" or "thinking outside the box" that produces great breakthroughs. A hunch can lead to an insight, a kind of grasp of the structure or order of relationships in the subject under study, with the evidence filled in afterward. Scientists examine the evidence, then come to insights, then see how well they explain the evidence, then come to further insights, then see how well those explain the evidence, and so on, in an unending process. This is how normal science proceeds. More importantly, this is how new models, which become new paradigms, emerge.

John Snow's work began with the knowledge that miasmas couldn't reasonably be the explanation for the spread of disease: if they were responsible, then night-soil workers, people who removed human waste and lived in the smells constantly, would have died off quickly. Moreover, cholera travels in a puzzling pattern, skipping some people, including the old and weak or impoverished, such as the residents of St. James Workhouse, and killing others, some of them young and strong, such as workers at the nearby Eley Brothers factory. Why did workers at the Eley Brothers factory die, while those at the Lion Brothers Brewery (who drank beer provided on the job) went unscathed? Snow visited the epicentre of the disaster and realized that the Broad Street water-pump stood in roughly the middle, and perhaps could be the source of the problem. He pursued the idea, in spite of the fact that the water itself was clear, both to the naked eye and to the microscope. Moreover, it was known to be the best water in the area; people would travel substantial distances to get it. The latter fact provided a clue to how the mystery might be solved: if he could find people who used the water but lived outside the immediate area, then he could demonstrate that the cholera might be travelling with the water. Snow proceeded from an intuition about the solution to an idea about how his intuition might be tested. Where strict logic was generally understood to be on the other side, Snow found a different way to approach the problem.

Intuition is a natural and necessary part of scientific and philosophical inquiry, just as reason is not alien to religion – and both are perfectly capable of falling into error. What of the claim to divine revelation? The first difficulty with this criterion is that it does not apply to all of those things that we often treat as religions: Taoists tend to recognize immortal beings and revere ancestral spirits, but many Taoists do not claim that its central texts are divine revelations in the sense that we mean when we think of Allah giving visions to the Prophet Muhammad. Buddhists also honour sacred writings, but many do not regard them as divinely revealed; since Buddhism does not necessarily hinge on the existence of gods, this is only to be expected. Tribal religions tend to rely upon stories that have been passed down through the generations; the narratives are understood as a means to explain reality, including the spirit-world. However, the relationship with the spirits is not really a vertical relationship – as between the transcendent Christian God and lesser, mortal humans – but is a horizontal interaction that permeates daily existence. Thus, the stories do not have the same kind of metaphysical authority that we expect of a divine revelation: neither are they "true," nor are a neighbouring tribes' stories "false" in the cosmic sense. The tribe's stories are simply that – the tribe's stories, which represent the tribe's way of knowing the world. The assumption that every religion turns on a kind of universally applicable divine revelation is simply not true.

This is only a small peccadillo beside the second, larger challenge, which is that divine revelations cannot be treated as if they are intrinsically better than other forms of evidence; they simply cannot be treated as exalted and unquestionable. These sorts of texts (the Torah, Qur'an, Bible, Book of Mormon, and other such divinely inspired books) provide a specific kind of evidence that helps us to respond to the sorts of questions that religions ask, which, as we have seen, are not necessarily the same sorts of questions that hard sciences ask.

That some people treat religious texts as divine revelations does not free them from the usual academic expectations that they be studied, critiqued, and required to answer for their own limitations. This is true for a variety of reasons. Most obviously, there are many religions in the world, great and small, which lay claim to receiving or having received divine revelations, and they (both religions and revelations) don't always agree. Humanity has too many different "divine revelations" to be able – and I do mean able – to privilege one over the other without serious investigation. The assertion that mine is true because it is the one that my ancestors passed to me is not sufficient, or even defensible. My parents were no more profound or trustworthy than anyone else. Why should I take their word as the final truth about the most important questions, especially when I disagree with them about many lesser matters? Yes, tradition has value as evidence – people do the same things time after time because they believe that they are following a right, true, and valid course of action – but the mere fact of longevity hardly proves that a way of acting is correct. Humans are perfectly capable of repeating foolish mistakes many times. After all, we still go to war and gain nothing by it but more destruction.

Of course, the fact that I possess certain opinions is no better ground for accepting that those opinions are true. I have been wrong before, and undoubtedly will be again. Besides, anyone can tell the world that God has revealed truths to him or her. Did an angel from God dictate the Book of Mormon to Joseph Smith, or did he write it himself, possibly copying bits from elsewhere? Not having been there, we cannot say with absolute certainty; all that we can say is what seems to be reasonable and likely.

The most important reason that claims to divine revelation must be subjected to close and critical analysis, though, is that texts as encountered are always texts as understood. A text is only a text if someone reads it; its meaning emerges in the reading. Therefore, the way that we understand the text is decisive. The Bible, as such, is merely black marks on paper – and even this assertion depends upon the ability to recognize "black," "marks," "on," and "paper," and all of these recognitions require significant feats of intellectual effort. We don't automatically know even these most basic things; they are part of our training, the introductory bits of our educations. Therefore, we need to learn to understand the Bible, from these starting points and through the most complex feats of relating terms to one another and to larger concepts. But our educations are not simple, neutral, and beyond debate. The Bible becomes important because people understand it in particular ways, and those ways may be more or less true to the intention of the text, and more or less true to the nature of things. That is why feminist readings of the Bible (for example) have come into being: the text has been used as an instrument of power against women, and women are now pointing out that this is sometimes a misrepresentation of the biblical message; liberating possibilities can be found if the text is differently – better – understood.[20] Claiming that the text is a divine revelation and should not be subjected to such indignities as critical assessment is merely an effort to put one's own understanding beyond criticism, a way for one person to say "my education is perfect because it's mine." That's not debate. It's just escape.

By itself, the claim to divine revelation is meaningless, except as a statement of personal or communal attachment ("we find the Word of God in this text"); its only use in the general conversation about religion is as a final defence, when all others have failed. When my arguments in favour of my views have proven to be weak, I can always say: "But my views come from God and yours do not. Therefore, mine are correct." This does not move the discussion forward in any way; it is merely a rhetorical tactic for shutting down investigation. This tactic relies on force to resolve conflict ("you don't want to go against the power of God, do you?"), instead of doing the hard work of being intellectually convincing. It is, in short, a way of saying that one is a fanatic, not especially different from any other sort of fanatic. The real question must be the truth (or not) of my arguments, rather than the power wielded by the putative source of the words.

Revelations, therefore, must be subject to the same kind of critical analysis that any other theories or collections of data (of the same kind) must face. We must bring to them the same tools of investigation that we would use in relation to any similar information that does not claim divine origin. The process must move forward in love, of course, and with both respect and humility, in the knowledge that our tools may be inadequate, our motives false, and our theoretical principles incommensurate with our goals. Love, respect, and humility are, however, just as necessary to the study of particle physics as they are to the study of religion.

In short, the claim to possession of a divine revelation is often a red herring, an attempt to conceal that religions belong to the same class of systems of thought as other worldviews. Similarly, scientific and philosophical ways of knowing are not intrinsically greater than, or even vastly different from, religious ways of knowing. The claim to disinterested rational inquiry disguises both the intuitive character of these sorts of reasoning and the degree to which they are driven by all of the same kinds of forces that may drive religious investigation. The only real difference might be, but is not necessarily, in subject material.

5 Values

When a religion assembles an understanding of the cosmos and its purpose, together with a statement about the nature of human predicaments and their solution(s), and calls for a faith commitment, then that religion will inevitably define values for its adherents. This is why people who believe that they have no religion and are proud of it fear explicitly religious people: religions prescribe values, and values lead to actions.

The word "values" really means nothing more than "things that are regarded as important." My values are the things that matter to me. My hierarchy of values identifies the order of importance that I ascribe to the things that I regard as important. However, many of my values are not created by me. I learn them from other people. For example, I value good literature (or even bad literature, which I call "brain candy" and like to relax with, sometimes), for reasons other than personal enjoyment. I have been taught to appreciate literature and to find worth in what it accomplishes; I think that it has real value for me and society. This value is neither inevitable nor beyond debate. Many people find no value at all in books , while others believe that much of what I like is simply evil.

Like literary appreciation, other values are taught. Many values are passed on by people who have given them no particular thought. Formal religions, on the other hand, tend to put substantial effort into thinking about the ethical implications of their understandings of the world. Having a sense of what the world is all about encourages us to believe that some things are more valuable than other things, and that some ways of acting are superior to other ways of acting. So, religions tend to encourage, even demand, that their adherents hold particular values and make decisions about the way they behave on the basis of those values. Religions teach values and patterns of behaviour.

Religions differ in their emphases. One could argue that Shinto has less of a formal account of the world and call for faith commitment than some other religions, and that it focuses more specifically upon people's actions (including specific ritual actions) and the way that they affect the world. Respect toward creation and the community, including one's ancestors, is at the centre of the Shinto way of life. In contrast, one could argue that Protestant Christianity, rooted in Martin Luther's emphasis upon faith before works, has more of an overarching account of the cosmos and less of a focus upon action. One of the challenges faced by the Western world is its Protestant heritage that comes with a more limited set of theoretical tools for determining ethics than are available in the Catholic, Buddhist, Confucian, and some other traditions. Note that this is a difference of emphasis, of degree, rather than a great distinction between kinds. Shinto does say something about the meaning of life, focusing upon harmony and order, while Protestantism does have a history of ethical reflection and of mandating moral priorities.

One of the reasons that political leaders try to suppress or dominate religions, or create their own, is precisely that religions define values. Voters may also vote on the basis of religion, for the same reason. China has been rather brutal in its treatment of Falun Gong, a Buddhist/Taoist/Confucian syncretistic religion, because of fears that its priorities of truth, kindness, and forbearance would collide with the Chinese government's strategies.[21] The Dalai Lama and Tibetan Buddhists have encountered similarly heavy-handed treatment because they are understood to have commitments that differ from those espoused by the Chinese Communist Party.

It should be noted that this sort of political / religious tension is not solely a product of authoritarian regimes. In the 1960 US presidential election, John F. Kennedy had to assert his commitment to the separation of church and state and his independence from Catholic Church authority: "Whatever issue may come before me as president – on birth control, divorce, censorship, gambling, or any other subject – I will make my decision in accordance with these views, in accordance with what my conscience tells me to be the national interest, and without regard to outside religious pressures or dictates. And no power or threat of punishment could cause me to decide otherwise."[22] Kennedy said these things because people – especially Protestants, before whom he made this famous speech – assumed that Catholicism would dictate Kennedy's values and, therefore, the country's fate.

As is evident in the Kennedy example, most people have a basic expectation that a religion will define the values of its adherents and make an effort to ensure that they are followed, even if only by employing a strategy of gentle encouragement. Not only is this a basic aspect of a religion, but it is generally assumed to be so; if a person claims to be Jewish but does not behave in any of the ways expected of a Jew, then people begin to question that person's commitment to Judaism. Of course, the reason that someone can claim to be part of Judaism and behave rather differently from the assumed norm is very likely to be that person's syncretism, which varies from other Jewish syncretisms. Something of the sort happens to a Muslim woman, Ranya Idliby, in *The Faith Club*, which will be discussed later in this book. Having a variant syncretism can be a challenge, as it is for Idliby; it means that one will have values different from those commonly expected of people bearing one's label. However, this merely re-emphasizes the point that a religion defines values for its adherents. The point applies equally to an ultra-Orthodox Jew in Jerusalem and a Reform Jew in New York, a Wahhabi Muslim in Mecca and a Sufi Muslim in Indonesia. Our religions set our values.

ANYTHING CAN BE A RELIGION

Where does this leave us in relation to Buddhism? Buddhism has temples, sacred writings, ritual ceremonies, and monastic communities. In other words, it has forms of organization. More importantly, Buddhism provides a general explanation of reality, focused upon the superiority of spiritual and psychological being over material limitations; it also defines the values of its practitioners, with an emphasis upon transcending the desires of the ego in order to be free to care for others. Buddhism explains life in exactly these terms, so that its purpose becomes clear: the aim is to escape samsara, the control of the birth/death/rebirth cycle, so that one can stand against the pain that desire imposes and be free to show compassion. I think that Buddhism counts as a religion.

I know. All of this is probably important to scholars, but the average person could not care less. I am sure that is true, except that we have now reached the tricky bit: anything can be a religion, including such surprising candidates as capitalism (and its popular sect, consumerism), Communism, fascism, imperialism, nationalism, liberalism– anything that provides lives with meaning and defines ultimate values. If it is my account of the meaning of life and my way of reflecting upon large questions, then it is my religion – whatever it might be. If the same is true for a group of people who support one another in belief and develop the five characteristics that we have talked about, then we have a religion in the fully fledged sense. This is true even if I do not regard my value system as my religion – a common arrangement in the world of modernity, where people are firmly committed to denying the presence of religious beliefs in their lives.

Of course, I may not altogether understand the account of life by which I live; in fact, I'm fairly sure that I do not, in spite of all the efforts I give to investigating myself and my world. I make too many complicated decisions, influenced by too many factors, to say with straightforward honesty that I fully understand the creeds by which I live. Moreover, my religion probably is not always the one that I espouse publically, whether as a consequence of active and intentional hypocrisy (which happens more often than I care to admit), or as a result of decisions that I make without fully realizing their religious implications. Precisely because syncretism is ubiquitous we do not always realize when we have switched fundamental orientations. The truth remains: whatever defines our values, directs our understanding of the world, and causes us to worship, is our religion.

This is probably a bit different from the way that you usually think about religion. You might well agree with a more traditional approach to thinking about religion, such as that found in a standard textbook. The authors recognize that religion has to do with "explanations of the ultimate meaning of life, and how to live accordingly," but also insist that religion must be based on a notion of the transcendent – by which they seem to mean God or the gods. For the authors, all other viewpoints are subsumed under the label "ideology," though they may bear all of the same characteristics as religions.[23]

As I have noted above, this puts Buddhism into an awkward spot. Either it cannot be regarded as a religion because of a definitional problem, or the meaning of transcendent must be opened up. We can broaden the category that we label "transcendent" so that it refers to any force, set of laws, or given requirements that are understood to be universal and to provide direction for people's lives. That way, we can easily include Buddhism, but then we must also include other accounts of life which people use to explain, order, and direct existence. Buddhism is a category-bender that helps us to realize the weakness in common assumptions, because if Buddhism is a religion, then so are a number of other systems that we do not always call "religions." Any set of criteria broad enough to include Buddhism will also include Marxism, for example. Marxism provides an account of the meaning of life and the nature of good action (communal and individual), along with scriptures, creeds, and institutions. Indeed, one might argue that Marxism is more precisely religious than Buddhism, because Marx (following Ludwig Feuerbach) was prepared to be clear and explicit about God – regarding God as merely a human projection and a means of sustaining class-based oppression – while the Buddha and many of his followers have largely abstained from defining ultimate reality, preferring to emphasize the ethical and psychological more than the metaphysical. That is part of the reason that John E. Smith opts to call Marxism (along with humanism and nationalism) a "quasi-religion"; it has the core elements of religion, though its atheism has caused this to be overlooked.[24]

There is another problem with the effort to limit the label "religion" to movements that specifically talk about "God" or "gods": we often treat forces as transcendent even when they are not apparently defined that way. We can function as if the natural were really supernatural. In capitalism, the "invisible hand" of the market is often treated that way; it is regarded as part of the natural order and an object of deference, even worship. In Marxist circles, "history" possesses a similar status: it is the final arbiter and judge of all human action and the justification for many forms of behaviour that would otherwise seem irrational. We will examine the role of history in the context of Marxism-Leninism, and its place in the theology of "scientific materialism," later in this book. In liberalism, "freedom from limitations" can attain such a mystical and supernatural status that Americans would rather have a street full of dangerous, concealed firearms than reasonable limits on gun possession.

This process is called "supernaturalization"; it is the activity of transferring a force or object from the natural sphere into the supernatural sphere, whether this is done intentionally or not. This means asserting that something has powers greater, and often more mysterious, than it naturally possesses. Supernaturalization can include naming that force or object as something sacred. The word "sacred" carries echoes of a kind of set-apartness that is attached to a deep sense of mystery; academics use the word "numinous" to describe this feeling. The greatest practical implication of treating something as sacred is that it takes on the character of a determinative first principle. The sacred becomes a standard by which the truth of all assertions is measured. Supernaturalization transfers something from nature into the supernatural sphere, granting it powers that it would not otherwise have, and giving it greater moral significance than it would usually have. Another way of talking about this, popular with Karl Marx and Marxist thinkers, is the term "fetishization," which Marx used to describe the function of capital in capitalist systems; fetishization means essentially the same thing as supernaturalization.

The significance of supernaturalization for this discussion is that it plays an important role in our ability to identify religions made up of more limited principles or parts of life. From a sociological perspective, apparently non-religious viewpoints can take on all aspects of a religion, however religion is defined. From a theological perspective, the refusal to recognize the process of supernaturalization is an important failure. In the eyes of many religions, supernaturalization leads to idolatry, the worship of that which is not divine.

None of the challenges that we have encountered so far is the greatest reason to part ways with the definitions of religion that we see in standard textbooks. Syncretism is. The distinction between religion and ideology, or any two other, similar labels encourages us to miss something fundamental: the complex and syncretistic nature of human religious outlooks. As I write, the Prime Minister of Canada, Stephen Harper, is an avowed Protestant Christian. Yet, I know a great many Protestant Christians who disagree with him about most matters of any significance, including what it means to be a Protestant Christian. For purposes of scholarship, the distinctions between Protestant and Catholic, or Christian and Hindu, are both helpful and important. They cannot be lost. However, in concrete daily existence – life as it is lived – people's religions are complicated mixtures. Thus, Harper declares an allegiance to a kind of synthesis of Christianity with individualist liberalism and free-market capitalism. That is his religion, defining his ultimate values, including his relationship with God, his notion of the human situation, and his understanding of salvation. We cannot separate Harper's Christianity from this mixture, as if it were merely about what he does on Sunday or believes about death; the result would be a grave distortion. All aspects of his theology have something to say about the nature and purpose of the whole universal order; Harper and others with his religious inclinations have welded them into a particular syncretism which is, itself, in an ongoing process of development spurred partly by further syncretistic shifts.

We cannot dismiss the religious character of movements like liberalism simply because of their self-proclaimed "secular" nature. This is really a cover story, designed to hide the implications of the larger system – and I say this as one who has quite a sizeable dollop of liberalism in my outlook. All serious political philosophers have been aware of the religious nature of their work; that is why Socrates was willing to accept death as a penalty for atheism (a failure to respect the gods of the city), as well as for corrupting the young (by teaching them things that did not accord with the public religion). The decisive moments in Plato's *Republic* – most notably the cave metaphor, which calls the reader to contemplation of the ideal (which Plato regards as the really real) – cannot be seen as anything but religious. Likewise, John Locke, founder of modern political liberalism, was also quite explicitly a theologian.[25] He knew that liberalism as a political system depended upon liberalism as an account of the whole, a statement about ultimate value and the meaning of life. Francis Fukuyama has taken this so deeply to heart that he has proclaimed the victory of liberalism to be the end – the fulfilment – of history, declaring that the fall of communism in Eastern Europe has completed the story of human aspiration for the world.[26] Fukuyama is using explicitly religious language; technically this is called "eschatology" – speech about the last things, the completion of human life and purpose. It is, in fact, Smith's primary criterion of religious thought: there must be some sort of assertion about human completion or deliverance for a system to count as religious in nature.[27] This is an instance of supernaturalization. Liberalism is a religion; those who espouse it and claim not to be religious are merely fooling themselves, often by maintaining a shallow understanding of both liberalism and the state of their own souls. When liberalism gets mixed with other religions such as Christianity, syncretism is occurring.

AN EXAMPLE: CONSUMERIST RELIGION

Suddenly, he had seen it all, revealed in the broad rays of the future. Shopping was indeed our new religion. Consumer choice, in a post-industrial society, was our area of free-will, informed perhaps by grace. He would participate in the new faith, as priest, as confessor. He would set up his stall in the Temple.

God, how right he had been, how horribly, uncannily right. Nathan the prophet. Even he would not have predicted the degree to which shopping as a full-time pursuit would have caught on in the last fifteen years. The supermarket and shopping-centre as fun-fair, family outing, parkland, playground, stately home, temple, youth club, and people's refuge: the shopping arcade as the forum of assignation, rape, abduction, murder, riot. Oh fountains, oh palaces, oh dreams and aspirations.[28]

Margaret Drabble

On a slightly different note, let's think about consumerism a bit, both as an example of a religion and as a powerfully syncretistic force. Consumerism has all of the characteristics of a religion. Moreover, it tends to be at the heart of most forms of religion in the contemporary West; even people who claim another label often function as consumerists.

Consumerism is a very popular form of capitalism in today's Western world; it is often the religion of people who claim to have no religion at all. On Sunday morning, these people are clear about not going to church. Instead, they get up and go to brunch. Then they go to the mall, the big-box stores, or the fancy clothing boutiques. Their shopping is an act of worship in the temples of consumerism; we do not notice that these are temples because they are everywhere and seem ordinary. Step back, though, and think about the Mall of America, the West Edmonton Mall, or the new mega-malls in Southeast Asia. Better yet, think about the role of Wal-Mart in North American psyches – especially as it seeks to become upscale and "aspirational," as they say in the marketing business. These are not just places where people get what they need to survive; no, these are temples where people go to spend time with the great god, "stuff," and to find out what they want.

Behind these visible structures, consumerism has highly complex forms of organization. From efforts to identify potential demand (demand is usually generated, rather than recognized), through systems of production, distribution, and sales, the entire corporate world is oriented toward feeding consumers. Indeed, government today is largely taken up with the concerns of wealth generation and distribution, and most of the tools that governments have at their disposal are oriented toward ensuring stable and continuous production and consumption. The Western commitment to the form of society that Weber so aptly named "legal-rational" means that the consumerist world is built around tightly structured bureaucratic systems in which law serves as the main ordering tool and the ground on which battles over the limits of producer and consumer behaviour are commonly fought.

Consumerism, as a kind of capitalism, even has its seminaries: business schools serve this purpose admirably, with courses on how to organize businesses, create demand, and extend the values of the marketplace into all spheres of life. Marketing specialists serve as highly trained and well-supported missionaries; Nathan, the character who proclaims himself "priest" in the quotation at the head of this section, is in advertising. Movies, books, magazines, websites, and catalogues all function as attractive scriptures, the instruments of the marketing missionaries, proclaiming salvation through accumulation.

In the consumerist world, life is understood in the context of acquisition; it is always about that next goal (house/car/RV/boat/ clothing item, etc.). This is the overarching, consumerist account of the meaning of life. The media and Internet bring the consumerist church into homes, complete with sermons and opportunities to make an offering. Numerous magazines serve the religion, giving advice on purchases and whetting the appetites of the faithful. All of life is determined by societal and individual acquisition, and the aspirations that lead to it.

Consumerism defines the value of all things, accounting for them in terms of their sale and purchase possibilities and the social standing that they will provide. It places a dollar (pound, euro, yen, etc.) value on everything, including escape from the problems of life. That is the fundamental purpose of advertising: it declares that any troubles people have or limitations they face can be removed by the simple expedient of purchasing the right stuff; it conveys a clear sense of the human challenge and how it can be resolved. As though to put an exclamation mark on this point, an email message has arrived in my inbox as I write this section. The email's subject line says, "How saving money could buy you happiness," and the message comes courtesy of the bank which holds the mortgage on my house. Apparently, happiness is what comes when we use our money in a way that serves the interests of our banks. The bank is encouraging me to save by offering me the chance to earn a higher interest rate with a different kind of account; I can then use the saved money to purchase something bigger and better. Meanwhile, the bank uses my money to acquire stocks or some other financial instruments that will increase bank profits. The result, apparently, is happiness all around.

The role of consumerism in defining values is evident at the individual level, of course, but it also applies to whole societies. The leaders of the Western world proclaimed the "Let's get out there and shop" gospel after the 11 September 2001 attack on the World Trade Center. Rudolph Giuliani declared that New York needs "the best shoppers in the world" to get out, spend money, and save the city.[29] "There's a way that everybody can help us, New Yorkers and everybody all over the country. Come here and spend money, just spend a little money ... New York is back up and going again ... so please come. We need your money. And we would like to take it from you."[30] The message is that shopping will save your soul and the soul of the world. This is the consumerist account of life and its meaning.

The success of consumerism depends upon a faith commitment, a fundamental commitment to acquisition as a way of life. For the system to survive, people must do at least two things: (1) believe in the system, and (2) act as if the system is the truth about the world. If people, en masse, were to cease believing in consumerism, then they would buy only what they need. The desire to accumulate more and better things would die as people turned their ambitions in other directions. Clothes, houses, and cars would simply be clothes, houses, and cars, rather than being visible symbols of status and self-worth. Thus, a car which simply fulfils the necessary tasks would be deemed sufficient; the brand name would become irrelevant, as would many of the included gadgets and comforts. Such a shift in belief in the system would permit people who have long disliked consumerism to be free from the need to participate. As the world currently runs, the only way to show disdain for consumerism is to purchase items designed and marketed for people who dislike the system; this is one of the ironies that attends any religious system that fully dominates a society. If people were to stop believing in consumerism, the whole arrangement would fall to the ground quite rapidly. Production would drop, which would create unemployment, which would trim purchasing power, which would exacerbate the decline in demand, which would cause further drops in production, and the cycle of decline for the consumerist world would take over. In the process, innovation would disappear from the production/consumption system because change in this form of economics depends upon the possibility of material reward for the development of new products which can be marketed to people who did not know that they had any need or desire for new things. Society would either have to return to consumerism by encouraging people to start buying stuff, or would need to find a different way to organize itself.

Consumerist capitalism, therefore, sets values and propagates them so that the system can operate. It has highly sophisticated forms of organization which permeate any society built on the Western model. Consumerism specifies the goal of human existence – accumulation

– and the means by which it may be reached, as well as the nature of fundamental human predicaments – scarcity and insecurity – and the way to escape them. Consumerism also has an all-embracing account of reality: the assertion that the material is what really matters and the natural order exists to serve as a resource for human consumption. At the root of consumerism is a faith commitment, a belief that acquisition will make life better, without which the whole system collapses.

Consumerism is a thoroughly syncretistic religion; it will sit happily alongside any religion which can serve or be turned to its purposes. There are even Christians who proclaim something called "the prosperity gospel," which argues that God wants everyone to be rich, with the associated idea that those who do not have enough (like many Zimbabweans, for example) simply do not have adequate faith. This is, of course, fundamentally different from the proclamation of Jesus of Nazareth, who told the rich man to sell all that he had and give to the poor, but it works nicely with consumerist religion – a successful syncretism from the consumerist perspective, though perhaps less so from the standpoint of Christianity. In addition, every religion – whatever its name and whatever its proclaimed meaning – if it wants to be successful, must submit to the wishes of the consumer. Thus, every religion needs its sales and marketing professionals; every religion must enter into a syncretism with consumerism.

Many people will deny that consumerism is religious. This is partly because they want to deny that they have a religion or, alternatively, insist that they have a religion and consumerism is not it. However, one of the main reasons that we deny the religious import of consumerism is that we simply regard it as the way things are and have always been. That, however, is not an accurate account of history. There have been cultures in which material goods were thought about differently, precisely because those cultures had different values. For example, Indigenous cultures of the Pacific Northwest in North America have traditionally held potlatches, large social events at which the hosts would dispense their personal goods as gifts to people in attendance. Historically, social standing in the community was partly dependent on the ability to host and to give away; those who could part with large quantities of valuables were esteemed. The role of goods here is the direct opposite of what we see in consumerist religion; possessions have social value insofar as they can be given away, rather than accumulated.

Indigenous societies are not alone in this attitude. In some medieval cultures, the accumulation of wealth of any kind had relatively low priority. If one had material resources, one commonly gave them away in order to establish alliances, thereby obtaining power and social standing; or one endowed various church activities, improving one's position in the eyes of God and the community; or one simply went on pilgrimage, which was simultaneously holy and fun. Though money was, undeniably, an important asset, it was not the only or even the greatest determinant of social standing; plus, the combination of ever-present theology and the lack of banking systems made accumulation difficult. The medieval approach had a sort of holdover effect in Britain, where people would use money to buy honour rather than material goods, until quite recent days. In the sixteenth century, money could buy social position, including a highly desirable, official family crest or coat of arms. Even in the nineteenth century, one purchased an officer's commission in the army and spent considerable sums keeping up one's social position as an officer thereafter. One might, of course, have seen some sort of profit on the sale of the commission when one wished to retire, but one might not – so the point of the whole activity was certainly honour rather than material gain.

Consumerism is indeed a religious sect (a kind of capitalism) and a dispensable one. The world need not run like this; if we were to choose otherwise, we could find a variety of alternative ways to structure our world. We are, however, sufficiently committed to it that any effort to remedy its limitations – including the syncretistic introduction of government regulation of safety and quality – must be sold as a benefit to the consumerist system.

Notably, we do not ask that religion be removed from the public square when government sees itself as the handmaid of consumerism; for many people, the real task of government is to support the economy. This sort of religion does not need to be kept separate from daily life. Consumerism serves its parent religion, capitalism, and anything that serves capitalism helps to keep our insecurities at bay. After all, very few of us really want to starve or freeze. In contemporary Western society, one is hard-pressed to distinguish politics from economics, and both are intensely religious.

Public consumerism can do us harm; the priority of accumulation can have undesirable, immediate, and long-term consequences. Governments participated in stoking the housing market by making the purchase of bigger, unaffordable houses possible and were, therefore, instrumental in creating the housing bubble that exploded in 2007–08. This crash has put a dent in what people can afford, but I have noticed that it has not changed their religion at all; even the calls for governments to regulate markets more stringently proved to be quite temporary. Public consumerism is also a prime catalyst in our mistreatment of our physical environment; we are becoming aware of these implications, but we do not really cut back significantly on what we buy and throw in the dumpster (or on the plastic packaging that all these things come in). People still want more money so that they can buy more, because "the person who dies with the most toys wins," as the popular slogan goes. Life really does have a purpose, after all.

Religion, then, is what defines our purpose in life, giving us a sense of meaning and a belief that we understand what life is about and where it is going. That is the fundamental characteristic of religion. It is also the reason that religion is ever-present; we cannot get rid of our reasons for being. We may claim to be non-religious in the sense that we do not believe in the Christian God or undertake Shinto veneration of the ancestors, but that never really means that we do not believe in anything at all. Equally, we may be non-religious in the sense that we ignore the deeper questions. How many consumerists really investigate capitalist economics, the deeper theology of their religion? How many really want a deep knowledge of the market system that is so decisive for everyone who lives in capitalist systems? Regardless of our lack of interest in such investigations, our ignorance of the deeper meanings of consumerist religion does not prevent us from believing in it and participating in its rites.

Should we try to live without religion? I hope I have demonstrated that this cannot be done; it is impossible. We all have some sort of religion whether we admit it or not. Yes, but should we try? Would the world be a better place if we give up any sense of meaning and purpose, and simply live in the moment, so to speak? I rather suspect that cows get away with it, more or less; I am not convinced that their preoccupation with food, shelter, and the other basics of life reflects a religious choice, since it seems to be instinctive and largely invariant. The point of this example is that the truly unreligious human is exactly like that cow, having only the most limited sense of purpose and history. Dispensing with religion may seem superficially attractive; living in the moment, without the human doom of knowing history (including the fact that we will all die), has a certain appeal. However, we have the awful knowledge and cannot let it go, if only because we know the consequences of any attempt. The human world is a constructed world; we build it and direct it. We have power over all that we encounter. If we are not sensitive to the uses of that power, or if we try to abrogate it, then disaster will inevitably ensue. Being non-religious means having no compass, and no ability to make any decisions. Life becomes pointless and we lose any reason to live, but have no more justification for dying. Indeed, this is worse than the lot of any cow, because cattle certainly display a desire to live.

We are religious beings. That is an unavoidable fact. Moreover, it is a good thing. Our capacity to change the world means that we must try to understand it; we need to know the truth about our world. We must also make decisions about the best actions to take, and those are not always clearly, obviously, and inarguably identified by the information that we have. We need larger accounts of the meaning of life, the purposes that we serve, and those we ought to serve. We need religions.

I do not mean that we need to be either simple-minded or closed-minded; indeed, the need for religions is rooted in precisely the opposite assertion. Religions are valuable only insofar as they participate in the larger human conversation. We need the influence of wisdom that comes from other people and other heritages. Religions need to have what I call "soft boundaries."

3

Soft Boundaries

It is all very well for historians of religion to think, speak, and write about Islam, Hinduism, and Sikhism, but they rarely pause to consider if such clear-cut categories actually found expression in the consciousness, actions, and cultural performances of the human actors they describe.[1]

Harjot Oberoi

THE PROBLEM OF EDGES

Where do religions begin and end? This is not just an academic question. It haunts every faithful believer. It is part of why the US presidential election in 2008 included a fierce debate over whether Barack Obama is really a Christian or a secret Muslim and whether he is a capitalist or a socialist in disguise. When we are attached to a particular religion, we genuinely care about whether we are being faithful or changing tracks, perhaps unawares. We are always engaged in debates about traditions and the degree to which they change or may be changed. The who's in/who's out question is often framed in precisely these terms: Are you a genuine follower of my religion? Do you share my attitude to the traditions of my religion?

This conversation about traditions arises because religions do not usually have hard edges. Certainly, every religion has its black-and-white thinkers who see only the purity of their own approach and the impurity of every other way of bearing what they regard as "their" label. As we have seen, though, the traditions to which they hold so strictly are themselves usually products of an interaction with other thought systems in other times. Even the firmest boundaries have had moments of softness. The most insightful thinkers tend to be aware of this; they are open to wisdom from other people, contexts, and, indeed, other religions. Plus, of course, there are always people who are not especially determined to be purists about the thought systems to which they give their allegiance. This happens for a variety of reasons, including curiosity, social context, marriage, or business. Sometimes, just plain laziness does it; purity can seem like a lot of unnecessary effort. In the chapter on development, we will discuss what might be the most profound reason for soft boundaries: the need to answer questions for which inherited traditions have no solid answer. One way or another, religions tend to influence each other.

The all-encompassing nature of religion is one reason for the existence of soft boundaries. Thanks to John Locke, we tend to distinguish between political matters and religious matters when we discuss the public sphere. In *A Letter Concerning Toleration*, Locke argues that religion is concerned only with "the public worship of God and, by means thereof, the acquisition of eternal life" (for Locke, this means life after death).[2] Contemporary Westerners often assume that this is a normal, indeed natural, way of thinking about religion. As we have seen, however, it does not reflect the understanding held by most of the world. Instead, it reflects two things particular to Locke's context: (1) a stormy seventeenth century in England, full of strife and political instability, much of which was connected to differences over Christianity; and (2) a particular way of thinking about Greek society and the rise of philosophy that allowed for a distinction between the mythical/religious, on the one hand, and the philosophical/natural, on the other.

The difficulties of the seventeenth century were the proximate cause of Locke's stance, but the more decisive factor for Western thought is certainly the way that we understand the Greeks. We tend to accept that myths function as "noble lies"; they order and direct the masses of people who are incapable of ascending out of the cave of dark ignorance to gaze on the blinding sun of truth. We believe that the means of ascent is the human mind, working without the aid of inherited wisdom or divine assistance and without the influence of emotion or any other power that might cloud our judgement. This is the Enlightenment reading of Plato's cave metaphor (from Plato's

Republic) and it sticks with us today. Because of it, we glorify the purportedly "objective" knowledge – by which we mean machine-measured and mathematically expressed knowledge – of the hard sciences over and against the merely "ideological" positions of religion.

I have already suggested that this is both a misunderstanding of science and a false portrayal of religion. It is a fiction that survives only as long as populations are largely homogeneous, living off a mixture of Christian heritage and Enlightenment values while denying doing anything of the sort. This works while it remains the consensus. It fails when challenged, because its deepest foundation is a lie. My intention here is not to criticize. Instead, I am reminding us of the starkness of the distinction that is part of Western mental furniture precisely because everyone else has traditionally thought quite differently. Western mindsets are causing shifts elsewhere, but we cannot travel the world of syncretism assuming that everyone is making the Western European and American distinction between natural knowledge and religious knowledge.

Indeed, that distinction is irrelevant to Indian thinking, which may be part of the reason that India has always been a centre of syncretism. Hindus (still most of the population of India) do not have a word for "religion." Instead, all of life is religious. Their priority is to follow right teaching, which depends upon following good teachers. Religion is fluid and ill-defined, partly because it must suit all circumstances. A belief-system is more easily kept pure in a compartmentalized life; if religion can be left behind when one enters the political arena or the laboratory, then it need not be modified to fit the concrete situations of life.

SIKHISM AND THE BOUNDARY PRINCIPLES

The openness that characterizes much, though not all, of Indian religion results in soft boundaries; indeed, the boundaries are so soft that scholars are forced to invent harder boundaries in order to study and describe the religions that they claim to find – which is the point of the quotation from Harjot Oberoi with which this chapter began. Oberoi points out that Western thinkers tend to define Hinduism as the religion of the Vedas, a set of sacred writings. However, much that is central to the various ways of being Hindu (such as the pantheon, forms of worship, and temple cult) does not come from the Vedas, and the reasoning behind such activities is likewise not particularly traceable to that text. Moreover, treating the Vedas as books is potentially misleading; the texts that compose the Vedas existed for many centuries in oral form before being written down.[3] Hinduism – insofar as there is such a thing – cannot be so simply and easily defined. It is not a "Religion of the Book," like Judaism, Christianity, or Islam – and even they are not adequately described by this kind of essentialist definition.

Instead, Indian religion must be described in multiple forms, as a variety of syncretisms – and even the whole mass of syncretistic labels cannot adequately explain the bewildering complexity of Indian life. There are many Hindu/Buddhist syntheses; mixtures of tribal religion with Hinduism, Islam (Sunni and Sufi), Buddhism, and/or Christianity, and also an intriguing group of Syrian Christians who carry elements of their Jewish heritage along with Hindu influences.[4] Jainism is also mixed in, fitting into various syncretistic relationships.

Sikhism follows the general principle. Indeed, its origins are essentially syncretistic: Guru Nanak, founder of Sikhism, drew heavily upon the Sant tradition of Northern India, which was itself a mixture of Indian religious viewpoints. The Sants drew upon Vaisnava (Vishnu-worshipping Hinduism), Nath (tantric yoga, which would be heretical Buddhism if one could be a Buddhist heretic), and Sufism (mystical Islam, often condemned by orthodox Sunni Muslims), though the Sufi influence may have been limited.[5] The heart of Sikh beliefs comes from the Sant tradition: there is one transcendent God, the Creator, who may be known through meditation on His Name, His creation, and through human experience within His creation. The one who follows this path can rise to complete unity with God, escaping human limitations, including the cycle of death and rebirth.[6] Adopting and adapting the Sant tradition, Guru Nanak created a very Indian sort of religion – one that is notably different from the surrounding religions, but is rooted in syncretism.

Syncretism has been an important part of Sikh reality for most of its existence, partly because of Sikhism's close geographical relationship with the variety of religious traditions that we label "Hindu." Sikhism may have come into existence with Nanak, but its character has changed decisively with further developments. One of these was the compilation of the Adi Granth (in 1603–04), a text which became central to the life of Sikhs. The fifth Guru, Guru Arjan, assembled the first edition; further material was added by the tenth Guru, Guru Gobind Singh. The Adi Granth is a thoroughly syncretistic text: along with material composed by self-identified Sikhs, it contains song-verses by a number of traditional, medieval writers who did not regard themselves as Sikhs and who were under the influence of various forms of Hinduism, Buddhism, and Islam.[7] In other words, at the heart of Sikhism is a text which clearly and unashamedly draws upon many other traditions of Indian religion. Moreover, this syncretistic text is now decisive for Sikh religion; in 1708, the tenth Guru, Gobind Singh, declared that there would be no more human Gurus and the Adi Granth (now called the Guru Granth Sahib) would serve to guide the faithful.

The consequence of this history is that the boundaries of Sikhism are soft and unclear. We might easily begin by asking: "Is Sikhism really Santism?" After all, Guru Nanak appears to have relied heavily upon an existing tradition in his religious formulation. Equally, we might ask, "Is Sikhism really a unified form of various Indian religious traditions?" If so, then Sikhism is probably something more than that, because it now has its own history of development. It may have started out as Santism and grown by incorporating other traditions, but in this process, it has become a religion.

Progress, in religion as in anything else, depends upon the possibility of reformulation at any time. The principle of progress, then, seems to give licence to the Guru Nanaks of the world. The principle of progress states, "Religion is always developing and must develop in response to new circumstances and new questions." Progress is the product of a genuine effort to understand the world in new, more accurate ways, and to find courses of action more appropriate to the challenges that life presents. The principle of progress is an assertion that every religion includes people who are making this kind of effort, who are prepared to challenge existing points of view, structures, and ways of acting, in order to accomplish some kind of improvement. This is an essentially democratic principle because significant change may come about as the consequence of small changes made by ordinary participants in a religion, or change may be the result of obviously substantial modifications from the top.

Anyone is free to redesign an existing tradition, thereby starting something new which may take on its own life. This is a part of the task of growing up, not only in highly mobile, liberal, Western cultures, but also in more conservative and traditional cultures. Indeed, part of the challenge of life, for both individuals and communities, is the task of continually reformulating our understandings of the world. Standing still is neither possible nor desirable. Stasis is not possible because tomorrow will not be the same as today. Stasis is not desirable because the valuable insights of the past will be lost if they are not continually recovered and rethought in the face of contemporary challenges.

Thus, Guru Nanak brought about something new when he drew together strands of existing religions. He posed Islamic/Santic monotheism as the answer to the question of freedom from the cycle of death and rebirth, which had dominated the Indian religious conversation. Guru Nanak was seeking religious progress. One consequence of this creation of a new thing was the establishment of difference; immediately, there came to be something that was not Sant, nor Muslim, nor Hindu. Moreover, in the act of rejecting both Islam and Hinduism on the grounds that both were in error, Guru Nanak created apparently hard boundaries immediately. "Although Guru Nanak's message was ecumenical in spirit and clearly influenced by the context of Hinduism and Islam, his followers viewed his insights as revealed by God in a wholly original manner."[8] Today, the community (*Panth*) of his followers lays claim to firm boundaries of orthodoxy. A religion that comes into being because of syncretism will not necessarily accept syncretism as an ongoing principle, even though syncretism will continue to happen. Can a tradition rooted in another tradition, rooted in a syncretism of several traditions, fairly insist upon control of its own boundaries?

A challenge arises because there is another principle involved: the principle of preservation of insights. We want to keep what we already know. If an insight is correct, then it is not necessarily refined by being diluted. Moreover, we do not want to lose sight of it. Therefore, the principle of preservation of insights states that, "We must always seek to retain the valuable wisdom of the past and present if we are to face the challenges of the future." The possibility of genuine progress, in the sense of moving forward rather than simply moving, depends upon our ability to sustain existing insights. If they are lost, then we will go backwards rather than forwards because we must continually return to an earlier starting place. Any mathematics teacher will remind us of the need to remember the basic operations of arithmetic if we wish to do truly advanced mathematics. An addition error will produce a wrong answer even in the solution to a highly complex and advanced calculus problem. As we shall see in our further discussion of helpful and unhelpful syncretisms, deciding what should be retained is a problem, and the answer is not always obvious.

Some people are clear that they have all of the essential correct answers; these people tend to wield the principle of preservation of insights as a shield against the principle of progress. They deny the necessity for syncretism, for further change. As a Greek Orthodox Christian believer said when questioned about ecumenism (Christian inter-church relationships), "We have preserved the True Faith, so of course we are not going to start compromising it with Churches that have deviated from it. We don't want to lose our treasure of the Truth."[9] Most people feel this way about something, and that something tends to be religious in exactly the sense that I have defined religion: the overarching account of reality that defines our core values and commitments and around which our lives are built. Whatever that is and no matter how ill-defined it is, we do not want to part with it. We want to retain what we regard as the great insight that gives meaning to our existence.

The principle of preservation of insights raises an awkward challenge, because it is the rational one of the two principles that causes us to create (what appear to us to be) hard boundaries. We erect walls, usually figurative ones, but sometimes perfectly literal ones, to defend the truths that we have found. Rules, organizational structures, membership commitments, holy texts, training institutions, customs, and an almost endless list of other things can be used for this sort of defence. Such attempts at creating boundaries can contribute to a kind of sclerosis, a religious hardening of the arteries. However, the validity of their purpose must be recognized; we must understand that a commitment to truth generally leads to the creation of structures that can maintain and sustain that truth, keeping it alive and enabling it to have a transformative effect in the world.

Unfortunately, there is another principle that causes us to attempt the creation of hard boundaries, and it is not so laudable. The second principle is fear of the other, and it is the irrational counterpart of the preservation of insights. The attempt to maintain and live out an insight tends to foster an often irrational sense that the other (person, organization, cosmic power, etc.) is out to undermine us and our great insight. Consequently, the two principles are routinely, often inextricably, mixed. In an effort to hold on to what we have found to be true and helpful, we are prepared to fight off all change and anyone who proposes it. The mixture is a complicated one. Rational principles, such as the need to preserve received wisdom, can be explained and justified in discussion. Irrational principles, such as fear of the other, cannot be justified except emotionally, though they can be recognized and understood. Consequently, we find ourselves in awkward tangles, with our intellectual commitments so involved with our gut fears that we can only take refuge in what we have always thought, what we have always done.

The challenge, then, is to find a means that will enable us to retain the wisdom of the past while helping us to be clear about a way into the future. The principle of preservation of insights is important to us, and rightly so. When we find what seems to be an important and correct answer, we do not want to see it slip away. Nor do we want others to misunderstand the answer because it is conveyed by someone who has only a limited or confused understanding of the issues involved. We are aware that half-right answers are wrong answers, and may be more dangerous for being half-correct. Besides, we cannot make decisions today based on conclusions that may be reached tomorrow. We need touchstones that provide us with some degree of reassurance, a sense that the past will not be lost, if we are to accept changes in our ways of thinking and acting.

One tool that we think will accomplish this is the creation of sacred texts; these tend to look encouragingly static – if carefully handled, they seem not to change – and individual. The Qur'an is not the Bible. Texts appear to give permanence to insights while clarifying the borders of identities. That is exactly the assumption that we see in Kraemer's work and in fundamentalist Christianity. However, we have also seen that appearances can be misleading; the look of permanence and individuality given by a written text is always illusory.

So it is in the case of Sikh scripture. The appearance of an authoritative text for Sikhs, which might seem to resolve questions of individuality and the preservation of insights – we can now define Sikhism as a religion of the Book, and therefore distinct both from Santism and from other Indian religions – seems only to make the boundaries question more complex. When the defining text is heavily syncretistic, as is the Adi Granth, the religion appears to suggest that syncretism is a basic characteristic of that religion's identity. The text may be seen to open doors as much as it closes them, precisely because the text becomes an exercise in mutual self-definition. Sikhism, by including writings from Muslims, Buddhists, and Hindus in its foundational text, is saying that it regards those traditions (at the very least) as sources of wisdom. Consequently, Sikhism cannot easily retain an identity separate from the conversations that occur in those contexts.

In contrast, the existence of a written, sacred text can reinforce the authority of the principle of preservation of insights. A sacred text locates the basic insight(s) of a religion in time and space, contributing to the formalization and refinement of religious identity. The text can, therefore, become a tool for the creation of hard boundaries; the appearance of permanence and individuality can be used to reinforce the kind of clarity that fear prefers. However, the existence of a sacred text is not necessarily sufficient by itself to cause such boundaries to emerge. Casting the Vedas into written form has not made Hinduism into a closely defined, clearly bounded religious tradition.

So it is that when Sikh efforts to declare hard boundaries emerged, those efforts depended upon two entities: (1) the Guru Granth Sahib, as the intellectual core of the tradition; and (2) the *Khalsa* (the word is rooted in the Persian/Arabic for "pure"), an order of especially disciplined Sikhs, established by Guru Gobind Singh at the end of the seventeenth century as a formal institution to defend and maintain the Sikh religion.[10] The Khalsa can usually be identified by ceremonial regalia, including the *kirpan* (ceremonial dagger), and by their uncut/unshaven hair. Significant efforts have been made to declare Khalsa Sikhs as the real Sikhs, and all others as faithful insofar as they approximate Khalsas, resulting in substantial controversy. Nevertheless, not all Sikhs are Khalsas, and Sikh boundaries have remained soft. This is partly a function of geography. As we have seen (and the development of Sikhism shows), the Indian home of Sikhism is not congenial to rigid distinctions.

Steven Ramey identifies significant examples of Sikhism in syncretisms in Sindh, an Indian province neighbouring largely Sikh Punjab. Ramey notes that "a disciple of a Muslim Sufi advised a community of Hindus in Lucknow, India, to install the Guru Granth Sahib in their community center."[11] The Hindus followed the advice, installing the text under a canopy, just as it would be in a Sikh *gurdwara* (temple). They put up a picture of Guru Nanak and named the room "Harmandir," after a famous Sikh temple, the Golden Temple in Amritsar. This room became central to their religious and cultural practices, and a reminder of Sindh, the home from which they had been driven by the partition of India that created Pakistan.[12]

The effort to create hard boundaries tends to challenge the products of soft boundaries, however. In this example, the room called "Harmandir" had its name changed to Hari Om Mandir in the 1980s. The Bhagavad Gita was added, as were images of various Sindhi spiritual teachers, including Sufi Sant Rochal Das (also defined as a Hindu). These changes clearly dilute the Sikh nature of the shrine. Why would that happen? The answer is that Rajiv Gandhi, Prime Minister of India, promised to pass the All India Gurdwara legislation which would place all public gurdwaras – the word means "Gateway to the Guru," which is the Adi Granth, and designates a place of Sikh worship and instruction – under the control of a group of Punjabi Sikhs, the Shiromani Gurdwara Prabandhak Committee. Out of fear that their room might be regarded as a gurdwara and placed under the Committee's control, the Lucknow group changed the nature of the shrine. As it happened, the legislation did not pass in Parliament and the Lucknow shrine might have avoided official gurdwara status, anyway.[13]

The whole episode raises many questions about boundaries. We are forced to ask whether people who are officially Sikh, and in some sense guardians of the tradition, should be allowed to control the uses to which the tradition is put and to define who constitutes a Sikh. Who owns the tradition and what does ownership mean? How far does the principle of the preservation of insights extend? Should purity of Sikh understanding, as sustained by guardians of the tradition, take priority over efforts to incorporate Sikhism into other syncretisms? The mere fact that a defining aspect of the tradition is that it is syncretistic (like all other traditions) tends to undermine its claims to control. If Guru Nanak had the freedom to create a new religion out of an existing syncretism, and the tradition has accepted a thoroughly syncretistic text as its touchstone of authority, then the claims of any group to establish definite criteria of identity are compromised by the nature of the religion itself.

This is a fundamental criticism. It raises the decisive question: Can there be any kind of authority in religion? Westerners hasten to say that there cannot; the conscience cannot be compelled. Yet, we take this position because we have accepted Locke's distinctions, which are basically faulty. We can reject communal authority in religion because religion is assumed to be separate from matters of public policy. Religion is understood as being solely a matter of individual concern, having to do with otherworldly matters. That is not really true, even in the most determinedly "secular" state. We therefore find ourselves routinely abridging religious freedom and compelling consciences in order to serve what we believe to be the public good. More pertinently, religion is clearly not separate from public policy in India, where control of gurdwaras is a matter for Parliament and where partition was precisely intended to create two distinctly religious nations and to separate the largely Muslim portion of India (now Pakistan) from the remaining, largely Hindu portion (still India).

If the people of Lucknow are carefully attending to the words of Guru Nanak, might they count as Sikhs, even if they are partly in and partly out of the Sikh community? Are the people who have created this syncretism really Sikh, or Hindu, or something else entirely? Who gets to decide? These questions go to the root of our sense of community, because they tend to help us define our communities and erect walls around them. We want hard boundaries, and we justify them with the principle of truth. However, every time we learn something from a source regarded as outside the community, we undermine the very act of labelling. The principle of progress meshes with the principle of preservation of insights, and there is growth in understanding. The boundaries turn out to be soft and permeable, and a new syncretism comes into being.

Chandu Ram was a Hindu guru in Sindh until 1977, when he left for Lucknow. There, he created the Shiv Shanti Ashram, which intentionally melds a kind of Hinduism (Ram's particular tradition) with the Sikh tradition. Devotional activities are focused alternately on Chandu Ram and on the Guru Granth Sahib. Nonetheless, there have been shifts in the religious order at the ashram. Originally, the Guru Granth Sahib was flanked by the Bhagavad Gita and Ramcharitmanas (a Hindu text) under a central canopy, but the latter were replaced by translations of the Guru Granth Sahib in 2001. Even though the Hindu texts remained accessible in a separate cabinet, the Guru Granth Sahib became the decisive text, indicating the centrality of Sikhism in the ashram. However, an important balancing factor, which shows the power of Hinduism in this context, remains: when the Guru Granth Sahib is read, Ram interrupts to ensure correct understanding of the text, indicating his respect for the text and its integrity. Nonetheless, Ram's ability to interrupt indicates his own priority over the text; his is the authoritative voice through which the text speaks.[14] Also, "an Om in raised brass adorn[s] the top of each section of the central canopy, emphasizing the Hindu identification directly above each copy of the Guru Granth Sahib."[15]

In the Shiv Shanti Ashram, we see layer upon layer of complicated syncretism. The boundaries are so soft as to be nearly nonexistent. We cannot identify a point at which Hinduism stops and Sikhism begins. The Hari Om Mandir arrangement is similar, with the added complication of a Sufi presence. These places are about religious worship. However, they are also seen as a means of attaining truth. Indian religious devotion assumes that the life of worship is integral to the journey toward understanding. The underlying premise, evident to the Indian mind, is that truth is discovered best in community, and communities are not rigidly defined and labelled. Rather than giving priority to identity, Indian people have tended to focus upon religious goals and the means by which they may best be attained. Labels are a complicating factor in a fluid religious world, but labels do not prevent the emergence of new syncretistic structures, whether institutional ones or structures of thought. Soft boundaries are a fundamental reality of this religious situation, and so, Sikhism emerges as a syncretism and continues as a component in various syncretistic arrangements, even as efforts are made to delineate fixed boundaries around a defined Sikh religion.

JUDAISM AND SOFT BOUNDARIES

In a sense, we have chosen the easy route to demonstrate soft boundaries by turning to an Indian example – even one as particular as Sikhism – because a lack of definite limits and membership tests is one of the fundamental characteristics of most Indian religions, at least historically. Nonetheless, the challenge of soft boundaries and the appropriateness of outside influences produce lively debate in circles that have traditionally been less amenable to syncretism. We will now examine this challenge in Judaism, one of the most firmly and clearly bounded of religions and a religion that may be moving in a trajectory precisely opposite to that followed by Sikhism.

Judaism is profoundly defined by its focus on the Hebrew people as chosen by God, and by its tradition of ethics associated with life in covenant with God. Also, Judaism has never been especially oriented toward proselytization. Membership tends to be defined by birth and by rituals that begin early in life; these engage the whole family and the larger Jewish community. Far from focusing upon bringing new people in, Jewish communities tend to be rather difficult to penetrate; being Jewish without Jewish relatives is a partial experience at best. Plus, of course, there is the challenge of language; you do not need to know Hebrew to be Jewish, but some familiarity certainly helps. These are internal forces that tend to create a sense of set-apartness, of unique identity. The non-Jewish world (especially Christians, but also Nazis and others) has reinforced these impulses with repeated efforts at persecution, including book-burning, deprivation of goods, and even mass slaughter. Thus, non-Jews have tended to insist upon clear and defined boundaries between Jews and themselves, and have enforced those distinctions with threats and violence. A consequence of all these elements is that Judaism is arguably the most distinct and bounded religion in existence. "Today Jews are virtually the only group that possesses a religion, a culture, and a sense of kinship specifically its own, distinct from that of other peoples."[16]

Yet, even the boundaries of Judaism are soft, in surprising ways. Even in this bastion of the principle of preservation of insights, the principle of progress creates intriguing syncretisms. One of the most fascinating examples is the mutual influence between Islam and Judaism (and, to a lesser degree, Christianity) from the eighth to the tenth centuries, that Steven Wasserstrom identifies.[17] Various sects of both Islam and Judaism had an impact on each other's theologies, and, at times, gave rise to shared prophetic figures. Wasserstrom even argues for the sustained existence of religious groups that explicitly participated in both traditions.[18] While animosity certainly played a part in the symbiosis between these religions, a remarkable degree of intentional borrowing seems to have occurred. Some of today's greatest enemies have a history of common development.

Jewish syncretism is not solely a historical phenomenon, buried in the distant and largely forgotten past. Soft boundaries in Judaism exist today, as we see in the distinction between Orthodox and Reform Jews, perhaps especially in North America, where that distinction is routine, but also in European Judaism, where the differences arose. Orthodox Judaism holds to some very carefully defined rules, a number of which make the Jewish identity publically evident. An Orthodox Jew is usually identifiable in a crowd. This is especially true of the *haredim*, who are particularly strict in their attention to past interpretations of the Torah (the written law believed to be given to Moses by God, sometimes combined with bodies of interpretation), as well as the written and oral traditions that Judaism inherits. For these people, careful attention to the rules is an important part of their commitment to the central principles of the faith. As A.J. Jacobs demonstrates in *The Year of Living Biblically*,[19] this is not mere empty legalism; even a distinctly secular person can undergo real transformation by making an effort to follow the Torah in a strict and determined fashion.

To the Orthodox and the haredim, Judaism consists of uncompromising efforts to follow the tradition as it is handed down. In their eyes, it has not changed, in any significant way, and it must not. At the heart of Orthodox Judaism is "the fundamentally conscientious and meticulously exact fulfillment of precepts as handed down in the written and oral law according to Rabbinic interpretation."[20] This is divinely given law, the means by which God's people live their side of the ancient covenant. Any development in the Torah is merely a matter of explication: new questions give rise to expansion of ancient principles, as they serve new purposes. The Orthodox and haredim do not see themselves as anything but really and truly Jewish; they regard themselves as a distinct people whose faithfulness to the covenant marks them out from other people.[21]

This is a strong interpretation of the principle of preservation of insights. If, indeed, the Torah provides the way that Jewish people can sustain a right relationship with God, then there can be no real justification for change. Any change must be for the worse, because it will dilute the original insight and cause decline in the covenant relationship. This stance denies that there is a principle of progress.

There are questions about how successful Orthodox Judaism has been in sustaining this approach. Even in nineteenth-century Germany, there was not merely variation in Orthodox forms of conduct, but also increasing breadth of variation, making Orthodoxy during its defining period difficult to characterize with precision.[22] Also in that time, some Orthodox Jews distinguished specifically religious innovations, on the one hand, and technical innovations, on the other. The latter were to be embraced, while the former were shunned.[23] That is reasonable enough, if one is prepared to accept that technological change has no religious significance. However, people as widely divergent as nineteenth-century Polish Orthodox Jews, various Mennonites, and today's theorists of technology reject such an innocent notion. The spirit of faithfulness may remain, but a computer culture simply does not allow for the same kind of religion as a premodern peasant culture or even a book-oriented, literate culture like that of nineteenth-century Germany. This point is important, but pales in significance when compared to the fact that the long and complicated history of Judaism has involved plenty of change, some of it fundamental. Jewish history displays numerous examples of the principle of progress winning – if only because of the vicissitudes of life which have rarely allowed extended periods of peace and stability. Thus, Efraim Schmueli, for example, distinguishes seven different Jewish cultural periods with quite notable differences among them.[24] The principle of progress is at work in Judaism.

Partly because of the discovery of history – the recognition that all things develop over time – some Jews believe that a significant degree of flexibility is part of following the spirit of their religion. Those who take this explicit position are in the Reform camp of Judaism, which now constitutes at least half of North American Jews. As a Reform rabbi, Edward Klein says, "Reform Judaism ... looks back to the beginnings of our faith for its inspiration. It finds that throughout the history of Judaism there has been adaptation to changed conditions."[25]

Klein goes on to list many different developments and viewpoints within the Jewish heritage, including the roles of Pharisees, Saducees, Rabbis, and Essenes. Most significant for our argument, though, is his mention of the Maimonists, who drew their inspiration from the writings of Moses Maimonides, who was influenced by the Arab Muslim reception of Aristotle; of Philo, who melded Judaism with Platonism; and of Nachman Krochmal, who brought Hegel's philosophy to bear on the Jewish tradition.

Klein recognizes that his religion changes under these influences. "When the needs change, when the times change, then the ritual, the ceremony, must be adapted to changed conditions."[26] Klein points especially to changes in worship that happened when Reform Judaism came into being precisely to make these sorts of modifications to Jewish liturgy in nineteenth-century Germany. Reform Jews modified some prayers and started using prayers in German, and they introduced a new service. While striving to preserve the basic insights of Jewish religion and thereby respecting the principle of preservation of insights, the original Reformers committed themselves to the principle of progress. The growth of Reform Judaism has been extraordinary. What began as a small German movement is now a large and powerful version of Judaism especially significant among the substantial Jewish community of North America.

This is, by most standards, a highly successful exercise in syncretism. It certainly demonstrates the softness of Jewish boundaries. Today, many Jews look no different from their non-Jewish neighbours. They may sustain central insights of the Jewish religion, but much that other Jews have regarded as necessary has been ruled optional and largely vanished. Examples include wearing the *kippah* (skullcap) and the *tefillin* (small, black boxes containing verses from the Torah), though use of the kippah during prayers may be increasing. Judaism has navigated the problem of authority that we have seen among Sikhs by creating different communities of rabbis to make necessary decisions. In an important sense, there is not one Jewish community, but at least two (Orthodox and Reform), arguably three (add Conservative to the list), and possibly more (depending upon how one names the various strands, such as Hasidic Judaism which also has its own variants, born of the importance of particular Rebbes to their own followers). While the outside boundaries of Judaism may be firmer than those of Sikhism, Judaism has various kinds and degrees of soft boundaries, and different groups of rabbis to mediate syncretistic developments. This is a common approach in major religions; it has parallels with the various forms of Islam, Christianity, and Buddhism.

The complexity, though, is in the true meaning of the principle of preservation of insights. We will discuss this at greater length in the chapter entitled "What is it now?" However, the problem bears mentioning because a Conservative rabbi, William Berkowitz, challenges Klein's argument. To Berkowitz, Reform Judaism's ability to distinguish between essentials (which Klein calls "eternally valid"[27]) and matters that can change without affecting the heart of Judaism is open to question: "But tell me, Rabbi Klein, did Reform Judaism not aim mostly at esthetic regeneration rather than doctrinal readjustment? Did Reform Judaism not lose all of its vision and thus create the great weakness that marked the Reform movement, limiting Judaism to universal teachings and ethical precepts? Did it not give up the Law and advance the argument that it sought to preserve the essence of Judaism?"[28] Berkowitz is suggesting that the truly valuable insight of Judaism is the recognition of the Torah as God's gift to God's people; at the heart of Judaism is fidelity to the Law. Klein, of course, rejects the charge that Reform Judaism has dispensed with what really matters about Judaism. He insists that Reform Judaism merely seeks to carry forward and live Judaism in a new time – which is precisely the aim of Conservative Judaism, though Conservatives place a greater emphasis upon the traditions of the Torah. To Klein's eye, the core of Judaism, its beliefs about God and life, have not merely survived but thrived in the Reform context. We have come to the crux of the debate: Does the Reform syncretism betray Judaism?

We cannot mediate the debate. It depends upon a detailed and abstruse knowledge of Judaism which I do not possess and is well beyond the boundaries of this book. The question is important, though, because it raises the issue of whether there can be a successful syncretism. Is every syncretism really the creation of something so new that the valuable old is inevitably lost? Can there be a good syncretism? Why might it happen and what might it look like? Our next chapter will examine some cases in which syncretism appears to be a good thing.

4

When Syncretism Is a Good Thing

Syncretism is a good thing when it results in an improvement to one's existing religion. How is that for stating the obvious in a wholly unhelpful way? Progress is, by definition, change for the better. The problem with such a simple statement has to do with two questions: (1) Who makes the judgement about what constitutes an improvement? and (2) According to what criteria does that judgement get made? The answer to the first question is, I am pleased to say, quite easy: ultimately, you do. In the final analysis, you make the decisions about how to understand and live your life, subject, of course, to the myriad limitations and conditions that life places upon you. Historically, the same principle has applied; people have always made their own judgements about the best things to think and do.

We all know, however, that the situation is not quite as simple as I have made it sound. Systems have an impact on us. They give us options, ascribing rewards for welcome choices and punishments when we make unacceptable or unpopular choices; they educate and form us; and they do much to determine the value of the things that we do. In other words, they affect every part of our lives, so that we are socially conditioned creatures. Our religions, therefore, are always a product of decisions made by the societies in which we live. I am a Christian partly because my parents were Christians, which is true, in turn, partly because Christianity is an available option in Canada.

Nonetheless, the basic point remains; people make up systems and are able to modify and replace them to a surprising degree. Some-

times the shift comes through the application of violence. Forced conversion is an undesirable but significant part of much religious history. It is one of the major reasons, though certainly not the only reason,
for the transformation of much of Eastern Europe into a communist
empire; most of the countries had been officially Christian and, while
some welcomed the ascendancy of communism, many resisted either
passively or actively. Violence is not the only reason that people
change religions, however. The most radical proponents of capitalism
are often in former communist countries and have not necessarily
been forced into their new beliefs. Georgia touts itself as one of the
most open and unregulated capitalist countries in the world, when
something more amenable to Russia's state-directed system might be
more comfortable. People change and systems change, and not only
by violence.

Syncretism tends to be less dramatic than these examples of overwhelming shifts in systems; it commonly occurs more quietly. Indeed,
often we barely notice it happening, which is why many people are
not aware of it at all. How, then, can we address our second question?
How can we speak of criteria for judgement about whether a syncretistic shift represents an improvement of an existing religious
belief? Some will say that we cannot and that this is the problem with
discussing religions in the first place: we have no way of judging which
is better and which is worse.

As you may have noticed, I reject the assertion that we cannot make
any judgements about religious truth claims. I think that we can ask
and answer questions about whether any particular religious statement is more consistent than a statement made by another religion
with the data that we have. This is the first criterion of what constitutes an improvement: the new answer must appear to be more accurate, more consistent with the information that we have about all reality. Moreover, I think that we can ask and answer questions about
whether any particular religious activity is likely to be helpful in relation to our vocations and other aspects of our lives. This is the second
criterion for an improvement: the new answer must be genuinely
helpful in the world in which we live. Note that this is not necessarily the same thing as being convenient – which is how pragmatic
thinkers tend to handle the question. The Muslim call to unity is no
more convenient than the Jewish call to live according to the Law, or

the Buddhist call to release self-oriented desire, or the Christian call to self-sacrificial offering, or the liberal call to submit to majority rule while caring for the rights of minorities – all of which can end up looking remarkably similar, or at least prove to have much in common, when fleshed out and lived attentively. The point is not to make life easier but to make it better; this is the ethical dimension of any change.

There is a third criterion for any improvement that makes it a syncretistic improvement rather than some other kind: it sustains and even expands upon some important part of the religion as previously held; insights must be preserved in syncretistic progress. This criterion of syncretism is necessary, but can be astonishingly difficult to recognize in practice. The problem has to do with identifying the significant aspects of a religion, because people will differ about what these are. No religion has an essential character that remains unchanged through history. All religions develop, even in their most precious characteristics.

Jacques Derrida, vividly aware of this challenge in relation to systems of thought and action, speaks of inheriting a spirit of Marxism (one of many such spirits); intriguingly, he also inherits a kind of messianic expectation, a belief in a future deliverance from oppression, out of the Jewish tradition.[1] Derrida may be correct in his assertion that a spirit of a religion is most precisely what we inherit and what we most need to retain or even rediscover. However, every religion has beliefs and activities that its adherents value deeply. If some of these are (or even one of these is) maintained in the new formulation, then the result is most definitely a syncretism.

The point here is that syncretism comes in many different forms and degrees. If I give up whatever I regard as central to Christianity and adopt Islam, for example, I will almost inevitably live in a syncretistic fashion. Even the most determined effort to root out Christianity from my life and the life of my family is doomed; my life and world are too deeply bound up with Christian ideas, symbols, and ways of being. On a larger scale, this is one, though not the only, reason why centuries of determined Christianity has failed to root out significant aspects of pre-Christian religious traditions in Western society. As we have seen, these traditions appear even in Christmas and Easter celebrations, which are at the heart of Christianity. Simi-

larly, centuries of determined liberal capitalist secularism have failed
to eliminate important elements of Christianity which still haunt central institutions of liberal society such as law, government, and education. The reality is that any religious change will be syncretistic in this
way. Even if I or my society tries to convert, the resultant actions will
be syncretistic. The inevitability of this kind of syncretism is important and must not be forgotten.

Nonetheless, intention is also significant. If I am intentionally trying
to be Islamic, then I am not attempting to improve my Christianity by
syncretistic methods; instead, I am converting, which is a different
kind of change. Though the result will be a kind of syncretism, I will
not be aiming to meld Islam and Christianity; my purpose will be to
eliminate Christian elements from my life and replace them with
Islamic elements. Thus, we can distinguish unintentional syncretism,
in which people retain traditional beliefs without trying to do so, from
intentional syncretism, in which people are explicitly working to create a new, syncretistic religion. Either can be helpful; a syncretism is
not necessarily destructive simply because it happens accidentally. However, in this as in many other matters, real benefits can be derived from
knowing that different traditions are being woven together. The deliberate effort to eliminate traditional religion from the lives of North
American Indigenous peoples has resulted in a very real effort to
destroy all of the wisdom that was carried by those traditions. The survival of elements from Indigenous religion in various unintentional
syncretisms cannot be said to compensate for the tremendous losses
incurred as a result of the effort at radically and completely converting
these people. Consequently, the focus of this book's discussion of syncretism as beneficial (current chapter), destructive (chapter 5), or unfortunately avoided (chapter 6) will be upon intentional syncretism,
the deliberate effort to unite or prevent the unification of multiple religious traditions.

The easiest way to discover whether important characteristics of the
religions involved survived the syncretistic process may be to ask
whether goals present in both are still being served. If two religions
have complementary goals, then they can be woven together in a helpful way, and the value of the syncretism can be tested. I suspect that
this describes the basic dynamic behind the whole process. People in
a religion discover that the ends they are seeking are also sought by

other people, with other religious views, and that these other people have different, potentially helpful, means of reaching those ends. Dialogue, of whatever kind, becomes the ground upon which a new religious combination can built – one that does a better job of accomplishing what both religions hoped to be able to do, before the syncretism emerged.

As it happens, this is the reason that practical issues are the easiest matters for people of various religions to collaborate on. Often, we agree on a specific course of action even when we disagree upon the justification for it. Thus, we find a common end, such as disaster relief, and are able to justify combining our efforts. Many of us care about those who suffer as a result of earthquakes, though such relief efforts may play a different role in our various kinds of religious thought; thus, we get the unity of the Red Cross and Red Crescent societies. The process of syncretism picks up on the same dynamic. A number of religions value human peace and calm, as well as physical health. Therefore, we encourage people to take up t'ai chi or yoga, recognizing their religious roots while understanding that they suit the goals that we wish to accomplish better than anything that we have in our own heritages.

A few examples of beneficial syncretism may help us to understand the process. The first comes from Buddhism, its movement into China, and its encounter with Taoism and Confucianism. The second is from Islam and its meeting with Greek thought as Islamic warriors from Arabia conquered ancient Byzantine territory. The third comes from Christianity's entry into Western Europe and its incorporation of Celtic religion.

I am going to distinguish these examples by placing them in a set of categories: symmetrical syncretism, asymmetrical syncretism, and reflexive syncretism. Symmetrical syncretism is a kind of balanced syncretism in which two or more religions become effectively one and the prior identities are more-or-less neatly carried over into the new arrangement. Asymmetrical syncretism is the much more common type in which Religion A grafts into itself elements from another religious viewpoint – call it Religion B; Religion A retains its general identity and is the controlling partner but is, nonetheless, significantly changed by its incorporation of elements from Religion B.

Reflexive syncretism is perhaps the most complicated of the categories that I'm using. Reflexive syncretism is a subset of asymmetrical syncretism, in which the elements taken from Religion B are a reminder of lost or buried aspects of Religion A. The result is a syncretistic change: Religion A is genuinely modified by the inclusion of elements from Religion B. However, some part of Religion A has previously held similar or entirely compatible views to those brought from Religion B. The result is a syncretism that, from some perspectives, looks more like a revitalization of traditional views in Religion A than like a syncretism.

These categories are very far from being absolute or obvious. They are, first of all, a matter of judgement: whether a syncretism is symmetrical or asymmetrical is going to be determined by the observer, based upon the evidence that she/he has. Tracing and quantifying shifts in ways of thinking and acting is a challenging task, affected by the evidence at hand and by the amount of emphasis that one puts on any particular piece of evidence. Thus, scholars specializing in the religions and time periods that we discuss may argue with my judgements. Second, the categories have soft boundaries: there will be groups and individuals within the overall religions to whom the suggested categories apply quite precisely and other people for whom the categories do not apply in any way that we can see. Religious labels are always generalizations of limited usefulness. Third, the degree and nature of any syncretism will shift from moment to moment: the relationships between two or more religious heritages change, so that a symmetrical syncretism can turn into an asymmetrical syncretism and vice versa. In short, the differences among syncretisms are very difficult to pin down and categorize.

This set of categories, therefore, should be understood as an aid to understanding. Scholars call this kind of model "heuristic." It is neither absolute nor especially precise. However, it points to some significant truths. In this case, the categories point to some real differences in the kind and degree of syncretisms: the relationship between Buddhism and Taoism in China is significantly more integrative, more fully transformational for both heritages, than that between Islam and Greek thought; Buddhism and Taoism become something more akin to one religion, while Islam remains Islam, though with enormous Greek influence. The reflexive category reminds us that an insight drawn from another heritage may not be entirely new to one's own heritage; it may serve as a renewal of a viewpoint with a long, native history. These categories also help to remind us that the process of syncretism goes at least two ways: the impact of Christianity on Celtic thought and life is different from the impact of Celtic understanding on Christianity, but both are significant. The categories will help you recognize these things, but will neither cover all possible kinds of syncretisms nor fully explain any of the stories that we are about to encounter.

BUDDHISM AND TAOISM IN CHINA: SYMMETRICAL SYNCRETISM

Buddhism has always been syncretistic. That is its nature; Buddhism has no intrinsic opposition to syncretism, which is why Hendrik Kraemer chooses it as one example of the kind of religion in which syncretism is treated as legitimate.[2] The formal acceptance of syncretism in Buddhism means that we have more examples to choose from than we can possibly investigate. Buddhism "has aptly been called 'The Vagrant Lotus'; for its history has been one of transmigration from one culture to another ... Buddhism has always accommodated and adapted itself to local beliefs."[3] One of my favourite examples of this tendency happens with the entry of Buddhism into China. In the Chinese acceptance of Buddhism, we can see how the new syncretism is an improvement upon existing religion and is widely accepted as such. It answers questions about the universe, life, and order, which were pressing at the time. The new syncretism is able to take root because its value to all parts of society, including rulers, enables it to find structures of organization which both propagate and sustain the new ways of thinking and acting.

In the Chinese reception of Buddhism, we can see symmetrical syncretism at its purest. Two or more religious traditions – in this case, Buddhist and Taoist – blend seamlessly. Each offers its priorities, practices, and texts, and the result is one religion incorporating all of the roots. A syncretism is symmetrical when it receives approximately equally from participating traditions, rather than leaving in place one strong tradition modified by others. The symmetry comes from balanced sharing, in which participants function as partners instead of feeling like conqueror and conquered.

The origins of Buddhism are in the Indian subcontinent. About five hundred or so years before Jesus appeared on the scene, a boy was born to the Gautama (the Sanskrit version; Gotama in Pali) family in what is now called southern Nepal.[4] His name was Siddhartha (again, Sanskrit; Siddhattha in Pali), which means "goal-accomplished." Although we do not know much about his early life, we are told that his father was of royal stature and significant wealth. Siddhartha, therefore, grew up a pampered prince; numerous legends surround his early days, describing a young man with everything that he might want, including several palaces, numerous concubines, and marriage to the most beautiful woman in the land, who gave him a son. Be that as it may, eventually (age twenty-nine, according to some late sources) he renounced his comforts for the life of a wandering ascetic. This was not an unusual path: numerous spiritual teachers travelled the roads, often following very rigorous regimens and seeking a way to be free of the endless cycle of death and rebirth. Belief in this cycle has roots deep in Indus Valley civilization, out of which grew Hinduism, Buddhism, Jainism, and other religious traditions of the Indian subcontinent. Siddhartha tried various traditional methods of attaining enlightenment, including severe ascetic practices such as non-breathing meditations and starvation diets, but he did not find the end that he sought. Meditating under a tree, he developed the "three-fold knowledge: memory of previous lives, seeing the rebirth of others according to their karma, and the destruction of spiritual faults which fester in the mind and keep it unenlightened."[5] This third knowledge is that which enabled him to exit the cycle of death and rebirth, giving him freedom from the suffering that comes with more lives. At dawn, he had reached enlightenment (nirvana or, in Pali – the language of the primary Buddhist texts – *nibbana*) and become a Buddha. He began to teach his way to other people in India.

Thus, the story begins (although some texts start much further back, with Siddhartha's prior experiences of death and rebirth). Over the next five hundred years, Buddhism spread through India. Then it nearly vanished, a victim of Hindu success and Muslim invasion, as well as Buddhism's tendency to focus its strength in monasteries and universities rather than spreading through the general population. However, a small number of monks had been making their way to

China along the trade routes and into cosmopolitan trading cities, such as Chang'an.

Although Buddhism attained footholds in a number of places, it does not seem to have had great initial success in China.[6] Of course, Buddhism suffered from being Indian; not only was it from elsewhere, but also all of its primary assumptions came from older Indus Valley religions, and all of its texts were in Indian languages. Moreover, its initial competitors were strong: while Imperial China was ascendant (until 220 CE), official Confucianism served religious needs. It offered a sufficient explanation for the place of China as the dominant power in its world, as well as instructions in how to live so as to maintain the order necessary for dominance. With the downfall of the Han Chinese Ch'in dynasty and the loss of northern China to Mongol invasion, commencing in 220 CE, the religious world changed dramatically. Taoism, with native roots, connections to traditional folk religions, and a diffuse nature, had the initial advantage. Buddhism needed to become Chinese.

It did so rather impressively. The first task was the greatest and most significant. Chinese culture was exceedingly textual; the availability of written materials mattered. From the perspective of Buddhism, that was just fine; Buddhism did not have what scholars call a "closed canon," a limited number of writings that constitute the sacred text.[7] The Christian Bible and the Muslim Qur'an are now examples of closed canons, although the Bible took two-to-three centuries to reach that state. In contrast, when Buddhism reached China, it had numerous texts in circulation providing teaching and exhortation. As these were all in Indian languages such as Pali and Sanskrit, translation into Chinese languages was needed, and that was a challenge.

No languages are more different than those of India and China. Chinese is uninflected, logographic, and (in its written form) largely monosyllabic; Indian languages are highly inflected, alphabetic, polysyllabic. Chinese has no systematized grammar; Indian languages, particularly Sanskrit, have a formal and highly elaborated grammatical system. When we turn to literary modes, we find that the Chinese preference is for terseness, for metaphors from familiar nature, for the concrete image, whereas Indian literature tends to be discursive, hyperbolic in its metaphors, and full of abstractions. The imaginative range expressed in Chinese literature – even in the Taoist classics – is far more limited, more earth-bound, than in the colourful writings of the Indian tradition.[8]

The task was immense, but it was undertaken successfully, if not altogether accurately. Precise translation is hard to arrange, even with more-or-less compatible languages. One simply cannot assume that there will be precisely equivalent words in the relevant languages, because each language reflects a different way of thinking about life, the world, and everything, really. With two profoundly distinct languages, inaccuracy is inevitable; plus, of course, a translator may have reasons to make more changes than are strictly necessary. However, from the point of view of syncretism, all of this facilitates the process. The larger the chasm between Indian and Chinese languages, the more the final product will be Chinese in character, since a larger change occurs in translation. And it was so; the texts took on a decisively Chinese nature.

The linguistic shift was not the only change that Buddhism made as it entered the Chinese thought-world. Buddhism entered China from a variety of directions because Buddhism had reached a number of neighbouring countries, including Tibet. The result is that the Chinese received a number of different flavours of Buddhism, more or less on an equal footing, so that Chinese Buddhism was, initially, a kind of syncretism of Buddhisms. Indian thinkers debated, often vociferously, the question of whether one ought to seek the spiritual liberation of others as preached in the *sutras* accepted by Mahayana Buddhists, or whether one should simply attempt to reach nirvana, as indicated in the Pali texts. The Chinese simply received both views, and both entered comfortably into the Chinese tradition.

These changes notwithstanding, Buddhism was still a religion from the west, beyond China's borders. However, Chinese Buddhists had an even more effective syncretistic tool for making their religion truly indigenous: the Chinese sutra. The Mahayana tradition recognizes a variety of texts, called "sutras," as sacred. Many, but not all, of these consist of sayings attributed to the Buddha. Chinese Buddhists composed many of these texts, often relying heavily upon Chinese religious heritages. Thus, when the Chinese people looked at Buddhism, often they saw their own traditional religion looking back at them.

Indeed, Buddhism became so thoroughly a part of Chinese life that by the fourth and fifth centuries, stories were in circulation claiming that Buddhism was really a Chinese religion – Taoism exported to India![9] This is an immensely fascinating story of syncretism. Buddhism and Taoism grew up together and fed each other. Taoism is, if anything, more difficult than Buddhism to define: a loose collection of Chinese ways of being that emphasize harmony with the order of the universe, focusing upon compassion, humility, and simplicity. Its origins are in "The Way of the Heavenly Master," which started in the western part of Sichuan province in the fourth century and spread through all of China, though it has roots in Chinese traditional religions. The similarities between Buddhism and Taoism were evident early in the syncretistic process, with the result that thinkers in both traditions plagiarized from one another unashamedly. We have texts from both religions that are nearly identical, with only the modifications necessary to facilitate adoption. The medieval Buddhist *Sutra of the Three Interrupted Kitchens, Preached by the Buddha* (about a system of fasting) is an obvious reworking of the Taoist *Scripture of the Five Kitchens*, for instance. Related to this sharing of texts, and partly as a result of it, there was a tremendous sharing of ritual and practice. Important figures in one became significant in the other, so that a bodhisattva (one who seeks enlightenment or an enlightened one who commits to helping others attain enlightenment) revered in Mahayana Buddhism, Guanyin, "motivated the creation of one of the most prestigious deities of the Taoist pantheon, the Heavenly Venerable Savior from Suffering."[10]

The integration between Buddhism and Taoism was so complete that a new form of Buddhism, a new syncretism, came into being as a result; Ch'an (Westerners usually call it "Zen," from the Japanese) Buddhism is firmly attested in the seventh century CE. Ch'an Buddhism is, as Daisetz Suzuki put it, "the product of the Chinese mind, or rather the Chinese elaboration of the Doctrine of Enlightenment."[11] It is a meeting of Mahayana Buddhism with Chinese traditional thought, focusing upon Buddhism as a means of attaining the enlightened state of being (rather than treating it as a system of ethics, for example). Suzuki goes even further, arguing that Ch'an could only have grown up in China, because "it needed a mind which had already been steeped in the Laotzuan ideas and feelings and yet could not detach itself from the details of daily life."[12] He suggests that Ch'an is not merely Chinese by accident of history, but also as a consequence of formation and existing understanding; in other words, it is an example of preservation of insights in a new syncretism. The essence of Ch'an is commonly expressed in a four-line summary, formulated by Chinese thinkers (we do not know whom):

A special transmission outside the Scripture;
No dependence on word or letters;
Direct pointing at the Mind of man;
Seeing into one's Nature and the attainment of Buddhahood.[13]

These lines are intended to encourage a sense of unity between self and selfhood, the self and the other, the questioner and the question, a unity that is rooted in the Taoist sense of harmony. This is a knowledge of the oneness of all things, reflected in an elimination of the dichotomy between one and another. The specifically Ch'an way of finding this unity (known as *satori*) is most perfectly expressed in the love of paradoxes. We see this in the famous *koan*, which is a story or formulation of words that is intended to push the student beyond ordinary rationality and into a direct encounter with her/his own nature, and which may, therefore, defy logic.[14] The point of the koan is to jar the student into a sense of immediate relationship with the other, overcoming all sense of the subject/object relation that dominates our ordinary existence.[15] The *mondo* (Japanese name, but the idea originated in China) is a system of rapid-fire question and answer conducted between master and student (the master asks the questions); koans are often employed in this context, as the purpose of the mondo is precisely the same as that of the koan. Meditation is also profoundly important in Ch'an, as a means to overcome separation and discover the Buddha nature in one's own nature and in the nature of the other.

In Ch'an Buddhism, therefore, the Chinese found an approach to enlightenment which stated the problem of alienation in familiar terms. Rather than focusing particularly upon the life/death cycle which dominated Indian Buddhist thinking, Ch'an names the problem in Taoist terms, as a matter of finding true harmony. This approach is not inconsistent with Indian Buddhism, most importantly because it takes the experiences and words of the Buddha as primary, even paradigmatic. Ch'an is, however, quite noticeably different from Indian Buddhism, because Ch'an names the challenge to which Buddhism is the answer in a substantially different way. This change resonates through the whole structure of the religion, causing shifts in the way that Buddhism is lived. The system of Ch'an activity, employing techniques such as mondo and the koan, is particularly Chinese, serving the goals of the Taoist/Buddhist syncretism. This system may be serving something in the Chinese psyche also; certainly it gives China a kind of ownership of its brand of Buddhism. The resultant religion is both derivative of Indian Buddhism and original in its own right; it gives rise to the question that we will discuss in a later chapter: "What is it now?" Ch'an displays both the principle of progress, by restating the challenge to which Buddhism is the answer in Chinese terms, and the principle of preservation of insights, by carrying over Buddhist practices and thought forms.

Ch'an has been highly successful in China, Japan, and Korea. Most English speakers know it by its Japanese name, "Zen"; under that name, it has a high public profile in Western countries. It has inspired some quite substantial literary works, including the poems and songs of Leonard Cohen, and Robert Pirsig's classic novel, *Zen and the Art of Motorcycle Maintenance* – works which themselves represent new syncretisms, since they do not entirely fit within traditional Ch'an/Zen views.

Let us return to our original questions, "Why was all this Chinese syncretism a good thing?" And, "according to whom?" The official religion of the Han dynasty was a sort of Confucianism which was a syncretism of elements drawn from various parts of Chinese heritage (including Taoism). Its emphasis was on cosmic unity and order, with heaven, earth, and man working together in harmony. The emperor was central to the vision, as the one who ensured the maintenance of order. The whole structure, however, was logically weak. It depended upon a misunderstanding of Confucius, as well as modifications of history and inherited texts, in order to place the Han dynasty in the place of honour. Consequently, scholars began to question the accuracy of official Confucianism. Perhaps more significantly, however, in the latter years of the Han dynasty, Confucianism no longer reflected the current power relationships with any accuracy. China's real rulers were a number of powerful families who gave lip service to the emperor while acting more or less as they pleased. For them, Han Confucianism explained little, though it could be used to justify much. Their games of power and honour depended upon the work of a much-abused peasantry whose life of toil was dominated by poverty and uncertainty. For those who held land, taxes were unbearable. Others went to work for the great families, turned to banditry, or went on relief; there seem to have been a great many who relied upon communal support. Han Confucianism had ceased to serve anyone but the emperor, and was not helping him very much. When the Han dynasty fell, and much of China was overrun by Mongols, the official belief system of the Empire was swept away; it no longer had either justification or meaning.

Chinese Buddhism, on the other hand, served as a rich ordering and explanation of life. It picked up a variety of traditional Chinese elements so that it did not feel alien. As we have seen, traditional Chinese symbols and rituals continued to be employed so that Buddhism seemed to be a Chinese religion. Confucian principles of order were sustained so that public authorities were not alarmed, and Confucian adherents felt secure. Moreover, while Han Confucianism had official support, Taoism was growing in popularity. The Taoist concern for harmony and simplicity survived, indeed thrived, in the new syncretism. Important features of Buddhism survived the transition and provided a new ethic. Understanding life in relation to the cycle of death and rebirth, and progressing on the basis of a combination of meditations that enable a deeper understanding of Buddhist wisdom, on the one hand, while the performance of good actions, on the other, were (and are) much more satisfactory than the Han attempt at self-aggrandizement masquerading as an explanation of the whole.

The decision to undertake the syncretistic effort that rendered Buddhism available and helpful to the Chinese was taken by a great many people from all walks of life. Its effectiveness is evident in the degree to which it was embraced by rulers, scholars, and labourers. The Sui and T'ang emperors threw their weight behind Buddhism, investing resources in Buddhist projects and making public declarations of support for the religion. Indeed, the rulers established an official bureaucracy to promote Buddhism – and, of course, to control its direction. Buddhism has numerous characteristics that may tend in subversive directions, and the dynasties had no interest in losing their authority because of religion. That said, part of the reason for the usefulness of Buddhism as an official religion is that it was also accepted by the people. The immense work of translation and authorship that we have discussed is a clear indication that the learned Chinese populace found Buddhism attractive and worthy of their best efforts. Ordinary people also took up the new religion, finding that it spoke to their situation and their heritage far more helpfully than Han Confucianism had. Indeed, the rulers followed the people to Buddhism, rather than pushing them there. The result is that Buddhism fulfilled the goal of sustaining order for which Han Confucianism was formulated; moreover, it has been highly successful in China and was a major force in national life until it was forcibly replaced by Maoist Communism in the aftermath of World War II. This represents approximately one-and-a-half millennia of communal acceptance in the most populous nation on Earth.

This example suggests a number of lessons. The first is a reinforcement of my earlier suggestion that a new syncretism must retain that which is deemed most important in the previously existing religion. Without eliminating Confucianism, the Buddhist-Taoist syncretism sustained the basic priorities and activities of both Buddhism and Taoism. The second lesson is that syncretism will be helpful and successful – a genuine improvement – if it answers questions that people are asking; it must respond to particular needs in the life of the receiving people. This happens only if the existing religion is, in some way, inadequate to respond to the contemporary situation. Han Confucianism was failing, and Taoism lacked the strength necessary to obtain support in imperial circles. The third lesson is that the religion being received and drawn into a syncretism benefits from being flexible enough to become indigenous. It cannot continue to be seen as the religion of the other, but gains from being open to sufficient change in itself that it can fit into a new, syncretistic relationship with substantial elements of another religion. Buddhism managed this to a spectacular degree: its open canon and limited doctrinal commitments made it extraordinarily suited to the Chinese situation. The fourth lesson is that syncretism and general acceptance are more likely to happen with relative ease if the newly received religion can find structures to support it in its new context. Imperial support and widespread popular appeal ensured this.

Thus, a new syncretism – or, more accurately, range of syncretisms – came into being and survived. It responded to very real needs in a helpful way, providing a new overarching explanation of reality, including an understanding of the place and purpose of humanity in relation to the larger order (or disorder) which defined the meaning of life for practitioners; for both Buddhists and Taoists, the new syncretisms represented significant change. To the Chinese, whether Confucian or Taoist or some combination, the emphasis upon escape from samsara, the cycle of death and rebirth, was a new account of human predicaments and of the means by which they may be resolved; in Ch'an form, it was a shift for both traditions. Buddhism brought new structures of organization, including monastic life. It also brought new faith commitments and values. Ch'an Buddhism represented a culmination of changes in the relation between master and student (affecting forms of organization). Though much was inherited from earlier Buddhisms, Chinese syncretisms were truly new in important ways; their service to society ensured that they represented progress for Chinese people.

ANCIENT/MEDIEVAL ISLAM AND THE GREEKS: ASYMMETRICAL SYNCRETISM

The initial integration, within early Islam, was a fusion of primarily Jewish and Christian materials with local Arab traditions ... The second integration, at the time of the great conquests and their aftermath, brought local administrative techniques, legal practices, artistic forms, and religious tenets under the arch of the new empire. The third integration was the appanage of "the Graeco-Arabic renaissance" ... in the ... ninth and ... tenth centuries. In all three stages the legacy of Hellenism and of late Graeco-Roman antiquity plays a major, if not paramount, role.[16]

Joel L. Kraemer

Many of the characteristics of beneficial and successful syncretism that we have seen in Chinese Buddhism also come into play in our next example, which is the adoption of Greek thought into early Islam. However, this example represents a shift in Islam, so that we see a syncretistic version of that religion, rather than a wholesale merging of different traditions of the kind that we saw in the Chinese example. Syncretism affected Islamic understandings of the cosmic order, in addition to causing profound changes in forms of organization, and causing notable shifts in the values that Islam taught. However, the account of human predicaments and the means by which they could be resolved stayed largely intact, as did the Islamic call for faith commitment, which retained both its nature and its importance.

This is asymmetrical syncretism. The syncretism results in a clear imbalance of benefits, with less mutuality than appears in a symmetrical syncretism. In asymmetrical syncretism, one religion is the evident victor, succeeding at least partly by integration or conversion, though force and other measures may contribute. The result is a syncretism because the side which dominates is itself changed by the encounter. The transformation may be so significant that the apparent victor becomes a rather different religion. In this example, Islam certainly won, but the Islam that emerged from the encounter was, in many ways, radically Hellenized (in addition to having been changed by other traditions from places such as India). The Greek heritage gains the survival, renewal, and dissemination of principles and texts that might otherwise have vanished. This is a substantial benefit, certainly, but the religion after the syncretistic moment is definitely Islam.

When Islam was first born, in seventh-century Arabia, most of its followers had little, if any, education. By the end of the Middle Ages, Muslims controlled a broad swath of territory, including North Africa and most of the Byzantine Empire (eastern part of the old Roman Empire). Islamic territories were centres of learning equal or superior to any in Europe , especially in medicine, a discipline in which European thought hardly exceeded the level of superstition (and European treatment was as likely to kill its patients as help them). How did this come to be?

Muhammad was a teacher and ruler amongst warlike and largely illiterate Arabian tribes (who had a rich oral culture).[17] Though the small tribes were accustomed to fighting vigorously among themselves, Muhammad convinced or forced them to desist and, instead, work together in a basic kind of unity. He focused upon the oneness of God and, therefore, the *ummah*, the oneness of the Muslim community. As a common religion with unity at its centre, Islam established real bonds among the Arabian peoples, all of whom had possessed independent religious identities before Islam appeared. This did not, however, eliminate their warlike inclinations, which were manifested in battles over the leadership of the Believers after Muhammad's death. Two civil wars occurred in the second half of the seventh century. Nonetheless, a series of victories by various caliphs enabled the creation of a more or less united force, and the desire for battle came to be focused outward. In a series of invasions (starting in the CE 630s, accelerating in the eighth century and continuing until the middle of the tenth century), the Believers moved outward from Arabia. In the North and East, they found themselves at the gates of Constantinople, having overrun substantial, wealthy, and valuable portions of the Byzantine Empire, including Syria and Egypt. They brought with them a hunger for learning, and they found plenty of resources to increase their knowledge.[18]

The Eastern Empire had a massive intellectual inheritance from ancient Greece. Indeed, it had served as the main guardian of Greek learning after the fall of the Western part of the Roman Empire. The relationship between the Eastern Church and such non-Christian learning was ambivalent because it was, on the one hand, education – giving it value – and on the other hand, non-Christian – rendering it an object of suspicion for some people. In addition to the heritage of Greek thought, the Byzantine Empire had hundreds of years of Imperial greatness behind it and a tremendous store of wisdom about life – especially the life of administration and ruling – that the Arab invaders lacked.

Consequently, the invading Arabs' lives were transformed by the encounter with Byzantium. They learned much about settled domestic life, both urban and agricultural, and discovered how to live like emperors and rule great states. In the process, their religious lives took on a whole new shape. Legal matters became a major area of influence: "Byzantine law was taken up by early Islamic *qadis* or judges, contributing toward the body of jurisprudence that would become the *sharia*, or Islamic law."[19] This is a tremendously important example of syncretism because of the decisive importance of sharia in Islam.

At least as significant for our discussion is the creation of Islamic theology, which occurred as a product of the encounter with Greek thought inherited from the Byzantine Empire. "Islamic theology (*kalam*) was to a large extent a by-product of Islamic philosophy. To place Islamic philosophy in its proper historical context, one must first review the various stages through which its predecessor, Greek-Hellenistic philosophy, passed."[20] The Qur'an established the root principle of Islam, that God (*Allah*) is One. It also provided the basic teachings. However, the Qur'an is not a work of systematic theology; its emphasis is on how people ought to live, which is why law plays so significant a part in Muslim life. The encounter with philosophy fostered an inclination to think in formal propositions and to relate one idea to another – in short, to become systematic.

 The encounter with philosophy came through Byzantium, a consequence of the invasion of those territories that I have mentioned. Erica Hunter tells the fascinating story of the "school of Edessa," which left Byzantine lands for Persian-ruled areas, as a consequence of disagreements over the nature of Christ. Edessa was an important intellectual centre in early Christianity because Edessa had been the first state to declare the new faith as its official religion. Edessa's school was a firm supporter of what is called "Dyophisitism," a belief connected to Nestorius, a fourth–fifth century thinker who argued that Jesus Christ has two natures (which the larger Christian church accepted), and appeared to suggest that the natures were in principle distinct and separable (which was rejected by the church at Chalcedon in 451 CE). In the fifth century, Narsai, the principal of the school of Edessa, moved himself, a significant intellectual asset, to Nisbis in the Persian territories because he was a Nestorian who expected that his version of Christianity would be more welcome there than in the Byzantine empire. The move was complete by 489 CE. "A rich educational tradition at Edessa, which had nurtured the translation of Greek works, including philosophy, had come to an end. These activities were transferred to the Persian territories, with Aristotelian studies gaining a firm footing in the Sassanid empire by the end of the sixth century."[21] Until the late ninth century, this school was the leading educational centre in the empire. Only then did the school established by the Caliphate in Baghdad gain pre-eminence. "There, through the labours of trilingual Christian scribes, especially Hunayn ibn Ishaq al-Ibadi and his son, Ishaq ibn Hunayn, who translated numerous Greek works into Syriac and then into Arabic at the *bayt al-hikma* or 'house of wisdom,' Greek philosophy was transmitted into the international domains of the Abbasids."²² In short, Christianity brought Greek thought, with its rational and systematic approach to understanding, into traditionally Arab Islam.

This is but one example of an intriguing movement. Greek thought was sustained in a Christian context in a remarkable and in many ways successful effort at syncretism. Because their land was overtaken by Muslim Arabs, or for various other reasons, many of these Christians ended up in Muslim territories, where they passed on their Greek heritage along with something of their own Christian influence. In this case, the initial movement was into Persia, which was Zoroastrian at the time but was subsequently conquered by Muslims, so there was a double movement and a succession of influences. The texts that these Christians produced were picked up by Muslims, who used them to formulate their own philosophical and theological viewpoints. Indeed, the Christians earned a living by making translations into Arabic for their new masters.²³ This was particularly true of the Hellenized Syrians, who had been among the most significant intellectual figures in early Christianity. The result was a tremendously powerful strain of Aristotelianism in Islamic thought, and a lesser, but very real influence of Platonism and Neo-Platonism in Islam. Alexander of Aphrodisias and Galen also figured large.²⁴

Perhaps the greatest impact of Hellenistic thought on Islam can be seen in the appearance of *kalam*, which is the technical discipline of theology, generally employing philosophical tools (and distinct from the other primary mode of thought in Islam with its emphasis upon law). Kalam is generally understood as beginning with the Mu'tazilist school of Islamic theology in the eighth and ninth centuries CE. Members of this school are identified by some contemporary scholars as "defenders of reason in Islam,"²⁵ and this school was heavily influenced by Aristotelian logic, as was its successor, the Ash'arite school.²⁶ Incidentally, the Arabic word for "philosophy" is *falsafah*, from the Greek.

In Islam as in Christianity, the formal activity of reflection on revelation that has come to be known as theology began in the encounter between revealed tradition and Greek thought. This represents a profound and important shift in the overarching understanding of the cosmos in Islam. Indeed, we can more accurately say that this is the beginning of the elaboration of such a vision; previously, Islam had not gone much beyond a general assertion of the oneness and might of Allah, combined with the recitation of the stories from the Qur'an. As with earliest Hebrew religion and Christianity, Islam had been more or less narrative in orientation. The encounter with Greek thought brought Islam into the realm of systematic thought; the effort to understand the teachings of the religion and link them into a formal structure began with this syncretism. Greek ways of thinking encouraged Muslims to think more deeply and broadly about the world. The importance of this shift must not be underestimated. In very important ways, it changed the nature of Islam. Islam ceased to be a more or less entirely practical discipline built around allegiance to the one Allah, and became a much more fully elaborated intellectual edifice, capable of holding its own with other great traditions of thought in the world.

The implications of this can be seen in the medieval West. The Greek-Muslim syncretism would eventually add a further layer, creating a new syncretism. In the Middle Ages, the movement of Greek texts through Christian and into Muslim hands came full circle. Thomas Aquinas was heavily influenced by Aristotle. However, he did not have direct access to Aristotle or even access to Aristotelian texts within his own Christian tradition. Instead, he received Latin translations of the Arabic translations of the Syriac translations of the Greek texts – which is a rather long way around, and had some impact on the quality of the texts that he could get. Aquinas's arguments were built upon a variety of influences, but among them must be counted ibn-Rushd (1126–1198 CE). Indeed, Latin Averroism, influenced by Aristotle (a Greek pre-Christian thinker), and imbibed by Latin Christians, received through a Muslim commentator using texts inherited from and prepared by Greek Christians, is a syncretism, to be sure, and was at the centre of the thought-world in thirteenth-century Paris. Aquinas wrote his famous *Summa Theologica* (or *Summa Theologiae*; scholars love to argue over the Latin) in a way that represents a notable departure in Christian theology. He started with a discussion of God as one, focusing upon the characteristics of the one God, and then proceeded to talk about God as trinitarian, or three-in-one. This is a shift from Augustine or Athanasius, prior figures with a formative effect on the Western Christian tradition who had simply discussed God as Trinity. The change comes about because Aquinas is using Aristotle, who helps Aquinas to think about God as the Prime Mover who starts all action in the created universe, and is in conversation with Muslim and Jewish Aristotelians, who think of God only as one and not as triune. Indeed, what Jews, Christians, and Muslims have most in common is a conversation about the nature of God. Syncretisms beget syncretisms, as good ideas travel from one mind to another – a reminder of the soft boundaries that religions possess.

In the blending of Greek thought with nascent Islam we see another beneficial and successful syncretism. We are reminded of the centrality of need; the Islamic tribes had neither an understanding of government nor a systematic theology that could make sense of their new situation. Nor did they have many of the basic elements of learning that are necessary both to civilized society and to an overall account of life, its meanings, and its challenges.

In the second integration that Joel Kraemer names in the quotation at the beginning of this section, Greek thought provided the tools to make both government and formal theology possible and, therefore, to enable Islamic understanding to become more profound and complex. In the third integration, as Muslim Arabs picked up the whole realm of Greek learning through Byzantine Christianity, the Greeks provided structures of rational thought, combined with an explanation of universal principles of order that enabled Islamic scholars to think reasonably about Allah and about the whole of creation. Hence, we find them engaged in rational discussions of God's existence and attributes in the work of scholars such as al-Ghazali (eleventh–twelfth c. CE) and Ibn-Rushd.[27] We find al-Farabi (ninth–tenth c. CE) relying on Greek Neo-Platonists to help him reason from an understanding of God through to an elaboration of the ideal political structure, the "best state."[28]

From Greek (and Greco-Roman) thinkers as diverse as Plato, Aristotle, Plotinus, and Ptolemy, the Muslim Arabs drew materials that helped them to elaborate an entire worldview, with major contributions in every known specialty. They received Greek insights and worked to develop them, mingling them with learning from Roman, Persian, Syrian, and Indian traditions, to create an intellectually rich society that contributed extensively to the world's store of knowledge in diverse fields such as law, mathematics, architecture, and the understanding of God. Remember that these disciplines are all, to the ancient and medieval Muslim mind, either specifically aspects of religion or at least intimately related thereto; only to the modern Western mind are such subjects as physics and medicine regarded as separate from the issues of God's work in the world. I find the example of Nasir al-Din al-Tusi (thirteenth c. CE) both fascinating and instructive. Al-Tusi, whose work was important to Copernicus, tried to explain how a God who is absolutely single could create a universe that has more than one entity; in short, "How do we get many things from one Source?" He borrowed mathematical rules from the algebraists in order to explain and defend an argument that the multiplicity of being emanates (a kind of overflowing of being) from the One (Allah), which is a doctrine which he received from the Neo-Platonist Ibn-Sina (tenth–eleventh c. CE).[29] Math meets metaphysics!

Muslim use of Greek thought was a benefit not only to Muslim society. This is not solely a one-way transaction. In the process of being incorporated into Arab Muslim life, Greek principles (and the supporting texts) survived and were made available to be passed on to the rest of the world; indeed, these gifts became a part of a lively new tradition which transformed them and also made them relevant and placed them at the centre of popular debate throughout the Mediterranean world and Europe. Consequently, we can reasonably argue that significant parts of the Greek religio-philosophico-political heritage survived and even benefited from the new syncretisms. Nonetheless, on balance, Islam was certainly the greater beneficiary. It was the new, vibrant religion, with contemporary hopes and desires.

This sense of social need on the part of the Muslims, combined with the availability of a whole system of thought to be drawn upon from elsewhere, bears some similarity to the Buddhist-Taoist situation. Most notable, perhaps, is the support that Greek thought received amongst authoritative figures in Islamic society; many powerful or soon-to-be-powerful people were ready to pay for translations of Greek texts, to follow their precepts, and to develop the tradition of Greek learning in a fashion suited to the early Islamic world.

There are, however, some significant differences between the Buddhist-Taoist syncretism and the meeting between Greek and Islamic thought. In the Chinese synthesis, the religions were fundamentally similar in general outlook and highly flexible, for various reasons; certainly, their non-creedal nature and lack of a closed canon were among the causes of their successful new relationship. Symmetrical syncretism was possible and highly successful.

Greek and Islamic ideas did not meet on quite the same footing as Buddhism and Taoism. The body of Greek literature, while not officially closed, was no longer growing; the Greek world which spawned it had passed into memory. While Greek thinkers were hardly of one mind and certainly not attached to a formal creed, they had some common principles. The priority of human reason and the activity of *theoria* (rational contemplation) that reason undergirded were among them. Islam, by contrast, was in its infancy; the Qur'an was complete, but the collections of the Hadith were not. Significantly, Greek thought was especially diverse on the matter that Islam answered most clearly and decisively and on which it brooked no compromise: the question of whether there is a single, ultimate Source of all being. The spirit of Islam, in its origin, was not the spirit of Greek thought; these two were not similar in the way that Buddhism and Taoism were.

If there was a certain refined completeness to Greek thought, it was balanced by the Islamic assumption of the divine origin of the revelation to Muhammad preserved in the Qur'an. This established some definite limits on the syncretistic possibilities, as did the triumph of Muslim armies over the existing Greek Christian populations. However, Islamic schools of interpretation were in their nascency, which meant that the situation was flexible enough for these two dissimilar approaches to the world to join together in a mutually fruitful relationship. In short, two streams of thought need not have as much in common as Buddhism and Taoism for syncretism to occur, nor do they need to be as flexible as the Asian religions were. There must only be a need and substantial openness on one side of the relationship, combined with helpful answers on the other side. The result was a fundamental transformation of Islam and a much greater availability of Greek thought to the rest of the world. Both of these outcomes represent notable kinds of progress.

The less-flexible nature of Greek thought and Islam resulted in a different kind of syncretism – an asymmetrical syncretism. The forms of organization, the understanding of the cosmos, and the values taught changed in quite visible ways, but much else did not. Many Muslims had (as many still have) a deep commitment to the principle of preservation of insights. Although the community went through significant fractures as it spread, the core declaration of the oneness of Allah, and the assumption that it demanded oneness in the community, remained. The call for faith commitment, with a strong expectation of charitable works, continued to be at the centre of Islam. By extension, the teaching that polytheists and atheists are lost and will suffer, both during earthly life and after, remained, as did the assertion that salvation is with Allah.

The syncretism resulting from the encounter between Islam and Greek thought, therefore, is best understood as a transformed Islam – an asymmetric syncretism. Greek texts changed Islam for the better, providing a young religion with tools that it needed to respond to new circumstances. This is progress. It is, however, a less radical kind of development than the merging of Chinese traditions seen in the Buddhist-Taoist encounter.

CHRISTIANITY AND THE ANCIENT/MEDIEVAL CELTS: REFLEXIVE SYNCRETISM AND COMPLEXITY

We have seen that syncretism can transform a whole society, even producing a whole new religious tradition. We have also seen that syncretism can enrich a tradition, deepening it and equipping it to respond to new circumstances. In the encounter between Christianity and the Celts, we can see a further type of progress; a syncretism can force a religion to be more true to its own roots by reminding that religion of important aspects of life that have been forgotten. While Christianity brought an overarching account of the cosmos to Celtic traditional religion, the Celts reminded Christianity of the importance of the natural world and a religious response to it.

This example is complex and it offers us two significant insights. The first is that reflexive syncretism can happen. Reflexive syncretism is the importation of elements from another religion, which serve as a reminder of aspects of the importing religion that should not be forgotten. It is the experience of going abroad and learning how to value one's own country. However, the second insight modifies the first. The second lesson of Celtic Christianity is that a syncretism may look very different when examined from a different viewpoint. Assessing the degree and nature of the mutuality in a particular syncretism can be a complicated activity because the results may be very different depending upon where one stands. An analysis of Celtic Christianity undertaken by a Mediterranean Christian in the seventh century – or even five hundred years later, in the twelfth century – might have read differently from an analysis undertaken by a Celt.

For Mediterranean Christianity, the introduction of Christianity to Celtic society is a reflexive syncretism: it causes Christianity to emphasize aspects of itself that have been forgotten or suppressed. A reflexive syncretism may have any degree of mutuality. In this case, Christianity offered the Celts something that they truly could use: a vision of the world that encompassed their immediate surroundings and gave cosmic importance to their lives and their history. This gift was not really intended to have a substantial component of mutuality. The purpose of the Christian overtures to the Celts was conversion, a one-way transfer of wisdom. The extent to which Christianity was moulded and transformed by the Celts and handed back to the Christians as another way to consider their own traditions is a credit to the strength of Celtic society and a comment on the limited degree to which Mediterranean Christianity could conquer this distant region. Christianity was required to adopt elements of Celtic religion in order to enter the Celtic world and transform it.

From the Celtic viewpoint, however, this looks more like a symmetrical syncretism, with a significant degree of mutuality, or an asymmetrical syncretism in which Christianity dominates but in drastically altered form. Quite possibly, it is both, depending upon whom one is discussing and where in history that person appears. If much of Celtic religious belief and practice survives in the formal life of the church (and it does), then the common people may well have been more traditionally Celtic than recognizably Mediterranean Christian, especially in the early days of the transition. In formal ways, the Celtic-Christian syncretism preserved major Celtic stories, though modified; some Celtic gods, in the guise of saints; the sense of gods as having three manifestations, in the theology of the Trinity; Celtic closeness to the Otherworld; traditional feasts; traditional art and symbols; and the Celtic priority of nature. From the perspective of many Celts, the importation of Christianity may well have seemed to be nothing more than the addition to their religion of an overarching account of history and the cosmos, combined with new forms of organization.

The Celts formed a powerful set of societies, dominating much of Europe from about 800 BCE until about 400 BCE. From that time on, Celtic Europe was under more or less constant attack from Germanic tribes and from the Romans. Slowly but inexorably, the Celts either entered into alliances with the Romans or were crushed by enemies, so that the only surviving Celtic societies were in Wales, Scotland, and Ireland – the Western fringe of the continent. The result was that the Romans came to dominate much of Europe by the first century CE. With the Roman Empire came religious change, initially with the introduction of many of the cults that flourished elsewhere in the Mediterranean world. These tended to be matched with Celtic traditions, in a neat piece of syncretism. For example, the Celtic goddess Sulis, worshipped on the location of the Roman baths at Bath (known to the Romans as *Aquae Sulis*, "the waters of Sulis"), was simply conflated with Minerva; as a consequence, little change was necessary and both Celts and Romans could worship more or less happily.

Eventually, however, Christianity came to the Celtic world through the agency of the Romans. That, of course, already implies a significant syncretistic movement. Christianity began as a tiny sect of Judaism, and the Jews had little reason to love Rome. Plus, traditional Hebrew thought was significantly different from the Greek and Latin ways of thinking that dominated the Empire. Early Christians, with their rejection of other gods and insistence that everyone ought to worship the one God and that God only, were not much more comfortable with the Roman approach to religion. However, both Roman ways and Christian ways shifted as Christianity made a home in the Latin world. By the time that Augustine of Hippo wrote *The City of God* in the early fifth century, Rome was comfortable for Christians, and the decline of the Empire was cause for fear and trembling. In spite of occasionally vigorous official efforts to stamp out belief in Jesus Christ, Christianity found the *Pax Romana* to be an ideal context for growth and was able to reach out to all corners of the Empire and beyond. Thus, the Christian church found its way into the Celtic world in the early centuries after Jesus's death. In the fourth century CE, Constantine made Christianity the Empire's official religion, providing Christian missionary efforts with reliable access to conquered peoples beyond the Mediterranean region and giving a significant boost to the religion in Celtic areas.

Elements of old Celtic religion survived for a very long time, even into the Middle Ages, in a lively syncretism with Roman cults, Christianity, and other religions introduced by various invaders. The survival of the old religious ways is most evident in Ireland, Scotland, and Wales, the aforementioned fringe, where they could function beyond the reach of Rome and the Germans. Among the most important elements of Celtic life that survived in vigorous form must be counted the ancient tales of gods and heroes, and this is one of the places where the Celtic/Christian syncretism is most stunningly evident. The Celtic language was strictly oral; it had no written form. Consequently, surviving versions of the old stories, largely in Wales and Ireland, are products of a Celtic Christian age.[30] The writers were commonly monks, and they included a number of the greatest Celtic tales in their histories. Since book production was largely in the hands of the monastic orders until Gutenberg invented his printing press in the fifteenth century, copying of the texts had to be done by hand, usually in monastic *scriptoria*. Celtic Christianity, therefore, is responsible for the survival of stories from pre-Christian Celtic religion. This, of course, means that the materials have changed in both form and content. Nonetheless, they carry important elements of prior Celtic life with them.

It is dangerously speculative to make close links between Irish epic literature and the pagan Celtic society chronicled by Classical writers. The gap in space and time between the Celtic Europe of the later first millennium BC and the Ireland of the early historical period is too great a gulf to ignore. But there is, nonetheless, incontrovertible evidence that some of the Irish material contains records of a Celtic tradition that is pre-Christian. This archaism is especially apparent in the Ulster Cycle, which describes a situation prior to the fifth century AD when Ulster's political position within Ireland fundamentally changed. The early, pre-Christian, political organisation encapsulated here is explicable in terms of the function of the compilers, which was to chronicle the past. There are other factors which point to

pagan origins. Christianity is not apparent in these Insular legends, and a world is described whose perception of the supernatural belongs to a pre-Christian tradition.[31]

The last point is the most significant for us. These are tales told within a Christian context and mostly by people whose livelihood depends
upon the church. Yet, these people are passing on tales of great deeds
from a pre-Christian past, and not only to suggest the superiority of
the Christian present. These are formative stories in a time that is as
much Celtic as Christian.

Being Welsh and Irish, the surviving legends show only a sliver of
ancient Celtic culture. Nonetheless, they give us some access to a vigorous world of gods and heroes, and they show us the power of syncretism. Welsh legends have been substantially reshaped so that they
are predominantly Christian. However, they retain a definite tinge of
traditional Celtic religion. The stories are full of supernatural beings,
"enchanted or magical animals; metamorphosis from human to ani-
mal form; heads with divine properties; and cauldrons capable of res-
urrecting the dead."[32] Even aspects of the geography of the spiritual
world are specifically Celtic, with an Underworld that closely resem-
bles the Otherworld of Celtic thought.[33] This is not Mediterranean
Christianity; indeed, a significant number of today's Christians, raised
in other traditions that object to anything magical, would argue that
it is not Christianity at all. That is part of what makes different syncretistic traditions so important.

The three main streams of Irish story – the "Mythological Cycle"
(compiled in the twelfth century, with sixth- and seventh-century
roots); the "Ulster Cycle" (likely compiled in the eighth century, but
possibly several centuries earlier); and the "Fionn Cycle" (compiled in
the twelfth century) – are more traditionally Celtic, revealing an even
more significant retention of traditional religion in a Christianized
world.[34] The Mythological Cycle includes the "Book of Invasions,"
which describes how the Tuatha Dé Danaan, a race of divine beings,
came to Ireland and brought with them many of the skills that people need to live. They defeated the Fir Bholg (a legendary pre-Celtic
people) and the Fomorians, a local race of demonic beings who were,
nonetheless, still necessary to existence because of their agricultural
skills. One of the most significant of the Tuatha Dé Danaan, Lugh, was

also related to the Fomorians and was instrumental in their defeat, providing a kind of religious and cultural unity which is emphasized by Lugh's status as god of light and the Fomorians' role as Under-world demons. The Ulster Cycle is the mythology of the Ulstermen – including the superhuman hero, Cú Chulainn – and their battles with Connacht. Full of supernatural creatures (including two enormous bulls sent by the gods to cause war), semi-divine heroes, and magical weapons, the Ulster Cycle carries a full freight of traditional Celtic belief that was, undoubtedly, modified for Christian ears. The Ulster Cycle repeatedly names three goddesses – Macha, the Badbh, and the Morrigán – all of whom can appear in single or triple form, which is a common characteristic of Celtic goddesses that must have eased the reception of the Christian Trinitarian doctrine in spite of notable differences between the two ways of thinking. War and sex seem to have been the preoccupations of these goddesses, in a manner that hardly fits traditional (or, at least, pre-Latin) Christian morality. The Fionn Cycle is the story of Finn mac Cumhaill, a magical and supernatural hero and war leader, whose task is the defence of Ireland against enemies of all sorts. We need to remember that these narratives were still being told in great detail and a celebratory fashion, by monks in the twelfth century, which is the date of most of the earliest manuscripts. Thus, all of this conversation about gods and magic and supernatural creatures continues to be part of Irish Celtic religion hundreds of years after the arrival of Christianity, and the narratives are being passed on by the Christian leadership at that late a date.

Survival of these stories through the agency of Christian writers is, first of all, an indication of the importance of the stories themselves. These stories both described and defined Celtic culture for centuries. Thus, they were too important to be lost. Transmitted by bards in the past, the narratives of the people were to be maintained by the monas-tic communities of Celtic Christianity, the primary leadership in parts of the Celtic world such as Ireland. The willingness of monks to write down the old stories also indicates that Celtic Christianity was not seen as altogether in opposition to the Celtic non-Christian past; in-stead, Christianity was regarded, at least by some significant religious people, as continuous with the ancient heritage, incorporating sub-stantial parts of the older belief system. Thirdly, the monks and their society could not help being formed by the same tales as their ancestors had been. Passing on an ancient narrative and seeing the world through its eyes is the most fundamental and powerful way of creating and sustaining syncretism. Miranda Green goes so far as to suggest that "the early monastic scribes may well have been the *filidh*, the keepers of past knowledge, who were steeped in the ancient ritual traditions and whose purpose it was to preserve myth in written form."[35] If so, then the monks were intentionally syncretists, working explicitly at the task of blending the old wisdom with the new. As the new stories are told in parallel with the old stories, and by the same people, both sets of stories are used to interpret the other, and a syncretistic worldview emerges.

This is vividly apparent in the stories of Celtic saints, to whom some of the old Celtic tales became attached. Occasionally, the ancient gods, goddesses, heroes, and heroines found new life as saints of the church. This is rather difficult to prove, partly because of the lack of written historical documentation, but also partly because of the nature of the case. Christian writers have little to gain by suggesting that their saints are the old deities in new guises; plus, any visual evidence is inevitably ambiguous. Nonetheless, there is evidence that some deities and heroes of the early Celtic myths were sanctified and absorbed into Christianity by transformation into saints.[36] Of these, Brigit is the most famous and most obvious case; there are so many parallels between her life and work as a Celtic goddess and as a Christian saint that the continuity between the two is undeniable.[37] Others, such as the bishop St Ailbe, show definite signs of Celtic mythological influence; Ailbe was a divine war-hound of Leinster, and "mythological tales and attributes … attached themselves to the bishop."[38]

Some of the old holidays survived as well, indicating a real continuity of practice in the life of the community. Samhain, the beginning of Celtic winter and a night when the worlds of the dead and the living were understood to be particularly close and the barriers permeable, became Hallowe'en. The relationship between the two holidays is evident today in the ghosts, skeletons, witches, and other creatures of the Otherworld that walk the streets that night. This is a distinctly European way of recognizing the night before All Souls' Day; it did not happen in earlier Mediterranean Christianity, and is still rejected by some Christians who are wary of its roots in Celtic religion. Beltane, the beginning of Celtic summer (celebrated by Germanic peoples as Walpurgisnacht), continues to be celebrated as May Day, though in a much-attenuated form.

Perhaps the most striking evidence of syncretism is found in art and architecture, where the survival of Celtic approaches gives Gaelic churches and other Christian artefacts a distinctive appearance. Artisanal techniques, such as enamelling, survived along with some traditional artistic stylistic features such as the use of lines and spirals.[39] The influence of the Celtic world on Christian architecture is not limited to styles, however. Some of the most important symbols of Celtic religion appear on Christian churches, often in surprising ways. The clearest example is the use of the human head in ornamentation. The human head played an important part in Celtic ritual life. The practices of gathering the heads of defeated enemies and hoisting them on pillars or cleaning them and making ritual use of the skulls seem to have been common.[40] Heads carved out of stone were used as decoration in religious locations. Consequently, we should not be altogether surprised to find them surviving in Celtic Christian architecture, including on Romanesque churches of the medieval era, including that in Clone, near Ferns in County Wexford.[41]

More speculative is the question of the sheela-na-gig. "Sheela-na-gig" is the name (probably modern) given to mysterious female figures that appear on churches throughout Europe, but especially in Great Britain and Ireland.[42] These figures have enlarged and exposed genitalia, which seem to be their most prominent feature. On the Continent, such figures are often portrayed with a male counterpart, again, with enlarged genitalia, but the Irish examples rarely include males. The sheela-na-gig is evidently the product of syncretism; there is no specifically Christian history for anything like it – no roots in Christianity's Hebrew, Greek, or Latin heritages – and finding a place for it in Christian theology is exceedingly difficult. The sheela-na-gig is definitely a part of the European adoption and transformation of Christianity. However, the roots of the sheela-na-gig are difficult to trace, as is its purpose. Because the carvings are medieval (they appear on stone churches and other structures in Europe), they may have appeared as a consequence of any of the various belief systems circulating during the previous millennium. The sheela-na-gig may, therefore, be Germanic or Nordic in origin, as easily as Celtic.

Some arguments suggest a Celtic connection, with reasonable like-lihood but little solid proof. Religious carvings can serve a variety of purposes and represent different things to different people in disparate places – a point which may account for the presence of a sole female in some locations, while the female has a male counterpart in other examples. One theory is that the sheela-na-gig represents the survival of belief in a war goddess, common in Celtic thinking. This goddess, called the *Cailleach* in Ireland and Scotland, is the ruler of winter and a creator figure. Another theory is that it may be a Celtic fertility figure, a goddess who grants safe pregnancy and delivery. The grossly enlarged vulvas on these figures suggest a fertility connection, and the sex/war combination is a notable characteristic of Celtic goddesses such as those in the Ulster Cycle. Whatever the origin of these odd figures, the sheela-na-gig seems out of place on a Christian church, which is why many were destroyed in a spate of nineteenth-century purification.

The Celtic encounter with Christianity was decisively syncretistic. For a period of at least five hundred years (one-quarter of Christianity's lifespan) and perhaps as long as one thousand years (one-half of Christianity's lifespan), significant traces of ancient Celtic religion had a noticeable impact on Christianity in Wales and Ireland – especially the latter. The old tales were told and retold; the ancient personages took on renewed guises and meanings.

The appearance of Christianity in Celtic lands is a product of invasion. However, the syncretism that ensued served religious purposes. It was not simply a case of an invader appearing and imposing a religion. The Romans were definitely not pure Christians – if such a thing could be imagined. Besides, even vigorously Christian emperors would have had a difficult time imposing orthodoxy on the remote tribes of the European empire. Thus, there was room for a more innovative approach to religion, especially in the more far-flung corners of Roman lands. Plus, much of our evidence for the Celtic-Christian syncretism comes from surviving Celtic kingdoms where the Romans never ruled. These Celts did not become Christian in order to curry favour with the enemy; if anything the alien character of the religion and its connection to a mighty and dangerous opponent probably worked to the disadvantage of the new religion.

What drove the syncretism, then? Why did people with such a rich mythic history embrace the new religion and meld it with the old? A response to Roman power was undoubtedly part of it; a religion that brings such power over others would certainly have been attractive. The conquering power of the Romans was evidence of the capacity of their God or gods to overcome the old gods of Celtic and Germanic religion. If the question is "Who can defend this place?" then the answer was the Romans and the powers they brought, more often than not. The advantage of a syncretistic approach is that it does not entail dispensing with the old gods and risking an insult that may bring unfortunate consequences. Instead, one can simply honour both and slowly come to recognize a unity between them. The distinction vanishes.

Another reason is our old friend, "flexibility." Celtic religion was tough, but malleable, even fluid. Part of the challenge in tracing it and identifying its influence is precisely that it lacked a permanent form and defined boundaries. Celtic religion, therefore, could shift in ways that allowed the adoption of relatively inflexible Christianity. Where there were similarities, the joining was easy. The notion of one god with three manifestations is not Christian, but it is close enough to make the doctrine of the Trinity acceptable to people who might otherwise find it alien. In addition, the emphasis upon asceticism that had always found a place in Christianity fit neatly with the way of life of some of the more austere northern European tribes.

Need, however, played the biggest role. Both sides faced theological shortcomings that became evident in their encounter. Celtic religion, with its rich narrative form, could provide helpful explanations of local challenges such as crop failures, bad weather, or defeat in battle. However, once the Celts encountered or became a part of the Roman Empire, they became part of a larger world. Now, they needed an account of the world that went beyond the place or tribe and its gods and yet included the world that they knew. The syncretistic blending of Celtic and Christian answered this need quite well. The story of Brigit still explained much of Irish history. Now, however, Brigit was part of the story of the whole world, and a figure who deserved honour anywhere that Christians gathered, which was effectively everywhere, from the standpoint of the British Isles. Thus, the story of Brigit survived and even reflected greater honour on Ireland.

Moreover, Christianity provided a comforting and helpful account of life after death, which may have been welcome in Celtic lands – though this is only speculation on my part. The certainty of divine welcome played a role in Anglo-Saxon conversion, as is evident in poems such as *The Dream of the Rood* (by an unknown author, preserved in a tenth-century manuscript but definitely older), where Christ's sacrifice is understood as paving the way to the heavenly kingdom for all who believe. We can reasonably speculate that this notion would be helpful, both in response to the Celtic awareness and fear of the Otherworld and as an answer to the significance of life in a new, larger world. Christianity's clear and straightforward declaration that God is in charge of the Otherworld, combined with the assertion that an appropriate understanding can be reached with God, must surely have been welcome. Christian explanations of life after death would have provided a sense of security in an insecure world.

Another gift of Christianity, this one with the firmest of evidence, was the monastic form of organization. The syncretism that we have seen, especially in the survival of Celtic stories, is largely driven by the monastic tradition which became a fundamental organizing principle of Celtic society. Indeed, the Celtic monasteries became so strong that they began to export learning to Gaul (now France) and Britain.

Christianity had a theological and practical shortcoming, also. It lacked a strong connection to nature, including natural processes (such as childbirth) that people faced on a daily basis. The story of the Incarnation (God become human in Jesus) is an affirmation of the value of the physical world; that is how today's theologians understand it. Similarly, the Eucharist (the meal of bread and wine that reminds Christians of Jesus Christ's death and resurrection) focuses upon the value of the material world. Indeed, early theologians such as Irenaeus of Lyons (a second-century-CE thinker) understood salvation as God entering into the whole world and transforming it into God's kingdom so that all of history became valuable and meaningful. However, years of Stoic and Platonic influences weakened that side of Christian thinking in the early centuries of the religion's development. The rise of the Desert Fathers and a strong tradition of otherworldly, hermetic focus contributed to this movement also, especially since the Desert Fathers did not marry or have children.

Arguably, this culminated in Augustine's distrust of the body and the material world, though Augustine's position was also affected by his own history of Platonism and Manichaeism. In addition to all of these historical developments, we may note that a general, theological affirmation of nature's value provides little equipment for dealing with its vagaries.

In contrast, Celtic religion, like most pre-philosophical, traditional religions, placed tremendous emphasis upon the significance of nature. The emphasis upon supernatural presences in specific places and the existence of formal ways to relate to those presences gave people tools for basic existence, on a day-to-day basis, where they lived. Melding both goddess and saint in one Brigit, and honouring her well, enabled ordinary Celts to sustain their intimate relation to the particular and material world while simultaneously participating in the larger cosmic story. The same can be said for the incorporation of Celtic elements in Christian architecture. The presence of heads performs this unifying function, as does the sheela-na-gig – whatever its origin.

One of the reasons that Celtic Christianity is celebrated today is its focus upon the value of the physical world. Many people take up Celtic Christian forms of prayer and meditative exercise precisely because they challenge the modern world's tendency to suppress bodily existence (think of how we spend long hours in chairs, in front of computer screens and under artificial light, on schedules which do not vary with seasons). This inclination to praise the Celts can easily be taken too far. As Caitlin Corning vigorously reminds us, much of this thinking about Celtic Christianity is more a reflection of modern neo-Celtic romanticism than of anything in actual Celtic history.[43] Celtic Christianity was no more pro-environment or otherwise modern than any form of ancient or medieval Christianity. Popular modern assumptions about the significance of Celtic texts and practices should not be allowed to guide our thinking about what the past looked like.

Nonetheless, we can see elements of Celtic traditional religion in medieval Christianity, especially in Ireland, and this religion was certainly more nature-oriented than Mediterranean Christianity had become. The survival of nature-oriented feasts such as celebrations of the solstices, as well as physically oriented symbols such as the sheela-na-gig, emphasize the contribution of traditional religion to Christian tradition. This accomplishment is not likely to have been solely Celtic; other traditions contributed to European shifts in the nature of Christianity.

By picking up elements from both heritages, Celtic Christianity became a helpful syncretism, performing a service to Christianity in the larger world. By calling Christianity to recognize neglected meanings from within its previously existing heritage, Celtic Christianity functioned as a reflexive syncretism. It bent to its own purposes traditionally Christian understandings of the overarching order and of the challenges of life and their means of resolution, while making a powerful faith commitment. Celtic Christianity took monasticism, an already-existing structure, and made that form of organization its own. However, Celtic Christianity changed the value-orientation of received Mediterranean Christianity, calling attention to the created order in ways that Mediterranean Christianity had forgotten or ignored. The result was a reflexive syncretism in which the Celtic world enriched Christianity by forcing that religion to understand itself more deeply.

Underneath that larger viewpoint, inspired partly by a long-term understanding of the implications of Celtic Christianity, is the local Celtic reality. That reality is a religion that appears to be at least half composed of the old, traditional religion. In the common terminology that we are generally avoiding, the Celts were as much pagans as they were Christians. They moulded Christianity into the image of their own thought-world, using it as a vehicle to sustain their own gods, their own understanding of how gods operate (in three manifestations), their own stories, their own festivals, their own symbols, and their own art. They enriched this thought-world by adding a Christian sense of God as the ruler of the cosmos and source of salvation, in addition to accepting and developing a Christian form of organization – monasticism. The result, in this analysis, is a highly successful syncretism in which the new religion and the traditional religion both provide elements, while the resultant religion is indistinguishably both. In this reading, Celtic Christianity is truly both Celtic and Christian.

THE GOOD OF SYNCRETISM

These examples suggest that syncretism can have two sorts of benefits. It can result in a new religious framework, offering real benefits to people who find their existing understanding to be inadequate. The Buddhist-Taoist syncretism that became Chinese Buddhism and gave rise to Ch'an Buddhism was tremendously important to a China that found its official Confucian explanation for the world insufficient to address new social and political circumstances. Moreover, the values of Han Confucianism and the actions that it encouraged were no longer helpful; they suited a world in which the emperor was all-powerful, but said little to a reality in which the emperor was weak and the competing interests surrounding him were strong. A syncretism that fully integrated Chinese traditions into a new understanding of the world was truly the solution required. The symmetrical syncretism that was Chinese Buddhism met the challenge as perfectly as one could reasonably expect, with as neat a balance of progress and preservation of insights, and as great a degree of mutuality as any in history.

In a somewhat different way, Islamic Arabs were faced with the challenge of growing power and the demands of empire. Their religion was particularly oriented toward solving a prior set of challenges: (1) the relationship between disparate tribes of different religious viewpoints and one Allah; and (2) the relationship among those tribes at a human level. Very rapidly, those tribes became part of a larger world and then found themselves in charge of that larger world. The questions that arose required a kind of systematic thought at which the Greek tradition was adept and for which it had numerous tools. The challenges around values and actions were similarly new, especially when they concerned bureaucratic structures with which the Muslim Arabs had no experience. Given that a basic source of the impetus for creation of the empire came from Islam, the religion that provided the fundamental meaning and values for the Arabs, a new syncretism needed to sustain those meanings and values. Indeed, the syncretism needed to be altogether recognizable as Islam while providing solutions for the new challenges. For this situation, the asymmetrical syncretism in which Greek thought was accepted and digested by the Islamic tradition was appropriate: Islam remained, but in a substantially different and developed form, with significantly greater reach and power; the preservation of insights played a dominant role, as was evidently necessary, but real progress occurred, also. Islam gained from Greek thought, but with a lesser degree of mutuality than is evident in the Chinese situation, so that the non-negotiable aspects of Islam remained more or less intact even as they were newly understood.

The reflexive syncretism that the Celtic influence represented for Christianity is real, but less easily assessed. From the Celtic perspective, the result was a symmetrical syncretism or a very strong asymmetrical syncretism, a highly successful meeting of Celtic belief with Christian belief. Celtic religion, local by its very nature, might simply have vanished and left little trace had it not joined with Christianity. The effect of the syncretism was to enshrine aspects of Celtic understanding so thoroughly that people still revere Brigit today, in the mixed way that only a truly mutual syncretism can arrange. The larger perspective is more complex, because Celtic Christianity was an aspect of larger Christianity and was superseded by Anglo-Saxon Christianity in many places. However, we can fairly say that the reminder of nature's significance evident in the stories and symbols of Celtic Christianity survived in the religion of the British Isles and especially in Ireland. Both in Celtic and Anglo-Saxon forms, British Christianity has a history of emphasizing nature, even to the extent of being the home of a form of Christianity (called Pelagianism, after an Anglo-Saxon monk, Pelagius) that resists Augustine's strong emphasis upon God's divine action as overwhelming nature. Today, many people turn to Celtic traditions for inspiration of just this kind. To what degree modern notions of Celtic Christianity reflect the traditions of the Celts is open to question; a lot of modern "Celtic Christianity" may be little more than an exercise in imposing on the past what we wish to find there. Nonetheless, the power of Celtic witness – of the reflexive syncretism that reminds Christians of the value of the created world – is significant. That people turn specifically to the Celts, rather than elsewhere, for this sort of encouragement is a reminder of what they accomplished.

... And When It's Not So Good

DESTRUCTIVE SYNCRETISM

Unfortunately, syncretism does not always result in beneficial development. It can make a religion worse. This is one reason that some people hold so tightly to the principle of preservation of insights. The insight originally resulted in progress and its adherents do not want that progress to be lost. They do not want to see mutuality, the sharing of wisdom that occurs in syncretism, to have priority over the good that they see in their own religion. Such people are aware that choosing real progress can be difficult, if they are even willing to admit that it is possible; other people, such as the Jewish *haredim* (often called "ultra-Orthodox"), do not admit this possibility. Consequently, people hold firmly to the wisdom that they have received. They have a valid point: syncretism can be a bad thing.

Alternatively, and commonly, we sometimes see both progress and decline in a particular combination of religions. This calls for complex judgements about what constitutes progress and changes a religion for the better. We can reach out and participate in a syncretism, alive to the potential benefits but unaware of some of the pitfalls on our path. Even when syncretism is a good thing, it is not necessarily an unalloyed good.

In our discussion of processes of development, we shall see how Western Christianity benefited from incorporating Latin thought into its life, while Christianity also gained standing in the life of the

Roman Empire. However, this brought about an attachment to the use of violence (which extended with Christianity's penetration into Northern Europe) that had not originally been part of Christian life and thought. This example draws our attention to a significant indication that a syncretism is unhealthy: it fosters violence or other destructive behaviour. Even if violence can occasionally be justified – the point is debated, but Christian just-war theory (like just-war theories in other traditions) argues that violence can be justified under specific circumstances – no fair observer can deny that European Christianity became unhealthily committed to the use and glorification of war.

A syncretism can also be problematic if it lands in the wrong place in the delicate balance between concern for the self and attention to the needs of the community. Falling too close to one or the other end of this spectrum results in the second and third indicator of an unhealthy syncretism. Capitalism can, all too easily, fall into the trap of self-interest over communal interest and can take other religions with it; parts of Christianity and Buddhism have been hurt this way as, I suspect, have other religions. Some forms of contemporary Islam have, partly in reaction, landed destructively at the other end of the spectrum; this is most evident in examples that we have seen earlier, such as jihadism and strict Saudi Arabian theocracy.

All religions have a besetting sin, a natural inclination that is or can become unhealthy if indulged too freely. In the case of capitalism, it is a potent combination of self-interest and greed. For some people, like Gordon Gekko of the movie *Wall Street*, this inclination takes over entirely, so that "Greed is Good" becomes a motto or even a mantra. Ayn Rand is their theologian; in Nietzschean terms she proclaims the death of God and asserts the rule of humanity (and especially the *übermensch* or "superman") over everything. In Rand's theology, selfishness is the fundamental virtue.[1]

The emphasis upon self-interest grows logically out of one of capitalism's basic principles: the common good, insofar as there can be such a thing, is the sum of individual goods. Communal decision-making and communal ownership are not truly capitalist notions; when they appear, they are modifications of a capitalist system. Capitalism focuses upon my goods and your goods, my ownership and your ownership. The overall idea is that an improvement in the status of any one individual leads to an improvement in the whole body politic. This is the explicit principle behind the "trickle-down economics" so heavily touted in the United States during the Reagan era. If someone gets wealthy, then that person will purchase things and hire people and undertake various other economic acts which will improve the lot of other people. The problem of course, is that making the greater good hinge upon me getting wealthy tends to remove appropriate limitations upon my wealth-increasing actions. The results of that can be seen in all sorts of unhealthy situations: the housing bubble; immense quantities of valueless Asset-Backed Commercial Paper; and oil spills in Louisiana. The only good is that which helps me to get rich. If it hurts you or the environment, well, that's the way it goes.

This inclination to focus upon material self-interest without concern for the other can change other religions dramatically when they enter into a syncretistic relationship with capitalism. We can see it in the legendary caricature/stereotype of Judaism – perhaps most quintessentially represented by Shylock in *The Merchant of Venice* – but I am not aware of any real attempt to argue that self-interested capitalism is an integral part of Jewish religion. In contrast, Oral Roberts and his successors have made "prosperity gospel" theology into a noticeable force in North American Christianity. Similarly, Buddhism, traditionally a critic of materialistic and selfish impulses, has been turned by some into a set of techniques for business success. In both cases, fundamental and defining principles of the earlier religions – principles which have historically been understood as the best moral characteristics of those religions – have vanished and been replaced by the evil that both religions opposed from the very beginning.

PROSPERITY THEOLOGY IN CHRISTIANITY

Prosperity theology is an odd but highly successful version of Christianity. The basic assertion of this point of view is that God blesses those who worship Him and that many of those blessings come in material form. God wants everyone to be rich; everyone who is not rich simply lacks faith and commitment. As Kenneth Copeland (one of the leaders in the prosperity movement) argues in *The Laws of Prosperity*, faithfulness to God will lead to material wealth, if only we ask for what we want in the firm belief that we will receive it.[2] In *The Spiritual Millionaire: The Spirit of Wisdom Will Make You Rich*, Keith Cameron Smith (millionaire and self-styled inspirational speaker) is even blunter:

> The proven ways that people have become millionaires are based on truths about money. The Spiritual Millionaire follows proven plans to become financially rich and learns great lessons about money. Once you learn truths about money then God can give you new ideas on how to make millions. However, God cannot give you ideas on how to become a Spiritual Millionaire until you believe that you can. The proven ways of becoming a millionaire give you hope and teach you that you can. And when you believe that you can, then God can and will help you.[3]

Some preachers of the prosperity gospel even employ the "name it and claim it" line, which means just what it suggests: you tell God exactly what you want and claim it as yours, believing with your whole self that it will be yours, and God will deliver it. Copeland's children do this, giving their money to his ministry and claiming the financial returns that will inevitably come – and come, they do.[4]

The practical problems with this are immense and obvious. The first is that wealth is a receding target. By North American standards, I am barely viable financially; my family and I live a very modest life in a condominium townhouse in a small city. However, by the standards of much of the world, I am exceedingly wealthy – there are many places in the world where 1500 sq. feet of modern comfort would be a luxurious space in which to house four people. If everyone is rich, then nobody is, in a bizarre sort of twist. That is because we tend to think of wealth in relative terms; it is about whether we are getting ahead of the Joneses, rather than whether we have enough to live well. Of course, we also tend to think of living well in terms of the number and diversity of creature comforts and the variety of (the latest and greatest) tools that we possess, rather than asking the more basic question of whether we have what we need to accomplish our tasks and fulfill our vocations.

Moreover, if North American levels of production and consumption were extended to everyone on the planet, then Earth would soon be exhausted; it simply does not have the resources to support our way of life on a universal scale. So, if every human were to have the requisite faith, and if we were all to place our orders with God (the Cosmic Neiman-Marcus Department Store), the planet-wide shopping spree would come to an abrupt halt as supplies of everything simply ran out. And, I, for one, do not want to think about the garbage disposal problem; that one is already a nightmare for most North American municipalities and, I expect, for the responsible authorities elsewhere in the richer parts of the world.

So, clearly, we are talking about a kind of salvation for an elect few. On any larger scale, the whole idea is simply absurd; it cannot be coherently thought. It becomes even more problematic with serious consideration of the problem it creates for other Christians; the prosperity gospel implies that others, such as poor but dedicated believers in the *barrios* of Latin America and the drought-stricken villages of Africa (to name only two examples) are simply not faithful enough or do not really expect God to provide. This seems unlikely to me, as well as being a brutal calumny.

Perhaps the greater challenge is the degree to which this theology represents a fundamental undermining of all that Christianity stands for. This is what Friedrich Nietzsche calls a "transvaluation of values," in which that which is noble comes to be regarded as base. Nietzsche argues that Christianity and Judaism represent just such a transvaluation because they value the weak, the poor, and the needy, placing them ahead of the mighty warriors in the human line-up.[5] Curiously, in prosperity theology, Nietzsche wins, sort of, as the great of society (the wealthy) are placed ahead of the weak. At the same time, however, he loses because nobility is now defined in bourgeois terms: the truly successful are those who accumulate riches, which is hardly what Nietzsche had in mind.

This is not a syncretism that sustains the valuable things that Christianity has to offer; instead, it is a victory for capitalism, attained by using the very thinnest form of Christian disguise. The result is an asymmetric syncretism in which elements of Christianity are used by capitalism to further its goals. *The Atlantic* magazine finds this to be true in the most obvious and practical ways; Hanna Rosin, a journalist, investigated the growing phenomenon of prosperity gospel churches and discovered that they played a noticeable role in the sub-prime loans crisis – though the magazine's cover page probably overstates the impact, with the massive headline, "Did Christianity Cause the Crash? How Preachers Are Spreading A Gospel of Debt."[6] A bit strong, perhaps, but the magazine does find that loan officers pursued clergy and spoke at church-sponsored events, encouraging people to take out mortgages and offering donations to churches or charities as an incentive. Prosperity churches have grown rapidly in the areas where subprime lending was strongest. Fernando Garay, a pastor, served as the poster-boy for the headline. Garay had been a loan officer (working in Countrywide Financial's emerging-markets division) with the particular task of pushing loans within the Latino community; his ministry continued the work.

The Atlantic helps us to see the reason that this syncretism is not a good thing: it dismisses the most creative insight of Christianity – the priority of love over self-concern, a priority which manifests itself in care for the poor and needy – and replaces it with the ideal of individual possession of material wealth. Though Christians do not always live up to it, the example of Jesus as self-giving is one of Christianity's defining marks. Jesus told his twelve closest disciples to travel with a minimum of resources and clothing (Mt 10:10, Mk 6:8, Lk 9:3). He announced that the poor are blessed possessors of the Kingdom of God (Lk 6:20), which means that they truly know the love of God. In this spirit, some of the earliest Christians sought to live together in community, with common ownership of all property (Acts 2:44, 4:32). For much of Christianity's history, earning interest on money was deemed to be usury and was unacceptable for Christians. Focusing one's life on the acquisition of material wealth hardly accords with this spirit.

Moreover, the prosperity theology vision of wealth is essentially magical; one attains it by the pure effort of will directed toward a God who merely awaits one's order. The God of Christianity is simply not this sort of God. The fulfillment of human life is understood to be in the divine will, not at the direction of humans; this assertion is universal amongst Christian theologians, though understood differently by different thinkers. Christians enunciate this position every time that they say the Lord's Prayer, which is as universal a Christian practice as one can find: "Your Kingdom come / Your will be done / On earth as it is in heaven."

Ultimately, prosperity theology is destructive, which may be the clearest evidence of its theologically unsatisfactory nature. If the prosperity gospel could be successful for the many, then it would destroy the world through unsustainable levels of consumption. Since the message of success that this gospel carries is evidently false (having failed so spectacularly), it has merely destroyed many people and helped to cripple much of the world's economy for a time. The prosperity gospel is a destructive form of selfishness – a bad bargain in syncretism and an example of asymmetric syncretism at its worst.

PROSPERITY THEOLOGY IN BUDDHISM

Something similar has happened in Buddhism, with the emergence of a North American Buddhism that is very different from Indian and Asian Buddhisms in remarkable and important ways. James William Coleman speaks of "the new Buddhism" and recognizes that it is "fundamentally different from anything that has gone before;" yet he also tries to argue that "in the best tradition of Buddhist logic, it remains at its core completely unchanged from the moment of Siddhartha Gautama's great realization under the bodhi tree."[7] About the change, there is little doubt; one may question the assertion that the core, if there is such a thing, remains stable.

I shall never forget sitting on the beach with a couple of friends, one of whom had been to India and had gained an interest in Buddhism. He tried to interest me in pursuing Buddhism because it provides training in all sorts of skills that are useful in business. They make one much more effective in using time and pursuing one's goals, was his basic line of argument. I was merely confused, since I thought then (as I understand now) that Buddhism is about renouncing desire, especially self-oriented desire, rather than strengthening one's ability to pursue one's desires; this is, as it happens, one of the four fundamental principles of Buddhism and, arguably, the most decisive because truly renouncing desire is what makes the Buddhist goal attainable.

Coleman argues that the core of Buddhism has not changed. Yet, this example suggests that a radical shift has occurred, and this is not an isolated case. Search the Internet and you will find numerous people peddling Buddhist principles as a means to fulfill capitalist goals rather than Buddhist aims. Coleman discovers that a number of leaders among California Buddhists have made use of the religion in just this way, managing to get wealthy – or, at least, sustain a rich lifestyle – on Buddhism. Many have found Buddhism to be a useful adjunct to a life of sexual appetite, embraced in various ways; tantric practices are legendarily helpful in this way. To Coleman's eyes, these are aberrations – and so they are, in that they can hardly be said to follow traditional Buddhist principles. They are not, however, necessarily outside the norms of Western Buddhism, in which liberation may tend to resemble openness, even licence, rather than highly disciplined poverty and simplicity. Certainly, the poetry of Allen Ginsberg and Leonard Cohen, as great as it is, can hardly be said to celebrate the renunciation of sexual desire.

Capitalist Buddhism is strong enough that it could be said to have the status of its own sect, like Zen, except that its fundamental principles are so profoundly at odds with other branches of the larger religion. Michael Roach is a pivotal figure in North American Buddhism. He is a monk and the first American to attain the status of *geshe* (a Tibetan Buddhism academic honour awarded after long study of the tradition). Yet, Roach's first book, *The Diamond Cutter: The Buddha on Managing your Business and Your Life*, is all about how to use Tibetan Buddhist principles to get rich. The central focus is on how Roach participated in taking Andin International, a diamond company, from a borrowed $50,000 stake into annual sales of $100 million – and how you can do something similar. The principles that Roach teaches seem to be excellent – a superbly moral way to run a business. Insofar as these principles demonstrate something of the Middle Way, neither seeking a radical asceticism nor focusing upon attachment to material wealth, they seem to be consistent with the historical development of Buddhist ethics. Roach is attempting a <u>symmetrical</u> syncretism in which the core principles of Buddhism and capitalism are both sustained in a roughly equal balance.

The central argument of the book, however, betrays a victory for capitalism over Buddhism at the precise point where the two were bound to collide: the problem of desire, which has been a challenge from the beginning for those who seek to follow Gautama Buddha. Quite legitimately, Roach argues that money is not evil. Instead, it is empty, in the sense of being mere appearance and having no intrinsic reality, value-lading, or meaning; the technical term is *sunya*, which means something like "void."[8] However, that which is sunya can have great potential; it can be useful in progress on the right path. Money, according to Roach, is morally neutral; this means that it is open to good use by one whose karma (intellectual, spiritual, emotional, moral formation) is sufficiently good. Therefore, Roach is able to say, "You would like to make a million and meditate too. The fact is that for real success in business, you're going to need some of the deep insights that come with a spiritual life. So you can have your cake and eat it too."[9] This seems reasonable enough, except that the book is cultivating the desire for money; all of the good principles in it are presented as techniques for helping the reader to get wealthy. They may make for a person who will behave nicely while chasing money, but worldly riches constitute the desire that drives the process; money does not function as if it were empty, but serves as a powerful draw. One of the final chapters, following discussions of meditation, exercise, and various other healthy things, announces, "In short, we have learned where money really comes from, and we have been given a truly foolproof method for getting it."[10] Later in the same chapter, Roach emphasizes, "The goal is to (1) make a lot of money; (2) stay very healthy in your body and your mind so you can really enjoy the money; and then (3) use the money in a way that you can look back and be proud of."[11]

This seems to be contrary to the Buddha's path to enlightenment, which is ordered toward relinquishing desire for that which is perishable. "The Four Noble Truths" are a significant part of Tibetan (and other) Buddhist thought;[12] they are found in what is commonly known as Gautama Buddha's first sermon, although it is probably the result of later systematic thinking.[13] The point of these truths is that suffering is a common part of the human condition, but it need not be overwhelming or controlling. Suffering "originates in that craving which causes rebirth, which produced delight and passion, and seeks pleasure now here, now there; that is to say, craving for sensual pleasures, craving for continued life, craving for nonexistence."[14] We can put suffering in its place by cultivating detachment from those things to which we cling for safety and success: money, fame, sex, worldly comforts, etc. When we no longer find these things worthy of pursuing, and we become free of desire, then we attain nirvana. Nirvana is the state of freedom from being controlled by wants and needs; it makes doing the true good possible, because actions are no longer directed by these powerful yet fundamentally illusory forces.

If Roach is going in this direction, then he is not admitting it. As we have seen, his declarations of purpose seem to be leading the other way. Roach's argument is not merely simplistic thinking; in important ways, it is more thoughtful than the awful Christian prosperity gospel arguments that we have seen. Roach encourages us to attend to the needs of others, even to place them before our own needs, and has numerous concrete suggestions for how to cultivate attention to others. Moreover, Roach asks us to emphasize increasing the wealth and happiness of others as we make our own millions; one of his basic points is that these things are limitless so that we may have all that we could want and help others to have all that they could want (which is an argument that he shares with Christian prosperity theology – and it seems just as unlikely and unhealthy when a Buddhist capitalist says it). Even if it were true, however, this argument does not seem to elude the basic problem, which is that we are still controlled by the desire for money and happiness. By being universalized, the goal shifts a bit; it is not entirely selfish.

However, the book never quite relieves us of our basic goal orientation; we are doing it for the money, even when helping others. If the goal is a capitalist goal, then arriving at a Buddhist end seems unlikely. Buddhism may ameliorate some of the worst effects of capitalist acquisitiveness, so that Gordon Gekko-style behaviour is ruled out, but in Roach's book avarice is the mainspring of religious growth. The result is that Buddhist capitalism may bring about some definite goods, as capitalism most certainly can, but the root insight that Buddhism offers the world is lost in the process. The syncretism turns out to be asymmetrical in an unhelpful way and at the most fundamental point. If the purpose being cultivated is to make a million dollars and be able to enjoy it, then Buddhist priorities are likely to be retained only insofar as they serve those aims. This means that anything that compromises the possibility of riches is likely to be heaved overboard when it gets in the way. Self-centeredness wins this battle, and Buddhism loses.

CHRISTIANITY, ROME, AND EUROPE

Both of the above examples display syncretism in the service of self-interest so that the universal concern which is central to healthy religion is compromised. However, there is something of a balance to be found here – a balance that religions must always be seeking. A syncretism can also be compromised by unhealthy means of sustaining public order. This can happen because syncretisms may come into existence precisely to serve order. Part of the reason for the (largely healthy) Celtic Christian synthesis that we saw earlier is that Roman rule would be compromised by efforts to root out native religion; simply uniting the traditions is a much easier and safer strategy.

The Celtic example is a helpful pointer toward an unhealthy syncretism, though, because it is a reminder of the transformation that Christianity underwent as it became the Roman instrument of social order. Christianity began in the first century CE as a small, minority religion, with no discernible clout. At first, it was one type of Judaism, at a time when the Romans ruled Israel and Judea through client kings. Judaism existed in a kind of fragile compromise, as a monotheistic religion in a world where polytheistic religion was a primary means of sustaining common life; participation in the cults of the larger community, including the emperor cult, was an important way of demonstrating one's respect for the Empire and its diverse peoples. A form of religious pluralism dominated. In this context, Christians had no allies because they rejected the easy pluralism of the Empire, but were becoming cut off from the larger body of Judaism by beliefs that are heretical – even blasphemous – by Jewish standards, and by a developing rejection of aspects of Jewish law. By 70 CE, when a failed rebellion ended the client arrangement and the area was occupied by Romans, the split was well underway and religious boundaries were becoming defined.

Quite rapidly, Christianity spread throughout the Empire, in spite of sporadic persecutions (such as the first persecution under Emperor Nero, after the Great Fire of Rome in 64 CE, and the last persecution under Diocletian, an Eastern Emperor in 303 CE, after the Empire was split into two parts). Christianity's success can partly be attributed to its success at syncretism: the new religion employed the very best of Neo-Platonic, Stoic, Roman legal, and other intellectual tools as it formulated its particular doctrines and ordered its life. Christians might dismiss other religions but they did not necessarily reject their ideas.

Tertullian (c. 160–c. 220 CE) is perhaps the most famous Christian isolationist, known for his declaration of the permanent distance between pagan wisdom and Judeo-Christian revelation. "What indeed has Athens to do with Jerusalem? What concord is there between the Academy and the Church? What between heretics and Christians? ... Away with all attempts to produce a mottled Christianity of Stoic, Platonic, and dialectic composition!"[15] Yet, in spite of his powerful denunciation of ideas from outside explicitly Christian contexts, Tertullian was a syncretist of real importance. Perhaps most significantly, he imported Latin legal thinking into Christian theology in a manner that was to prove decisive for the Western Christian mind: God became the judge who gives the law, and sin came to be seen as a violation of that law.[16] This looks like obvious and straightforward biblical theology to the average Western Christian, which is merely an indication of how far this impulse has gone; Eastern Christianity has moved in a substantially different direction. Moreover, Tertullian did not hesitate to rely upon the Stoicism that he commented upon so scornfully. Indeed, the Stoics made important contributions to his thought, supplying his psychology and an argument for human knowledge of God without specific divine revelation.[17]

Tertullian was not alone in this strategy. Origen (c. 185–254 CE), a thinker important to the development of Christian understandings of God, was a Neo-Platonist and Neo-Pythagorean (with, perhaps, some Aristotelianism tossed in for good measure). Augustine of Hippo (354–430 CE), perhaps the greatest of early Christian theologians and the defining voice of Western Christianity, was influenced by Neo-Platonism and Manichaeism; the latter was a kind of dualism in which matter is understood to have been created by an evil Demiurge and the human task is to escape the material world, a viewpoint with Gnostic and Zoroastrian roots. The list of syncretistic thinkers goes on and on; it is decisive for Christian thinking.

Christianity was not really of significant size or importance until the fourth century, when everything suddenly changed.[18] In 313 CE, Constantine (ruler of the Western Empire) and Licinius (ruler of the Eastern Empire) announced a policy of religious toleration and declared Christianity to be legally acceptable within the Roman

Empire. Constantine became personally associated with the religion and began to give it the status of the Empire's leading religion. By 324, Constantine had become the sole ruler of the Empire. Though his personal beliefs are a matter of some dispute, he bestowed favoured status upon Christianity. Constantine built great church buildings, exempted Christian clergy from some laws, provided tax exemptions so that church money could be used for charitable purposes, and played a significant role in the resolution of ecclesiastical disputes.[19] He began a profound shift in the life of the Empire, integrating Christians into the ruling elites. By the end of the fourth century, the Empire would be officially Christian, the old religions outlawed, and their rituals banned.[20] Christianity went from being a relatively minor opposition religion to being the heart of the Empire in the course of a single century.

This was a challenging time to be in charge. Christian thinking needed to develop rapidly in order to respond to a whole series of changes. This was the period in which Christian beliefs about the nature of God and the identity of Jesus Christ were clarified as a result of internal pressures for consistency and also as a product of Imperial requirements for stability and order. Christianity was also forced to grapple with the phenomenon of mass conversion since infant baptism was becoming common. Moreover, Christian identity could now be a passport to the Emperor's favour. Here, Christianity's openness to syncretism served it well: a Christian aristocracy developed rapidly, and traditional Christian ideas were modified to incorporate Roman notions of nobility, friendship, and honour.[21]

Perhaps the greatest challenge, however, was that Christians inherited the Empire just as it was crumbling. The long northern and western borders had always been debatable, to be held by force rather than to be trusted as impermeable barriers. By the middle of the fifth century, they were very nearly porous. Goths, Visigoths, Vandals, Huns, and others invaded, appropriating land and sacking cities. By the end of the fifth century, the Western Empire had effectively collapsed. The Eastern Empire survived much longer, but we will leave its story behind because our concerns are with the West.

The Christian church inherited the problem of maintaining order over (and sustaining culture within) a vast area, even as order was becoming impossible. For the church, however, this was a different kind of challenge from that faced by earlier Romans. Christianity's basic task had not been defined in imperial terms; the Christian mission was not to rule. Instead, the church's job was to bring people to God and provide charitable assistance to the needy. When conflated with the work of ruling the Empire, this mission underwent a rather drastic change for the better and for the worse.

The church felt the increased burden immediately. We can see the church pressed for resources to help by the middle of the sixth century, when papal letters reveal declining income in the face of great destitution. Pope Pelagius I turned to Archbishop Sapaudus of Arles, begging for money, clothing, and food for the people of Italy, whose fields had been ravaged so that they could not survive.[22] Christian prelates became public authorities, but authorities whose job was to provide support for a society in decay, full of uncertainty, poverty, and violence. "Gregory, Bishop of Tours (540–94) and Gregory the Great (540–604), Pope and Bishop of Rome, ran the legal and financial affairs of their dioceses as well as the spiritual" and this was in a messy and difficult time.[23] Municipal authority flowed into the hands of bishops and, slowly but surely, so did resources. "At the end of the sixth century a Frankish king complained that all the riches were flowing into the hands of bishops at the expense of the royal fisc, and that royal authority was being eclipsed by that of the bishops of cities."[24] Thus, the bishops could carry out tasks that once belonged to other authorities such as "constructing new channels for a river, securing water supplies, maintaining fortifications, as well as the traditional tasks of organized charitable works: feeding the poor, housing the refugee, redeeming the captive."[25]

Out of this situation emerged the medieval order.[26] The church responded to the challenges by developing new structures. Under Gregory the Great, papal primacy was asserted very strongly. Archbishops, subordinate to the pope, directed the work of bishops. Bishops became rulers of dioceses, subordinate to archbishops. Priests became the representatives of bishops, while deacons and other ordained officers served under priests. This order varied in its application. Medieval communications were notoriously slow and unreliable. Plus, of course, there were always local interests at stake so that a priest might be more beholden to a local landowner than to his bishop, and a bishop might be more responsive to the wishes of his king than those of the pope. However, a basic order existed. As religious orders grew, they developed parallel, ordered structures. Gregory the Great encouraged the growth of Benedictine monasticism in the West, but ensured that direction came from the Papacy, which retained the real power.[27]

The church asserted its formal authority over monarchs and, therefore, over all matters of public concern. By the time that Charlemagne, King of the Franks, was crowned as Emperor by Pope Leo III (800 CE) Christianity had become the official force that conveyed political legitimacy in society. Popes even had their own troops, and papal elections could be bloody affairs driven by thirst for political strength. As the government revived from the tenth century onward, the church still insisted upon its formal superiority. Ecclesiastical persons were not subject to civil law or common law, but had their own system of canon law which covered any offences with which they might be charged. The church could also call the civil authority to carry out penalties that the church imposed. More potently, it could mobilize the community to serve its purposes, as in the Crusades.

The church was the home of learning, giving it added authority. Literacy was almost entirely found within the church hierarchy so that even monarchs and tradespeople were dependent upon clerics for their skills in reading and writing. Whole cultures depended upon monks and their ability to record events and stories to be passed on to future generations. Moreover, monks passed on agricultural skills to tribes that had traditionally survived on hunting, fishing, scavenging, and fighting, and thus peasant culture emerged throughout Western Europe.[28] The churches founded universities, creating a larger intellectual community.

This is a syncretism. While something of early Christianity may be found in the church's concern for social needs, its emphasis upon human salvation, and its continual efforts at refining Christian doctrine, the face of the church changed dramatically. New questions and people with different backgrounds transformed Christianity. Roman ideas about precedence, power, and order, Platonic ideas about hierarchy, and generally non-Christian ideas about the use of violence made Christianity into something very different from what it had been in the early centuries, when an intimate group came together to worship Jesus, share in the Eucharistic meal, and distribute alms to the poor.

In some important ways, this was a successful syncretism. It probably counts as a symmetrical syncretism, as it maintained extensive portions of Christian, Latin, and Germanic roots. Christianity grew in
numbers and intellectual sophistication. Christianity also served the
world, providing leadership in intellectual life, literacy, music, art,
architecture, agriculture, and law. Christianity provided support for
the poor and needy, and made available what little health care there
was. Without the church, life would have been a great deal more mis-
erable than it was for many people. In addition, Western society could
not have emerged as swiftly as it did and might have carried notably
inferior values when it finally flowered.

This is not the whole story, however. At times, Christians found
themselves involved in activities that were impossible to defend on
the strength of traditional Christian principles (and are generally
abhorred, today). Western Christianity has a just-war theory, traceable
to Augustine (and to prior Roman thinking), which allows for certain
kinds of wars – notably in defence of others. However, much of the
story of the Crusades is completely inconsistent with just-war principles. A case might be made for justice in the original justification for
the First Crusade: to free Eastern Christians from Muslim persecution
(rather dramatically overstated) and to liberate Jerusalem from the
Arab Muslims who had invaded the city.[29] However, profit and power
swiftly became motives, and, in significant cases, the dominant reasons for crusading. The crusades against Almeria and Tortosa proceeded on the basis of contracts between Spanish rulers who wanted
power, and Genoa, which provided troops in return for a portion of
the city under attack.[30]

Perhaps the most egregious example of crusading as an economic
and political activity is the Fourth Crusade, which was undergirded by
a Venetian investment. Unable to reach the Holy Land, the crusaders
were sent to invade Zara, a Western Christian city which owed money
to Venetian merchants, and then onwards to invade Constantinople,
in support of a deposed Byzantine Emperor.[31] The invasion of Zara
was specifically contrary to Papal instruction, and the invaders were
excommunicated (though that may have been an exercise in diplo-
macy and Pope Innocent may have been prepared to accept the invasion privately, but not publicly).[32] From the beginning of the crusades, relations between Westerners and the Eastern Empire had been

uncomfortable, as the Byzantines laid claim to lands invaded by Muslims and now by Westerners. However, an invasion of Constantinople hardly counts as just and it has no relationship at all to the original reasons for crusading. It may have come about as a result of a combination of factors such as Venetian desire for profit; Frankish desire for power; and Papal desire for union between the Eastern and Western churches, under Papal leadership.[33]

Crusading tactics are no more consistent with just-war ideas than were crusader goals. In the Fourth Crusade, fires were used as a weapon three times, destroying one-third of Constantinople's houses – the dwellings of people who had no choice, either corporately or individually, about finding themselves in a war zone.[34] But then, as early as the First Crusade, deplorable violence was a central aspect of the venture. The first armies to set out (in 1096 CE) did so with insufficient supplies, so they pillaged Hungarian territory in spite of support (including provisions) from the King of Hungary.[35] When later armies took Jerusalem (1099 CE), they slaughtered the Jewish and Muslim inhabitants, covering the streets with human parts, blood, and gore.[36] As troops of the Second Crusade marched through Adrianople, a Byzantine city, they torched a monastery to avenge a murder – and the same city was pillaged during the Third Crusade.[37] In short, the soldiers of the Crusades behaved as soldiers always had, by and large.

The point of all this is not to criticize the Crusades; plenty of people have done a thorough job of that. Instead, my argument is that the syncretism between Christianity, on the one hand, and the ruling mindsets of Rome and Northern Europe, on the other, was not altogether healthy for Christianity. The Crusades took place partly to deal with the challenges of ruling. Medieval Christian rulers needed to direct Mediterranean and European warriors toward Eastern Christian and Muslim lands as a way of moving violence out of Western Christian territory – a practice which echoed the reasons that Muslims had invaded Eastern Christian lands. Plus, the underlying values of strength and nobility that motivated medieval soldiery were rooted in Roman and European ways of thinking. Christianity had become indistinguishable from the world that it ruled, by a process of syncretism which changed all of the religions involved.

In the process, Christianity gained much, but it also lost something of value – something central to its very existence. The priorities of justice and peace that led Jesus to die on a cross rather than to fight his tormentors, were transformed by the exigencies of ruling in a violent world. Christianity, which began with a sacrificial life and death, found itself justifying the massacre of innocent Jews and Muslims in Jerusalem, the city where Jesus died. Moreover, as a matter of public order, Christians called people to kill others in wars that were manifestly unnecessary and unjust.

The same tangle among Christianity, the priority of public order, and values inherited from other religions has played into various other unsavoury episodes. The Spanish Inquisition certainly belongs in this category. Simply trying to maintain the sort of unity that society requires is a real challenge for any religion, let alone one that began as a small opposition movement. Central characteristics of identity can get lost, and the principle of preservation of insights can fail or be insufficiently considered. Social desires and needs can spur unhealthy syncretisms just as easily as individual preferences. Syncretism is not always a good thing, even when it is quite thorough and complete. This was not the sort of asymmetric syncretism where one religion was effectively undermined by another. Instead, all of the roots of medieval Western Christianity contributed and were fully on display. However, taken together, the contributions of Christian faith, belief, and fervour; Latin organization, civilization, and honour (including the honour found in war); and Northern European warrior culture, amounted to a dangerous religious force. In some very important ways, this was a bad bargain in syncretism, at least for Christianity.

THE DANGER OF SYNCRETISM

Syncretism is not an automatic solution to the challenges faced by any religion. Indeed, there are no automatic solutions to any challenge. Judgement is always necessary. We must make the best decisions that we can about the courses of action that we take, recognizing that our choices may be wrong.

The real value of syncretism is that it enlarges the pool of resources from which we may draw. If we insist that we must rely only upon the answers that we find in our own heritages, then we will almost inevitably encounter questions that go beyond our available intellectual equipment. That is why Buddhism was helpful to the Han Chinese, Greek thought to the Arab Muslims, and Celtic thought to Mediterranean Christians; these alternative sets of ideas provided solutions to the challenges that the Chinese, Arabs, and Christians faced. Mutuality proved to be enriching.

The central point of the principle of preservation of insights is a reminder that not every change is progress. Some changes initiate decline by causing the loss of the valuable wisdom that sustains a particular religion. The thoroughgoing capitalist versions of Christianity and Buddhism that focus upon riches as the end of life are examples of this kind of change. In the "prosperity" syncretism, Christianity and Buddhism lose core components of their overarching accounts of life and meaning. In each case, a shift in this account ramifies through the whole religious system, causing radical changes in the explanation of life's challenge (relative material scarcity) and its resolution (an order of life that leads to material riches). This changes the faith commitment, which begins to hinge on the degree to which the religion delivers relative material wealth. The values taught by the institution change, focusing upon increase in wealth, presumably for the leadership along with less powerful adherents. Even the forms of organization may shift as clergy attach themselves to money-making institutions (as we see in the example of Fernando Garay as preacher and sub-prime loan officer). This particular way of constructing a syncretism with capitalism is destructive of Christianity and Buddhism, leaving them as hollowed-out husks – an asymmetric syncretism of a particularly unwise kind. Note that this does not mean that no syncretism can be arranged with capitalism; it is a powerful and risky ally but it offers some notable goods. Giving in to the worst excesses of capitalism is not healthy, however, and Christianity and Buddhism need to take a firm stance against the "prosperity" syncretism.

The example of the syncretism among Christian, Latin, and Northern European ways of thinking and acting is more complicated. Although Tertullian and others were aware of the danger, they could hardly avoid entering into the conversation that was structured by Greek and Latin thought. The intellectual resources were really quite astounding; the theology that emerged from the time is vivid, rich, and powerful. More importantly, perhaps, the dominant thought forms of the Latin world enabled Christianity to answer its most pressing questions about God and salvation. Without these resources, Christianity would have remained in narrative mode, telling its stories but unable to respond to the larger questions those stories inspired. Returning to our earlier example of the syncretism between Celtic traditional religion and Christianity, we can add that Northern European religions strengthened the connection between Christianity and the natural world, balancing some of the limitations introduced by Latin and Greek thought.

At a practical level, the opportunities for good were tremendous. The chance to influence the lives of all Europeans must have been tremendously exciting. Moreover, the needs that very rapidly became evident could hardly be ignored. To have rejected the opening would probably have been unconscionable. Of course, the desire for power will have played its part also, so that people whose interest was in serving the public weal or attaining private enrichment were attracted to the church.

The complicated syncretism among Christian, Latin, Greek, and Northern European thought was in many ways a blessing for Christianity and the first step on its way to becoming the world's largest officially identified religion. However, the very same syncretism compromised Christianity profoundly, undermining some of its most original principles and causing it to live in opposition to its founder's example. This is a reminder that syncretism's great gift to the world is that it can strengthen intelligent, reasonable, responsible decision-making. Syncretism offers options. It opens up the world. In a syncretistic universe, mutuality means taking seriously other religions as having insights that can help us. However, those insights are not automatically beneficial. They may offer worse paths for us to travel than the well-worn roads we already know. Syncretism can be a means of progress and a way of discovering new possibilities. However, even as we consider the possibilities inherent in other ways of thinking and acting, we must give serious attention to the principle of the preservation of insights. What we already know may be more accurate and helpful than what others can tell us. As every parent has said at least once, "Following the example of others is only good if the other is a good example. You do not need to do what everyone else is doing. After all, if they jumped off a cliff, would you jump, too?"

6

When It Should Have Happened, But Didn't

OVERLOOKING THE POSSIBILITIES

The world suffers no shortage of a refusal to be open. Too often, we commit to our own paths and reject the possibility that someone else may have a better answer to the challenges we face. Or, the principle of preservation of insights can make us reluctant to listen and slow to change. Often, we come home from work angry at someone in the office who simply will not listen, who is simply determined to do things the way that they have always been done. The possibility of mutuality, of learning from others, never emerges.

Religions face the same challenge. Indeed, the difficulty may be greater when it applies to religious matters because they are profoundly important to us. Plus, the larger significance and impact of change can be tough to assess before the fact. If we modify the way that we pray because of insights that we gain from another religion, what will that change? Maybe almost nothing. Then again, maybe many of our traditional members will leave and our whole religious community will be hollowed out. Or, our traditional members will stay and a huge number of new people will join. Commonly, we really do not know what will happen before we try. The results of committing ourselves to the principle of progress are rarely discernible beforehand.

In retrospect, we can often analyze the effects of syncretisms that have occurred. We can say some things about the effects, good and bad, of the linkage between Arab Islam and Greek thought, for instance. However, assessing the impact of roads not taken is much more difficult. We can recognize failures, such as the unhealthy relationship between European Christianity and various Indigenous religions during the Age of Empire, but distinguishing between the consequences of Christianity's neglect of its own principles and its refusal of syncretism is a very difficult task. Even a careful historical and theological dissection of the dynamic will still face a large number of imponderables, because we cannot really say how history would have unfolded if another approach had been followed.

In other words, proving that avoiding syncretism gives poor results is very difficult. It requires us to make educated guesses about how history would have turned out if people had been more open, more interested in mutuality. Guessing about historical outcomes is a mug's game. One of my favourite novels is *Making History*, by Stephen Fry, in which people change the course of history by preventing the birth of Adolf Hitler. The experiment goes awry because another Nazi leader, much more powerful and effective, arises.[1] The lesson of the book, to my mind, is that the "what ifs" of history are manifold, so a course of action that seems better to us, looking back at history from a distance, might not have given better results. We might not be as good at changing history as we think we would be, even had we the power to do so.

Nonetheless, I think that we can point to cases where a failure to engage in syncretism produced such terrible results that we can reasonably assume an improvement would have been possible. The challenge is, of course, to find a test case. Fortunately for this book, though unfortunately for a great many people, we have a ready-made, almost laboratory-designed, example of the failure to accept syncretism and the implications of that failure. A simple and almost absolute rejection of syncretism killed the great religious experiment of the twentieth century: Soviet Marxism-Leninism.

SOVIET MARXISM-LENINISM

Soviet Marxism-Leninism is one of history's greatest experiments in closed-mindedness, a triumph for the principle of fear of the other. The story of Soviet Russia, from the Revolution in 1917 until the

advent of Glasnost and Perestroika in the 1980s, is a narrative of continuous efforts to limit freedom of thought. Communism was the
dominant religion, and its pre-eminence was built upon firm efforts
to stamp out all other religious viewpoints. As we shall see, Soviet
Communism was indisputably a religion: not only did it meet all of
the criteria that we have established for religions, but also it reinforced
its own religious character by trying to destroy all competitive religions. Unlike capitalism, which seeks to co-opt other religious viewpoints invisibly, Soviet Communism actively worked to close churches and synagogues, while making social advancement impossible for
anyone who gave allegiance to another religion.

The challenge set by the Bolsheviks, who constituted only one party
in Revolutionary Russia in 1917 (and a small one, at that), was to
establish a true Marxist state in Russia as a means of fomenting revolution elsewhere in the world. Indeed, the requirement for international revolution was among the core beliefs held by Lenin, who
swiftly established himself as the Bolshevik leader. In Lenin's mind,
Marxism could not survive in one country without support from surrounding countries. More especially, it could not hope to transform
Russia and its satellites, which were geographically enormous and
overwhelmingly agrarian. Marx's theories are not built around revolution in communal, peasant villages without any experience of capitalism or modern industry. Marx and Engels wrote in Britain, in
response to the Industrial Revolution. They had no reason to consider the Russian situation. This meant that Russia needed a wholesale
transformation; it had to become "an educational establishment," as
Isaiah Berlin neatly labelled it.[2] Stalin repudiated the international
vision of Lenin, but the problem remained: Russia needed to become
thoroughly Marxist, though it was hardly a natural candidate for such
thinking.

Lenin believed that the success of the Marxist revolution depended
upon society speaking with one voice. Though circumstances dictat-
ed ebbs and flows of policy, the basic direction of his government was
toward the elimination of other voices. Tsarists and liberals were
squeezed out quite rapidly, followed by more moderate socialists
(Mensheviks, Social Democrats, and Bukharinists) and more radical
socialists (Trotskyites and Left Socialist Revolutionaries). Stalin both
continued the process and increased the pace, focusing power in the

Politburo (which he dominated) and conducting the Great Purges of 1937–38, which eliminated all political enemies (including many Old Bolsheviks). Where Lenin had been reluctant to kill Bolsheviks, Stalin had no such scruples. Stalin reoriented and forcefully unified the Soviet Union, moving from a policy that supported the existence of many nationalities to a Russia-first approach. He also used the secret police apparatus to ensure unanimity of opinion, an approach that Khrushchev and Breshnev would inherit and sustain. Indeed, use of the secret police to maintain order became a standard part of the Soviet bureaucratic administration.

From the beginning, the Communists regarded other religions as enemies to be suppressed and rooted out. This policy applied especially to Russian Orthodox Christianity. On 20 January 1918, very shortly after the Bolsheviks came to power, the church was deprived of the right to own property or to act as a legal entity.[3] Throughout the Soviet era, churches were closed, clergy harassed and put to death, children firmly indoctrinated against Christianity, mass anti-Christian propaganda campaigns undertaken, and opportunities for advancement denied to those associated with Christianity. This was an intentional effort to wipe out Christian thinking and replace it with a new religion. Similar efforts were undertaken against the Catholic Church in places like Lithuania and Poland where there were significant Catholic populations. Islam suffered similar attacks, but the strategies tended to be different because the Muslim population was heavily concentrated in Eastern parts of the Soviet Union, where Islam dominated and could not easily be repressed. Instead, Muslims were deprived of their courts and other public functions. More effectively, though, they faced great population shifts, as Muslims were moved out and Soviet Russians moved in.[4]

The new religion that replaced Christianity and Islam was called "scientific materialism" or "historical materialism" (it was understood to be based in a science of history, so either term works) or "dialectical materialism" (history develops dialectically, which is a way of saying that forces produce their own counter-forces, until the final resolution). Its first prophets were Marx and Engels. However, they said little that could be helpful to resolve the concrete daily questions of life in the Soviet Union. Thus, successive leaders working through the Communist Party functioned as a living authoritative voice. Scientific materialism had specific principles which survived the vagaries of changing regimes, though many details shifted (sometimes, in contradictory directions). It was decisively atheistic, rejecting any notion of God or gods as traditionally understood. Scientific materialism laid claim to being verifiable on the basis of history. However, history here refers less to concrete historical data than to laws of history as understood by Marx and Engels. Indeed, at the heart of the new religion was a belief in the power of history. Through the process of supernaturalization, history was substituted for the Christian God. Marx's conception of history as possessing a definable process, by which capitalism would be undone and the socialist paradise be reached, was the dominant (and politically necessary) doctrinal basis. One way of understanding this eschatology (the conversation about end times and the fulfillment of the world's purpose) is a belief that history is a kind of force with powers of its own. Whether Marx thought this way is not clear; he may not have intended to treat history in this mystical and deterministic way.[5]

However, the Soviet version of Marxism depended upon the belief in History as an independent and decisive force. Only the twin promises that "History will judge in our favour" and "The perfect Marxist society is around the corner" enabled the Communist Party to urge on the workers in the face of manifest and repeated failure. That is why Roy Medvedev called his classic account of an important period in the development of Soviet life, *Let History Judge: The Origins and Consequences of Stalinism*.[6] The only judge of real importance to the Soviet mind was, indeed, history. Soviet society was, if anything, even more eschatologically oriented than Orthodox society had been. The same kind of mystical vision that had made Russian Orthodoxy a strongly and radically monastic religion continued to be at work in Soviet Marxism. However, the god had changed, as had the larger vision, forms of organization, accounts of life's challenges and their solutions, faith commitments, and values. In short, the whole religion had changed, but it channelled an ancient impulse in the service of the new god, History.

History was understood as being on the side of the working class, the proletariat, which came to mean the Soviet people as a whole, except for anyone who was being vilified by the Party at any particular moment. Soviet Marxism rapidly came to insist that the state should be understood as the communal mechanism that oppresses the working class. The state, therefore, withered away in 1917, when the Bolsheviks took control. The proletariat was in charge of society already. Therefore, the Communist Party, which ordered society, became the oracular voice of History. The Party was the voice that would lead the vanguard of History into the time beyond time, when capitalism would have fallen. Marx, the prophet of History, had said little about what would happen then. So, a new prophet was needed. Lenin, as the leader of the Communist Party, became that prophet.

Inevitably, worship life shifted dramatically from its pre-Soviet style. Lenin was the first figure to be elevated to what might be called sainthood. While he was alive, Lenin became the universal father figure. His picture was everywhere; people throughout the Soviet Union came to regard him as their protector. Upon his death, a fine mausoleum was prepared and he was ensconced in Red Square, in Moscow, there to be viewed by the faithful, who stood in long queues, awaiting their opportunity.

However, something more dramatic happened in Soviet religion, largely under the leadership of Stalin: the complete infrastructure of a religion was created.[7] Marx assumed that the arrival of the dictatorship of the proletariat would be the decisive moment in the history of religions. The destruction of public support for traditional religions would result in their disappearance. To his mind and the minds of his Bolshevik followers, traditional religions were nothing more than a cover story, mechanisms to obscure the oppression of the working class and even to draw them into participating in oppression. The anticipated vanishing act simply did not happen. Traditional religions, even when their leadership was thoroughly compromised, as was that of the Russian Orthodox Church, continued to exist and maintain a decisive hold on the hearts of many people.

Soviet liturgies for baptisms, weddings, and funerals were composed. The Summer Days of Youth, a week dedicated to preparation for the transition to adulthood (like Western Christian-style confirmation preparation – Orthodox churches do not perform a teenage confirmation rite) came into being, with a celebration that looks suspiciously like a confirmation rite. In 1925, the League of Militant Atheists was born. It survived until 1941, when it was quietly buried out of diplomatic concern for Western sympathies, though various groups were formed after the war in order to carry on the same activities. The League gave substance to Soviet religion. In addition to participating in drafting liturgies and publishing them, the League sponsored weekly services in factories. Workers came together to sing hymns, chant slogans, and listen to sermons on Soviet doctrines. These were, undeniably, Soviet church services.

Soviet religion permeated all of society. Religious formation was treated with deadly seriousness. Thus, education came firmly under Communist Party control. Children were trained to adhere to Soviet Marxism-Leninism and to avoid, even abhor, other religions. Public campaigns, complete with posters and radio broadcasts, discouraged people from going to churches or mosques and encouraged Party membership. The Party decided pedagogy. The Party controlled educational content, determining which specific psychology, biology, or physics lessons would be acceptable.

Courses explicitly promoted atheism "as a historically logical outcome of scientific development."[8] Indeed, university course syllabi are amusingly, even embarrassingly, religious in character. An example: "Physics: The place of physics in anti-religious propaganda. Connection between ancient myths and the endeavor of man to discover the causal relationship between various natural phenomena. The expression of primitive man's helplessness to establish the true, scientific reason for the phenomena. Scientific method in thinking as the true foundation of godlessness."[9] All curricula reflect religious priorities. However, Soviet curricula seem to have been blunter than most.

The same principles applied in the arts. The Party could make or destroy a novelist, poet, playwright, or filmmaker at any moment. Thus, Shostakovich found his work sometimes promoted, sometimes banned; at times, he was celebrated by the Party, while at other times he feared arrest. At the heart of the difficulty was always the question of how Marxism-Leninism should be represented artistically. What forms of art and kinds of representation would be suitable for the scientific materialist world?[10]

What we have been discussing is a totalitarian society in which a single religious viewpoint is absolutely authoritative and is imposed by force. The consequences of the totalitarian approach to society are profound and unhealthy, partly because syncretism is explicitly banned. A real and astonishingly thorough attempt is made to create hard boundaries and sustain them. Wisdom from other contexts, which might have encouraged the growth of democracy, expansion of human rights, or even the orderly rule of law, is simply inadmissible.

People begin to internalize resistance to alternative ways of thinking. Fear of prosecution causes conservatism. Initiative and innovation may prove dangerous, so the most advisable course of action is simply to follow the leader. "Follow-the-leader," as a pure approach to life, intentionally stifles syncretism. It does not prevent syncretism entirely; people will always learn from others outside the system. However, the fundamental question raised by people within the system is not "What is the best course of action?" Instead, the basic issue is always "Is this a safe course of action?" When a decision may lead to hard time in a Siberian gulag, one thinks very seriously before accepting it.

Concretely, Soviet society became a creaking bureaucracy. By the measures that matter to Marxism (the withering away of the state, social equality, worker liberation, and economic production), the Soviet system was an utter failure. The state was not dominated by the proletariat; it was a standard-issue civil service of a large and intrusive sort. Moreover, the working class did not control its own work; Five-Year Plans were set by the central authorities and rarely bore any resemblance to what could be accomplished in industry or agriculture. In short, the state certainly did not wither away. Instead, it grew. Renaming the state, calling it "the proletariat," changed nothing; it remained an overgrown and highly politicized bureaucracy.

Society was anything but egalitarian as social and economic privileges were strictly controlled by the Communist Party. Shortages of everyday items were commonplace. Shortages tended to reinforce social stratification because the privileged could shop in well-supplied stores or import goods from the West, while the lower classes simply went without. Even the accomplishments of dramatic increases in literacy, which aided social mobility and industrial capacity, which increased economic performance, could not hide the limitations of the system.

Other measures suggest failure also. The environment was brutally mistreated as industrialization occurred at record speed and without regard to larger consequences. While athletic accomplishments were extraordinary, arts and culture languished. For so large an area and so brilliant a people, the monuments of human creativity were few in number. The strongest evidence of the inadequacy of a system without syncretism is, however, a monument that the Soviets, themselves, erected: the Berlin Wall. From 1961 until 1989, the Wall stood as a means of preventing people from escaping the Soviet Union, stemming the flow through East Berlin to West Berlin. It was a visible symbol of Soviet determination to prevent emigration, generally described as "defection," to the West, a system that extended to careful control of all interactions between Soviet citizens and Westerners. A system has failed when it must build a wall to keep its people inside.

The religious point is significant. If people want to leave a country, why should one stop them? The answer may simply be practical: losing valuable skills can be a problem for a society. However, the wall was not there solely to contain people with particular skills or status; if it were, then those with less valuable skills would have been allowed to leave in a routine way, as would the more troublesome elements of the population. Something much more profound was at stake. On both sides of the East-West line, religious purity and competition were decisive social considerations. After World War II, emigration ceased to be about moving from one country to another. Instead, it was apostasy, a change of religion. Moreover, both sides understood that moving from East to West served an important role as evidence of the failure of the Soviet system. If the system failed, then Soviet Marxist-Leninist religion could be dismissed. Thus, emigration was treated as a matter of the utmost seriousness. Few were allowed to leave, in contrast with earlier periods (1917–38 and 1939–47).[11] Ultimately, this policy served as its own evidence of failure, and bottled up a population that would break out in the late 1980s and early 1990s, wiping away the religion of Soviet Marxism-Leninism and its theology of scientific materialism.

Logically, the fate of Soviet Marxism-Leninism is exactly what might be predicted on the basis of our larger discussion. Syncretism is an important means of growth. It allows us to reach out to other religions, to accept their wisdom, and to offer our own wisdom to others. When true hard boundaries are established, a single religion must answer every question about life and its meaning. No religion yet presented can do this, partly because religions tend to generate new questions. We need each other, so that together we can meet the complex demands of life. Soviet Marxism-Leninism failed to fulfil many of its own goals, even the most realistic ones such as a more egalitarian society, partly because it had to rely solely on its own resources. They were not adequate. Human intellect is limited enough that I suspect no single religion ever could be entirely sufficient unto itself.

7

The Problem of Labels:
What Is It Now?

A major lesson from the dead-end encountered by Soviet Marxism-Leninism is that religions need to engage in syncretism. One inevitable consequence of syncretism is change. When Islam learns from Greeks and Christians it ceases to be what Islam had been before. Something has shifted. Any change means an evolution, certainly, but a syncretistic evolution causes an important kind of change. If a Muslim is balancing the Qur'an and Aristotle, is that person a Muslim, a Greek, or something else entirely? The same question arises for a Jewish Freudian psychologist, or a Protestant Reformation-era Christian trying to balance the insights of the Renaissance with late-medieval philosophy, or a Marxist learning yoga. Simply quoting the Qur'an or Torah or Bible or Marx may obscure the problem, but that strategy will not solve anything. The categories become fluid and sometimes they break down entirely. The fundamental question becomes "What is it now?"

This ends up being a very personal sort of question. We live by labels that we assign to ourselves and other people, but the labels do not necessarily mean what we expect. A philosophical sort of Indian Buddhist may have a difficult time recognizing Buddhism in the Japanese Shinto/Buddhist syncretism. In a more pressing case, a Saudi Arabian Sunni Muslim with Wahhabi commitments may not see true Islam in an Iraqi Shia with Zoroastrian influences and expectations rooted in ancient Persia. People who are on the outside looking in have an even greater challenge, since they may have no idea what is at stake in all these differences. If you've grown up among North American liberal/capitalist/fundamentalist Protestants, then a Spanish Catholic, affected by a history of interaction with Islam, Judaism, and European folk religions, may not seem Christian at all. All of the labels are relativized.

Religion is not alone with the problem. Since Charles Darwin turned the world upside down by demonstrating that things evolve, we have had a real problem with taxonomy, which is the science of classification and naming. The categories that we have traditionally used to describe the living world around us are all derived from evidence provided by our senses as we encounter the world. This evidence is, unfortunately, worse than useless in the task of classifying creatures according to their evolutionary relationships. Hence, in *Naming Nature: The Clash Between Instinct and Science*, Carol Kaesuk Yoon points out that a group of scientists (called cladists) argue that fish do not exist as a category, in spite of the apparently obvious nature of this grouping. Of course, there are fish. Aren't there? Well, not necessarily, because their biological relationships are not with one another; various fishes are actually members of other evolutionary families. They all exist as offshoots of other developmental branches on Earth's biological tree. The result, for humanity, is another episode in the game that I like to call "What is it now?"[1]

As we have seen, human ideas also evolve. They become intertwined and their faces change. Contemporary evangelical Protestantism, with its emphasis upon heartfelt individual decisions for God, is at least as much a child of liberalism and Romanticism as of Christianity. So, which is it? Well, it is all of the above, but it seems to be its own thing – a kind of Western Christianity (which is just as much Western as Christian).

Under close examination, though, evangelical Protestantism proves to be rather difficult to grasp as a unity. It includes Jim Wallis, editor of *Sojourners* magazine, who believes that Christianity and efforts for social justice are inextricably linked. Wallis has wide currency in the evangelical world and his magazine is read by many. Yet, there has historically been a sizeable constituency of evangelicals who argue that Christianity is a private affair of the heart, while politics is a corrupt matter for earthly oriented people. Some of these people have been mobilized over the last two to three decades by various leaders, such as Pat Robertson and Jerry Falwell. However, rather than focusing upon social justice, they have tended to emphasize individual liberty and free markets, with the addition of restrictions upon biomedical research and the eradication of abortions. These last priorities have brought them into alliances with Catholics, who have been particularly active in the anti-abortion movement. Yet, one of the defining characteristics of traditional evangelical Protestantism has been a fundamental and visceral rejection of Catholicism; many earlier evangelicals rejected the notion that Catholics are Christians, calling them "Anti-Christ" and other unpleasant things.

From the time that the label "evangelical" gained currency, there has been a significant party of evangelicals in Anglicanism. These people have not always had the discomfort with Catholics or with politics that have been characteristic of other strands of evangelicalism. They have also been more comfortable with some level of ritual worship. Today, their churches are indistinguishable from other Anglican churches, by and large, and the latter, in turn, are indistinguishable from many Catholic churches. However, some critics insist that by being Anglican, these evangelicals have placed themselves within "mainline" Protestantism and, therefore, no longer deserve the label "evangelical," which is a categorization issue that the Evangelical Lutheran Church of America and the Evangelical Lutheran Church in Canada also face. Apparently, calling themselves "Evangelical" does not make them so.

Are you confused, yet? I certainly am, and I have hardly made a dent in the list of relevant complexities. Quite frankly, I cannot decide whether there is such a thing as evangelical Protestantism, or whether there are several such things, or whether the label is useless because of its fluidity and diversity. Do not even get me started on whether there is such a thing as a reformation (as in "the Protestant Reformation"). Somewhere along the line, our usual notion of discrete "thingness" began to seep out of this conversation. We are stuck with movements having various origins, influences, and affiliations. We are forced to play the Darwinian game, "What is it now?"

This would be the obvious moment to introduce the standard evolutionary analogy: the tree. I could talk about how this is a branch of that and how that is a branch of the other. I'd be all wrong. Employing an analogy from concrete stuff, like a tree, clarifies issues that really are not clear. It removes the complications that are a normal (and unavoidable) part of religions. Trees are helpful for timelines; they have definite beginnings and endings, with branches that lead to other branches. However, they have two characteristics that make them misleading for our purposes: (1) a branch always comes out of one other branch, rather than several; and (2) branches are discrete entities, meaning that they do not all meld together.

The first criticism might be fixed by switching from a tree to a flowchart or something similar that enables one to see multiple origins. That way, one can tell that evangelicalism has origins in the Judeo-Christian heritage, followed by the appearance of Protestantism, and enriched by liberalism, capitalism, Romanticism, and other contemporary strains of thought. One can recognize that "branches" of religions do not necessarily even come from within one religion (one "tree," if you will), but instead come from a whole variety of sources.

However, even flowcharting is not going to correct the second problem, because it is still too concrete an analogical process to capture what truly happens. Branches have specific diameters and circumferences. They do not have bits attached to various trees which prevent us from seeing how large the branches are or how they are configured. Instead, they are clear and precise; we see where one branch leaves off and another begins, more or less every time. This means that trees tend to inspire an unhelpful picture of how we construct the religions that we understand and live.

Flowcharts are not quite so awkward because we can add bits here and take them out there. Flowcharts do not need to have a single trunk with branches growing out from single places and concluding in single, clearly identifiable locations. Instead, flowcharts allow us to represent religions as interdependent systems, with a variety of arrows connecting different parts of the systems. Nonetheless, flowcharts are unable to capture the fluidity and complexity of human religions, because a system of boxes and lines still implies that religions are discrete entities with hard boundaries. We can represent mutual influences, but we cannot display the puzzles that challenge us. Any given religious structure, organization, person, or thought system is a blend of ideas and impulses from a variety of religious sources. The clarity of the flowchart is unhelpful in as many ways as it is useful. This is, of course, true of every analogy, which is why we need to be aware of the limitations of analogies.

An example of the weakness of the flowchart approach might help to clarify the point. In a book on religion for the general public, I recently came across a flowchart that tries to explain the different branches of Christianity.[2] Quite rightly, the authors distinguish between Calvinism, Anglicanism, and Presbyterianism. Equally correctly, they use a line to indicate that Presbyterianism grew out of Anglicanism. Fine, right? Well, not really, because anyone who seeks a basic understanding on the strength of such a chart will be rather misled. The problems – for which I do not blame the authors because the weaknesses are intrinsic to flowcharting – have to do with the complexity of relationships amongst these entities. Calvinism (a European Protestant movement) has always had a significant presence in Anglicanism. It was, arguably, the dominant viewpoint in late sixteenth-century Anglicanism, even as the Church of England differed from most Calvinist churches on some important matters such as the use of the term "priest" and the clothing worn by that personage. On these issues, Anglicanism tended to be closer to Catholicism. Plus, the person who composed the Anglican book of liturgies (rituals) is commonly thought to have been a Zwinglian (another kind of European Protestant), while many of Anglicanism's early leaders were manifestly Lutherans (a further kind of European Protestant – and one that appears on the flowchart). Presbyterianism, in contrast, has tended to be firmly Calvinist and combines a Scottish heritage (including substantial Scottish nationalism) with elements of this early Anglican Calvinism.

Confused, yet? So are many scholars who debate endlessly the nature of influences on various people and organizations in the sixteenth and seventeenth centuries, when this was all sorting itself out. Adding a line from Calvinism to Presbyterianism would help, but it would not clarify the Anglican question. Nor would it say much about the influence of Scottish nationalism, or the rise of religious freedom and natural religion (important elements of modern liberalism) that contributed so much to the appearance of Presbyterianism, Methodism, and various other parts of Christianity in the seventeenth century. In short, the flowchart is not wrong; it is actually quite good and helpful and I commend the authors for an excellent effort to give clear and thorough treatment to a very messy topic. No, the real problem is precisely that the topic is messy. Even a very good flowchart is a simplification that hides the complex, syncretistic nature of even small parts of any one religion. Think of trying to flowchart whole religions in a fair and honest way! The margin of error, already significant, will be vastly increased.

Biologists have found that evolution means that creatures are not discrete and permanent entities; the language of species has become impossible to use except with the help of genetics, because there are no static species in nature (causing biologists to wonder about the helpfulness of the tree analogy, too[3]). Creatures change in ways that defy categories. The result is the thylacine, a marsupial with adaptations and appearance similar enough to those of a wolf that European colonists dubbed it "the Tasmanian wolf," for example (so far as we know, the last died in an Australian zoo in the 1930s).[4]

Ideas do something similar. However, ideas are, if anything, more complicated because they are not in any way physical and they do not occupy space. One cannot even trace their genes in the way that one might trace the development of, say, a leopard. Ideas do not have DNA in any literal sense. We can follow some of the written history of ideas, but that does not cover the whole story of many human thoughts. It says little about what happens in non-literate cultures, which constitute an immensely complex branch of study that moves by analogy from non-literate cultures that we know to those about which our ideas are largely speculative. Scholars can trace linguistic developments which give hints about the transfer of ideas, and can examine surviving objects which reveal something of the way that people thought in the past. However, these clues are commonly insufficient to allow a full, or even substantial, reconstruction of the thought of an era. We have already encountered this problem in relation to Celtic religion, where we have limited records and those only in Christian documents, and especially the sheela-na-gigs, for which we have no written explanation.

Our understanding of literary development is of limited use in understanding what goes on in people's heads. Even in the cases where we have a few texts, such as ancient Anglo-Saxon religion, reconstructing the overall belief structure is exceedingly difficult. Specific practices, such as funeral rites, can be reconstructed from remains left by the culture. Scholars can, for instance, investigate burial sites and discover something about the ways in which death was handled. However, we really know very little about how death, itself, was understood. Indeed, we know very little about Anglo-Saxon understandings of the gods and how humans related to them. We are reasonably sure that the notion of fate played a central role, and we speculate that Anglo-Saxons probably retained a largely traditional Germanic mythology, although we are not richly informed about ancient Germanic religion, either. Again, what little we know comes largely through texts that have Christian influence and, therefore, suffer both from Christian recounting of non-Christian belief and from being of late origin. None of those (very few) texts can make a firm claim to include "pure" pre-Christian material. We simply do not know what Anglo-Saxon religion looked like. Monuments like the burial site at Sutton Hoo cannot inform us to nearly the degree that we would like because they simply do not explain the framework of thought in which they were constructed. We rely on a few clues in *Beowulf* and the items in the burial mound to try to understand. However, we cannot know what sort of afterlife, if any, was expected, or what relation the gods might have been understood to have to such an afterlife, if any.

In a sense, contemporary syncretisms face no such challenges. Our age of endless writing and rapid communication, combined with endless data storage and search systems, mean that religious developments can easily be tracked. Sitting at my computer, I can discover vast amounts of information about relatively small and obscure religious forces in remote parts of the world. Even African jungles and deserts are not hidden from me. However, the sheer multiplicity of religious influences and availability of masses of data are, together, making the history of ideas unimaginably complex. Attempting to flowchart the religious influences that I, myself, include at this moment would be simply impossible, no matter how narrowly I choose to define religion. I encounter too much data, from too many sources, too often. My religious views are now too complex and have too many points of origin for there to be a reasonable hope of tracing them and accounting for them. The result is that all physical analogies to the relationships among ideas will be limited in their helpfulness and must eventually fail.

The challenge that we are seeing is the difficulty of studying the history of ideas. If it were only some dry-as-dust academic issue, belonging in some imaginary ivory tower, then I would not need to introduce it here. However, this is an important part of the issue of group identity, something that starts to touch our lives when we are very young and only increases in importance as we grow and age. Humans, for better or worse, always want to know who is "us" and who is "them." It is a part of a basic psychological need for boundaries, direction, and order. We need rules and examples to follow, and we need to know whose rules and examples we should not follow. These things provide comfort, to be sure, but they also give us a path to growth and development. We are simply unable to sustain the effort necessary to choose from among all the possibilities every time a decision must be made. Just imagine trying to decide from among all the possible ways to learn, for example, each time that you need to discover something about mathematics! Or, if you prefer something more obviously religious, imagine trying to choose from among all the various ways to think about a Higher Power or Higher Powers and selecting from all possible ways to honour that Higher Power/Higher Powers every time the question arises.

We rely on our labels, the verbal symbols of our identities, to help us through these complexities. That is why we help our children to understand the way that we make decisions, as well as why we explain the particular choices that we make. Some people go further, sending their children to Sikh or Muslim or Christian of Jewish (or Sunni, or Shia, or Catholic, or Protestant, or Reformed, or Seventh Day Adventist – precision counts in these matters) schools. This is a choice of formation, where the issue is partly about beliefs and partly about being with people like us. We want our children to share our approach to the world. We establish labels and pass them on to ensure that our identities and those of our children are clear.

Every decision that we make limits the available options for the next decision, and we need to know something about the kinds of limits that we are choosing. What are the consequences of the choices that we are making? We need the wisdom of the past in order to face the present and the future. For that, we turn to others and others turn to us. This is a group process and a necessary one. It is what constitutes tradition, the creator of the principle of the preservation of insights and the content behind our labels and other identity markers. More to the point, though, the process of sharing wisdom brings into being particular traditions which are the outcomes of meetings between the principle of preservation of insights and the principle of progress. We cannot pass on to our kin (or to anyone else) all wisdom, since we do not have it all and much of it would be irrelevant. Instead, we pass on what we have, which is a combination of what we have received and what we have learned experimentally, sifted for relevance to the questions at hand. The former tends to be the larger part; we really learn very little experimentally. Most of what we know is stuff that we accept in faith from the group around us. Both in the passing-on and in the receiving, group identity is formed. That is a big part of what education, at school or elsewhere, accomplishes.

However, our ideas develop and thus our labels and other verbal and visual symbols of identity are not as revealing as we tend to expect. Having been raised in an officially Christian household, I was able to say, "I am a Christian," while still quite young. And, having become a priest and theologian, I can say, "I am a Christian" now. And, my wife's expatriate Lebanese friend can say, "Of course, I am a Christian. I am not a Muslim!" The three meanings of "I am a Christian" are all different. They may be attached to something of the same group identity in a global sense, but they are radically dissimilar in some very important ways. The kind of fundamentalist Christianity in which I was raised – the tradition that I received and group identity that I adopted – is very different from the kind of ecumenically trained, Anglican theologian that I am now. I have moved into a different tradition, intentionally drawing from a richer, broader variety of sources than my parents would have imagined existed. My parents would not have welcomed large portions of my library into their house. Then there is my wife's Lebanese friend, for whom Christianity has a whole socio-political resonance that is almost entirely distinct from either of my usages. For him, Christianity defines a place in society; in Lebanon, where he grew up, the label "Christian" even identified a particular set of voting choices, since Lebanese government is linked to religious identity. Where church attendance is a central characteristic of Christian group identity for me, it is secondary for him. Here are three distinct uses of the word "Christian," and all of them are perfectly legitimate. So goes the game of "What is it now?"

The difficulty that we face is that the muddle does not simply belong to ordinary folk like me. There are varieties of Christian thought, some with names and some without. The truly great and the truly reviled theologians end up with their own names attached to particular kinds of thought: Augustinianism (Augustine of Hippo); Pelagianism (Pelagius, a British monk who opposed Augustine); Thomism (Thomas Aquinas); Lutheranism (Martin Luther); Calvinism (John Calvin); and so on. People pick up the theologians' ideas, study them, modify them, and live by them. People become identified with the traditions that they inherit and become part of the communities that discuss these ideas. There is no "mere Christianity," though C.S. Lewis tried to convince us otherwise; one cannot construct a Venn diagram of Christianities and separate out a portion which has been held always, everywhere, and by all Christians.[5]

Ideas come to individuals. They are born in the heads of particular people. However, the measure of an idea's success is the degree to which it becomes a part of the working thoughts of other people. In other words, ideas end up belonging to communities. Communities employ them, modifying them in the process, and then pass them on, usually modifying them further in the activity of passing-on. Ideas are not like batons which do not change substantially as they move from one hand to another. Ideas travel through minds, where they interact with other ideas and are affected by capacities for understanding. Ideas are passed on through the notoriously tricky medium of language, and the idea itself is dependent upon the linguistic skills of both teacher and learner. What enters any particular mind is not necessarily the same thing as what exits it, which is not necessarily the same thing as what enters the next mind.

This process draws our attention to the ownership of ideas. They are ultimately personal. My religion is finally mine. It is not exactly the same as anyone else's. Thus, we have countless variations of what constitutes Christianity, and Marxism-Leninism, and Islam. Every single one of them is a syncretism, a mixture of various religious bits and pieces picked up in various times and places, for various reasons. They may seem to be especially beautiful, especially true or helpful. They may simply be things that we are required to believe. They may be so obvious to us that no justification seems to be necessary. In one way, the results include so much variation as to defy categorization. Our

"What is it now?" is uttered in tones of frustration, perhaps even despair.

As a matter of fact, though, taxonomy is not gone from the discussion of religions. I have defined myself in relation to our conversation. I am willing to bet that you have, also. We can say that the Dalai Lama is a Buddhist (of a particular kind, of course) and that his followers are Buddhists. This is because ideas are even more ultimately communal than they are personal. Our personal ideas always define us in relation to groups; they identify group allegiances. Moreover, the formation and transmission of ideas is really a group process. That is what all of our means of communication, including books like this one, accomplish. They enter us into a larger conversation, in which we think and learn together. This process is identity-forming. As we accept particular ideas, we become associated with others who accept those ideas and, in an important sense, distanced from others who reject them. We share a kind of intimacy with those who participate in our understanding of the world. Those with whom we disagree on most things of importance are outsiders to us.

Humans are not inevitably and unavoidably attached to specific identities; we can choose. This has always been true; it is far from being just a modern phenomenon. If it were, then how would new religions have started? The Hebrew scriptures portray the Hebrew people going back and forth in their worship, sometimes obeying the God named by the never-spoken consonants YHWH and sometimes following other popular religions of the Ancient Near East. In one of the most famous stories, Moses is on Mt. Sinai receiving the Law while the people down below are busy melting their gold to make an idol in the form of a calf, which they worship. Again, under the Roman Empire, the Mediterranean world was flooded with religions; people accepted one or many, as they chose. The only basic requirement, which caused trouble for Christians and Jews, was that one was expected to do obeisance to the Emperor in addition (though the degree to which this was required tended to fluctuate). There have been violently repressive regimes in many countries, at many times, forcing people to adopt particular views, which means that our choices are not always honoured. Even that is an awkwardly negative reminder that we are intrinsically able to choose.

Moreover, we are able to retrieve information from around the world more swiftly than anyone in history. The electronic universe makes the ideas of a great many people, everywhere on Earth, instantly accessible to someone with a computer or a smartphone. This accelerates the process of syncretism, since information about other points of view is incredibly easy to obtain. Not very long ago, we needed to have people or newspapers or books, all of which are physically cumbersome, as well as being defined by their own origins and preparation, in order to encounter other religious ideas. Now, they are instantly available, in all their variety. Everything is there, from the meditations of the deepest thinkers in ancient traditions to yesterday's ramblings from someone in dire need of psychiatric care.

I doubt that this changes traditional dynamics of religious interaction, except to strengthen them. The curious become more curious because curiosity can be rewarded quite rapidly. Technologically aware teenagers who set out to investigate the world can do so; indeed, they can do it without their parents knowing. The result is that those who want to be syncretistic, who want to incorporate all the wisdom that they can find into their lives, have remarkable opportunities. Their religions will not be their parents' religions even though they may opt to wear the same labels.

The phenomenon of easy syncretism inspires fear in the sort of people who would be insecure in any age of history. Some people are quite concerned about boundaries, about the who's in/who's out question. These people seek to create and maintain pure traditions, minimizing or even eliminating syncretistic elements. The age of instant communications reinforces this fear. Parents have very little control over what their children see and hear; community leaders have even less power over the investigations and conversations their communities will enter into. This certainly accounts for some of the oppressive measures undertaken by Salafi Islam. If a community (such as the Salafi) believes that there is a pure tradition and that the future of the world depends upon both the maintenance and ultimate victory of that tradition, then that community has little choice but to turn to violence. Though always present throughout history, syncretism is a more powerful force in a world of instant and unobtrusive communications.

The "What is it now?" question is always immediate because nobody really stands still. We learn and forget. We grow and decline. And, our religions are not always easy to label, nor are the changes easy to track. This demands that we approach the world with both a critical mindset and a high degree of openness. Categorizing people and things, associating them with a label and, therefore, with certain characteristics, is a basic human survival skill. It is as primal as distinguishing between friend and enemy or recognizing the difference between a person with good mate potential and one with poor mate potential. The problem, of course, is that we are liable to be both a little right and a little wrong with these sorts of decisions. Generalizations about people based on one label or characteristic have little predictive value, especially outside the childhood context, which is where many generalizations are born and nurtured.

The challenge, then, is to recognize that labels are helpful but not sufficient indicators of what people are like, especially when those labels apply to very large numbers of people. Westerners live with a fairly standard account of Muslims, highly visible in the media since the bombing of the World Trade Center: Muslims are, on the whole, backward and violent; sworn enemies of the West; and oppressors of women and other religions. Undoubtedly, there are such Muslims. The Taliban, with its destruction of the Bamyan Buddha statues, refusal to permit girls to go to school, violent hatred of Westerners, and exceedingly repressive treatment of the Afghan population, fits this mould. However, the Taliban of Afghanistan hardly represents all Muslims or even all Afghan Muslims. As a number of authors have sought to demonstrate, there is such a thing as progressive Islam.[6] Plus, Muslims whom I know, like Hamid Slimi (a Canadian Islamic leader), have a habit of being rather different from the stereotype. These Muslims have at least as solid a claim to the rich Islamic heritage as any wild-eyed, AK-47-toting extremist. If we want to understand people and religions correctly, then we need to be prepared to encounter complexity rather than simplicity. We need to recognize that every person's religion is the product of personal and communal histories of development with many influences, some of which are syncretistic. Practitioners of a particular religion have sufficient beliefs and practices in common that they can bear a common label.

However, developmental histories and life-contexts result in highly idiosyncratic ways of understanding, expressing, and living those beliefs and practices. We cannot assume that "A Muslim is a Muslim is a Muslim." After all, a recent *National Geographic* feature uncovered Muslims in Indonesia who combine traditional drumming, palm wine, and mysticism with Islam – all of which contravene standard Islamic prohibitions.[7] Then again, Indonesian Islam has developed in a complicated syncretism, especially in its relation to Hindu traditions, and thus it looks very different from Islam in North Africa, though there is quite significant variation across North Africa, also.[8] We need, therefore, to approach the labels that we and others wear with critical minds and careful investigation. To paraphrase *The Princess Bride*, "That word may not mean what you think it means." The decisive question must always be "What is it now?"

8

Critical Openness

The central challenge that comes with living honestly and in full awareness in a syncretistic world is attitude. Finding and sustaining the right attitude can be difficult because attitudes touch both emotional and intellectual parts of us. They call forth "gut" responses that may not agree with what we hope to feel and think. Moreover, attitudes are often a product of deep training, going back to the earliest days of childhood. They are not easily understood, and to recalibrate them can be the effort of a lifetime.

Recognizing that each of us is a syncretist of some, usually indefinable, sort is difficult, no doubt. Similarly, discovering that the religions that we value so highly all have a syncretistic history can be disorienting. Some people who take pride in abstaining from religion entirely will likely be a bit irked at the suggestion that they are religious – often, intensely so. These, however, can be treated as personal considerations, especially since we are accustomed to treating religious matters as individual concerns. We may need to make some internal adjustments in response to these attitudinal challenges, but they can be kept out of the public sphere.

However, syncretism is communal by definition. It depends upon the existence of multiple points of view, which are shared and intermingled. It is, therefore, both an accurate description of what happens in our world, as we have seen, and a helpful goal for our age. In the world of instantaneous information sharing, we stand to benefit greatly from the insights of other people. We need to transcend our assumptions about hard boundaries. We need to adopt an attitude that I call "critical openness," an approach to life that combines a willingness to hear other viewpoints with recognition that anything we hear will likely include both some truth and some error. In order to live syncretistically in a way that is helpful to ourselves and others, we need to go beyond being personally attracted, disoriented, or irked, into a desire to recognize syncretism and cultivate it. Regarded properly, syncretism can be a force for good in the world.

OPENNESS

Openness, in this case, is a commitment to resist easy generalizations. Openness denies kneejerk reactions and rejects simplistic assumptions about what labels mean. A Jew is not, purely and simply, a Jew. A Muslim is not, purely and simply, a Muslim. For that matter, a Marxist is not, purely and simply, a Marxist. Everybody is a mixture and, if not altogether unique because ideas are shared, is unlikely to be exactly the same as other people with the same tag. We cannot say, "Osama bin Laden is a Muslim. I think that bin Laden is evil. Therefore, all Muslims are evil." Likewise, we cannot say, "Jim Bakker is a Christian. I think that Jim Bakker is corrupt. Therefore, all Christians are corrupt." We cannot be sure what another person believes or does solely on the basis of the label that he or she wears. More information is necessary, and that information is only available to someone who is willing to understand. If we ask only to bolster preconceptions or, worse yet, hatreds, we will never get beyond the oversimplifications of labels.

Openness, therefore, is about a genuine commitment to understanding. We need to be attentive to all of the available data. We need to be open to considering all of the information that we have, or can reasonably be expected to have, about other people and their viewpoints. This calls for an honest commitment to learning, all the time, while constantly resisting our natural assumptions and inclinations. The reason that prejudice has such a bad reputation is that it involves judgements that are made prior to reception of relevant data. Prejudice means, purely and simply, to prejudge in the absence of some necessary information. Prejudice is the product of relying on inherited or learned categories rather than making the effort to understand the particular case, the specific person, before us. Openness explicitly rejects prejudice and makes a serious effort to overcome it.

Prejudice decides that a Muslim person is automatically untrustworthy and likely to be violent. Similarly, prejudice decides that a Jewish person must be a rapacious capitalist and part of an international Zionist conspiracy simply because that person is Jewish. Openness is the quality of seeking to avoid this kind of prejudice. Openness means gathering all of the information, which may mean recognizing that the Muslim is a peacenik and chronically incapable of lying, or that the Jewish person is a bookish introvert with the soul of a poet and neither the capacity nor the inclination to enter into anyone's conspiracy.

In order to treat these people appropriately, we must slow down and try to understand them. That means trying to understand the people's own views rather than simply treating them as particular cases of a single category that we think we understand. I can fairly claim to be something of an expert on Christianity in many of its highly varied forms, but I still cannot honestly say that I know or understand the particular Christianity practiced by every person that I meet. I am, for instance, still working at trying to understand Ahmsta Kebzeh, the mixture of Christianity and Sufism that is practiced at a church in my own neighbourhood. Of course, the problem grows rapidly as I get further away from home ground. The vast number of different, and not easily explained, versions of being Hindu bend my simple, Western-trained, and category-oriented, mind entirely out of shape. Prejudging is not adequate if I want to know the truth rather than submitting to prejudicial reflexes. Openness means that we need to gather the information about every particular person that we meet in a real effort to identify her or his religion, rather than to fall back on inadequate labels and preconceived categories.

Simply gathering the data is not sufficient for a truly open approach to the other, however. We must make a real effort to understand it properly. Take the Judaism example from the previous paragraph and change it a bit. Perhaps the Jewish person in question is a highly successful businessperson, with strong international connections and a rich, complex history of government involvement. That is exactly the sort of evidence needed by someone who wants to paint a picture straight out of the scurrilous and ridiculous *Protocols of the Learned Elders of Zion*. Now we have all of the ingredients for an instant conspiracy. Openness, however, is the quality of seeking a deeper and more thorough understanding of that person's views and activities, resisting the inclination to assume that prejudices are correct. Alternatively, openness may require that judgement be suspended if insufficient data is available; we may simply be unable to know how honest and above-board any particular person is. One way or another, we need to be willing to approach others or think of them without prior suspicion, without prejudice. The complexity of religions is such that we cannot easily assume that a label is sufficient to explain the identity of any specific person whom we hear about or meet. The great danger of oppressive religions such as Soviet Marxism-Leninism is that they undermine the fragile structure of trust that enables us to encounter other people with genuine openness. This is immensely oppressive religion. Under the rigorous, totalitarian control of the Soviet state, nobody could trust anyone. Honesty was a sign of insanity or suicidal innocence. Paranoia was a way of life. Anyone who professed allegiances to authorities other than the Party and the state was immediately the other and dangerous. This is a dramatic, indeed paradigmatic, example of the sort of behaviour that destroys thought. It reminds us that the power that negates openness, which tends to eliminate the chance of love (and, therefore, insight) occurring, is fear.

We need a degree of confidence in our beliefs and ourselves to be able to sustain an attitude of openness. Those who react to disagreement with violence or extreme vehemence are commonly not people who really, deep down, believe in what they profess. If your system, your God, or your gods, is/are as powerful as you claim, then it/he/she/they cannot truly be undermined by human criticism. Only the fearful and insecure must destroy opposition rather than simply attempt to prove the error of opposing viewpoints. Being reasonable is a basic and necessary aspect of openness.

Openness goes further than merely listening to the other, though. That still leaves the other as other. Openness is not a simpleminded tolerance of the sort that says, "You believe what you want to believe. I will believe what I want to believe." Indeed, "tolerance" is one of the least helpful labels in use today. One can tolerate while ignoring; tolerance is not intrinsically transformative. The kind of openness that I am suggesting does not allow us to ignore the views of our neighbours. Those views may have the answers to questions that we have, and perhaps to questions for which we desperately seek solutions. That, really, is the point of this book: we ought to be syncretists by choice and not merely by necessity because no particular religion answers all the questions that will arise in the course of any particular person's lifetime.

The consequence is that openness must be about listening and learning. We need to be prepared to be instructed by those who wear religious labels that we may not find attractive. The possibility of constructing a viable religion depends upon hearing and understanding other viewpoints. Wisdom does not become wisdom merely by having a familiar name, nor does it cease to be wisdom because it has an unfamiliar or unwelcome name. Healthy religion is syncretistic religion.

The recognition that syncretism is both all-pervasive and necessary has a further impact on us: we must present ourselves to ourselves and others with a greater degree of honesty than we commonly prefer. This is an even more demanding (and delicate) sort of openness. One of the reasons that I am writing this book is that I have grown tired of listening to Christians insisting that we are wrong to listen to the rest of the world in our own discussions about ethics. I hear an endless round of a standard complaint: "But that is the world speaking. We need to make a Christian decision." The root of this argument is a false assumption that we can live in a Christian colony or in any other kind of religious colony. More to the point, we are already syncretists. This means that the dichotomy between Christian and non-Christian (or Muslim and non-Muslim, Buddhist and non-Buddhist, etc.) is, in important ways, an illusion.

Because syncretism is everywhere, the other is not other. We tend to assume that hard boundaries define our religions. We assume that we have things in common with people who share our label but not with people who wear another label. We expect that Hindus will believe more or less the same things, while Sikhs will believe other things, and Buddhists will believe something else entirely. We are us and they are them. However, the reality is that cross-fertilization has made all of us into complicated hybrids. We have been sharing wisdom around

for thousands of years, and that is not about to stop. We will continue learning from others because we have needs that go deeper than
our barriers. When our religions cannot provide the answers to our
questions, we go searching. That is how fundamentalist Christians
end up learning yoga; Indian religions may seem alien to American
Baptists, but Indian traditions offer something that Protestant Christianity does not. We all mix religions, and that is a good thing!

There are real differences between religions; I do not deny them.
Instead, I regard them as profoundly significant aspects of the human
conversation which must not be overlooked. I celebrate the differences between religions. The differences are what we have to offer
each other. Thus, my whole argument hinges on the notion that religions differ. Syncretism happens, and is beneficial, precisely because
religions have valuable insights and practices to share. If all religions
were really the same underneath then there would be no virtue in listening to others. We would simply hear ourselves echoed back, even if
the accent were slightly different.

My point, though, is that we are free to listen to other religions and
ought to do so. We must recognize that we have always lived in a kind
of meeting-place of views. We have always listened to people from
other religions, and we need to admit this to ourselves. Openness has
been part of our history. We betray it if we fall into closed-mindedness
now, or if we try to deny openness as part of our own formation.
Rather than being a fall away from traditional purity, openness is an
acceptance of historical reality. Openness means the honesty to admit
that we live and have always lived with soft boundaries rather than
with clearly defined and impermeable walls around us.

BEING OPEN, CRITICALLY

Absolute openness, however, is neither possible nor desirable. Pure
openness would include the acceptance of every opinion at face value.
Nobody I know is either able or willing to live with that kind of
approach. Inevitably, that would involve us in all sorts of impossible
contradictions and foolish actions. Consequently, we need to ask
questions, investigate viewpoints, come to our own understandings,
make our own judgements, and reach our own decisions. We need to
think critically. This requires us to attend to all of the available evi-

dence. In turn, attending to the evidence demands that we ask and answer as many of the relevant questions as possible. Underlying the possibility of this kind of questioning must be a recognition of the part that our own personalities and our own structures of knowing play in any effort to understand; in an important sense, the other is truly other and our task is to allow the other to be other instead of forcing the other to fit our expectations.

Critical openness means accepting all of the relevant evidence rather than rejecting material which may tend to disprove our preferred positions, but also means recognizing that all evidence is simply that: evidence. Our world is inherently ambiguous; in all its aspects, it may be interpreted many different ways. In each and every one of us, there is something of the detective, the inquiring mind that wants to know.

The primary challenge here is to avoid the intentional amputation of the mind that is so popular with children of the Enlightenment. The Enlightenment tried to convince us that the only useful data is measurable data, and the only objects worthy of study are those that, in principle if not necessarily in immediate practice, are open to measurement. This is an embarrassingly false reductionism. Trying to live that way, we lose some of the most important evidence about ourselves and the world around us. The language of "the heart" is lost, as if human emotions were merely irrationalities that need to be suppressed or destroyed. In some important ways, the history of the twentieth century is an encounter with the problem that this viewpoint has created. It has unleashed technocracy, based on the idea that there is a technological solution to every problem, while simultaneously releasing the emotional forces of racism, nationalism, and the like, from any assumption that they must be linked to a larger understanding of the cosmos. In short, the head and the heart have become separated, not merely as a historical fact (this is a standard human challenge, faced by everyone sometime), but as a basic assumption about human existence. Everything from advertising to art to radio and television has become a matter of trying to reach the emotions without engaging the mind. In the ancient analysis of rhetoric, this is known as the effort to convince using a maximum amount of *pathos* (emotional power), with a minimum of *ethos* (personal trustworthiness) or *logos* (reason).

We need to recognize that the data of the heart are, indeed, significant. Pascal's riposte to the Enlightenment, "The heart has reasons

that reason cannot know,"[1] is not altogether unreasonable. Pascal is
trying to suggest that the physical sciences are not always adequate
guides to the nature of reality. Humans are actually more wonderful-
ly constructed than that; we are better attuned to reality. We retrieve
and respond to information that no scientific study is swift or complex enough to recognize and explain.

Any scientific study is composed by a person, reflecting that person's limitations (including intellectual and emotional limitations) as
well as the shortcomings of existing theories, mechanisms, and technologies. No such study can ever match up to what you, as an ordinary
person, do on a day-to-day basis. That is part of why teaching can be
difficult. Teachers need to decide how they do something and then
create exercises that will enable students to put themselves into the
same position. Often, we do not really know how we do things; our
actions are a function of growing awareness that comes only with repetition, trials and errors, and a growing understanding of the best way
to act. Plus, our capacities for this process of growth are undergirded
by a whole host of variable conditions such as how well fed, clothed,
and educated we are; how well loved we have been; how our family
has supported (or not supported) us; and so on. We can come to general conclusions about the ways in which these variables affect people's abilities, but those can never account for how you, a particular
person, will engage the world.

Those responses that we call "emotions" or "feelings" are ways of
gathering information. They are not something that we hope to sub-
stitute with real knowledge in some glorious, scientific, "someday"
utopia. Instead, they are an important aid to understanding because
they recognize things that our minds need to know. Feelings, both
emotional and physical (the two are intimately linked), are a part of
our psyche trying to tell us things that we need to know. Our minds
need time to process that data, and may never fully understand it.
That does not render it invalid. We can all think of examples. The classic, of course, is the experience of falling in love with a person who
becomes a long-term partner. I can identify many reasons that I chose
to marry my wife, but even the total collection of reasons never
amounts to a thorough explanation; none of them is the reason, and
all of them together still do not add up to the reason. I am as aware as
anyone else that these sorts of relationships do not always work out.

That should not be a surprise; none of us is infallible at collecting data and understanding it, and we do not always make the best decisions based on what we could know at any given time. Plus, we have no idea of what will happen ten, twenty, or thirty years down the road. The miracle, though, is that an astounding number of our relationships turn out to be reasonably happy and productive. I see a lot of solid marriages around me – in spite of the rough spots that all relationships go through. They happen and survive because we know more than we think we know. Feelings are a useful guide to behaviour.

Ultimately, however, the challenge still comes back to the operations of our minds. Feelings are only helpful if they orient us toward answering the relevant questions about the religions that we and others espouse. Mobs often form and act on the basis of powerful common feelings. That is why the discussion of openness began with a warning that gut prejudices are dangerous. Critical thinking does mean thinking; it means rejecting the obvious answer in favour of asking the complicated and dangerous questions.

Indeed, critical thinking is all about what I think of as "the complexity fly." That particular fly buzzes around, reminding me that "It is always more complicated than that," where "it" is anything that I'm trying to understand. The complexity fly is both an invitation and a goad to ask more questions, to probe deeper into both the object that I'm trying to understand and into myself as the understanding subject. Critical thinking, therefore, depends upon two things: (1) the willingness to question; and (2) a recognition that questioning must also be quest, a search for the other as other rather than as a mirror reflecting the self of the questioner. This is why attitude is so important. We must be prepared to raise questions about those aspects of our identities that we take most seriously. We must be willing to risk our religious viewpoints, which encompass both our most deeply held views about everything and our most important values, in a constant effort to obtain the truest possible answers. Most importantly, we must do all of this in profound humility, in a recognition that the other – perhaps even the despised other – may have better answers to our questions than can be found in our own traditions.

The good news is that syncretistic critical openness can lead to greater wisdom, freedom, and peace. Syncretistic critical openness can lead to greater wisdom because it increases the likelihood of new insights into life, the universe, and everything. Conversation amongst traditions allows for sharing of wisdom, including advice about paths that have proven to be highly successful, other paths that have proven to be abject failures, and still other paths that have been somewhere in between. Syncretistic critical openness can lead to greater liberty because it frees us from the simplistic assumption that truth comes only in a particular colour and shape of package, with a particular label on the front – the correct label being defined by our upbringing. We are free to follow the trail toward truth, wherever it may lead. Syncretistic critical openness can lead to greater peace, both on the individual and on the communal levels. It can lead to greater peace on the personal level because it allows us to release the fear that causes us always to defend. I do not need to defend Christianity in conversation with a Muslim if we both bring the appropriate attitude to our interaction. Instead, we will both be there to learn from the other, weighing the value of our own and the other's words in a genuine common effort to understand as much of the truth as we can. Syncretistic critical openness can also lead to greater peace on the communal level because the need to police boundaries decreases. The responsibility of the community and its leaders shifts to a focus upon rational expression of the wisdom that it has inherited (the principle of preservation of insights) and an ongoing commitment to transformation through the reception of wisdom from other traditions (the principle of progress). Authority comes to mean the capacity to convince instead of being defined as the ability to state and maintain the kind of unchanging identities that we saw in our discussion of people who reject syncretism entirely. Such an attitude could contribute to world peace. At the very least, syncretistic critical openness could make life in our neighbourhoods much easier and more mutually satisfying. That is why I am committed to an advocacy approach to syncretism.

CRITICAL OPENNESS IN ACTION

Reflexive Syncretism: The Faith Club

There are people who firmly and intentionally support syncretism and the type of critical openness that fosters it in a healthy way. We see this in the encounters described in *The Faith Club: A Muslim, A*

Christian, A Jew – Three Women Search for Understanding, where some of the most notable syncretisms are of the reflexive kind. Trained theologians can be syncretists, also. Process theology generally comes out of a meeting between modern science and the Christian tradition and its focus on scientific thought gives its syncretism an asymmetric character; however, process thinkers have made a consistent and determined effort to formulate a syncretistic theology and call others to think in a syncretistic manner. The most symmetrical syncretism intentionally adopted by a public figure, having a real influence upon the world and inspiring followers, may be that of Mahatma Mohandas K. Gandhi. In their different ways, each of these examples provides us with some guidance in living a syncretistic life with true critical openness.

The Faith Club provides an intriguing example of syncretism. Three New York area women – a Muslim, a Christian, and a Jew – are brought together by the project of writing a children's book about religion, in the aftermath of the destruction of the World Trade Center, 11 September 2001. However, the complexities of each woman's relationship to her own and the others' religious identities force a deeper and more complicated relationship to emerge. As they encounter one another through a series of intensely honest and personal discussions about religious attitudes and beliefs, all three of the women find themselves transformed. The story of Ranya Idliby, the Muslim, is especially helpful for our discussion. Also, particularly valuable is the book's inclusion of advice on how to start a Faith Club which can assist people to move beyond recognition that syncretism happens and into an engagement with syncretistic critical openness on a routine basis.

One of the helpful aspects of *The Faith Club* is its existential approach. In this book, we encounter people as they are and their religions as the actual complex, syncretistic, identities that people carry through daily life rather than the abstracted generalizations that we often speak about in conversation. Life in *The Faith Club* is much more realistic than the oversimplified shorthand portrayals of religious identities that we commonly associate with the general labels "Muslim," "Christian," and "Jew." As Suzanne Oliver, the Christian, points out, "Ranya, Priscilla, and I had started out months earlier talking about what *Jews* believe, what *Christians* believe and what *Muslims* believe. We were like soldiers galloping forth from our camps carrying the standards of our people. We'd presented those standards to each other and examined them to see if they bore any of the same markings as our own. But now it was time to take off our uniforms and begin talking about the real people underneath. In other words, us."[2] Idliby, Oliver, and Warner start the way that people often start interfaith discussion, expressing what the women understand to be textbook representations of their faith traditions. However, the participants begin to recognize exactly what we have noticed about labels: they hide a multitude of specific, often complex religious identities. So Idliby, Oliver, and Warner chose to move beyond the labels and ask the question, "What are our religions now, in our lives?"

Right from the very beginning, we see Idliby grappling with her two major issues: (1) How is she, a modern, Westernized woman, to find an Islam in which she can relate to God?; and (2) How can she help her children relate to both their own and other religious traditions? Both questions emerge as Idliby responds to questions raised by her children about religious holidays from other faith traditions. Idliby admits to celebrating "a commercial kind of Christmas" even though she and her family are Muslim and regard Jesus as a prophet rather than the son of God.[3] Thus, we see that she is already a syncretist of a kind that is very common in North America. She mixes consumerism and a touch of Christianity with her Islam. More profoundly, Idliby feels lonely because she is a Muslim woman from a Palestinian family, but with a modern American identity formed by the kinds of feminism and liberalism that prevent her from wearing a headscarf or being comfortable in a mosque where women cannot mix on an equal footing with men. For her, the group (which the women began to call the "Faith Club") becomes her "mosque, church, and temple," her "surrogate religious community" and the heart of her quest for religious identity.[4]

The Faith Club takes what I have called "critical openness" as its central principle. While they "signed no official pact," they "lived by a certain code: honesty was the first rule of the Faith Club, and with that tenet as a foundation, no topic was off limits."[5] This commitment to honest inquiry is particularly evident as the women confront the challenges of prejudice that Jews and Muslims face. Naming, confronting, and investigating these issues enable the women to move beyond them into new appreciation for the other faith traditions; Warner, the Jew, starts out fearing and hating Jesus because of the abuse that Jews have received in Jesus' name, but comes to think of him as a friend and fellow Jew.

Idliby's quest is for an Islam that can participate in this spirit of syncretistic critical openness, but it is also a search for the power to declare herself openly as a Muslim.[6] Until she feels more comfortable with Islam, she cannot speak to the world as a Muslim. This is one of the roots of reflexive syncretism: the willingness to receive from other traditions different ways to know and value the best in our own traditions. As Idliby meets with Oliver and Warner, she becomes more deeply aware of the need to engage with a worshipping community; the intellectual community provided by the women's faith club is valuable, but insufficient. In precisely the right attitude, that of an offering, Oliver suggests that Idliby try attending the Episcopal church where Oliver is an active member.[7] Idliby does so because she grasps the significance and power of reflexive syncretism: "I had become aware that the more I learned about the common beliefs that link our three faith traditions, the more my belief in God was strengthened."[8] Idliby discovered soft boundaries. Although attendance at the service reminds her that she is truly a Muslim, especially at the moment of Holy Communion when she is reminded of the differences between Christians and Muslims over Jesus' identity, Idliby is vividly aware that she is growing as a Muslim precisely because of the influence of her Christian and Jewish friends. In the same spirit, she attends a Yom Kippur service which helps her to understand and accept death.[9] The others also shift; Oliver tells the story of rethinking Abraham and Moses (recognizing their Jewishness) and the doctrine of original sin (taking a different, but still Christian, position),[10] while Warner rethinks her relationship to the Covenant, the Promised Land, and contemporary Israel,[11] and finds true faith in an experience that she thinks of as being "BORN AGAIN" (emphasis hers).[12]

These changes are syncretistic. They are not merely discoveries of neglected aspects of each person's respective religious tradition. The notions of death expressed in a Yom Kippur service may be consonant with some Muslim views, and may help Idliby to be a better Muslim of her particular syncretistic type, but the feast itself and the views it expresses are undeniably Jewish in origin. Similarly, Warner's rethinking of the Promised Land as including non-Jews has a historical place in Judaism, but it is inspired by Idliby's Muslim insistence upon being there, too.

These examples function as reflexive syncretisms, though they also suggest that the boundaries between reflexive and asymmetric syncretisms are not always clear. An observer cannot always say with certainty which aspects of Idliby's new syncretism are Islamic with some nudging from elsewhere, and which are Islamic with Jewish and Christian elements. Because Islam, Judaism, and Christianity share much of their history and have central texts in common, the distinctions are not always easy to pin down. Both kinds of syncretisms appear to be present in the experiences of all three of the women; however, the predominant mode seems to be reflexive syncretism because their faith club intentionally works in that mode. Incidentally, Idliby did eventually discover an imam and Muslim religious community who were seeking to find and live an Islam rooted in aspects of the tradition which were more consonant with their American experience and with the kind of faith that Idliby discovered in relationship with her Christian and Jewish friends.

The Faith Club includes instructions on how to start a club like the one that Idliby, Oliver, and Warner created. While the book focuses upon the three religions commonly called "Abrahamic" (Judaism, Christianity, and Islam) the principles upon which a faith club rests are more universally applicable. The assumptions and guidelines are oriented toward increasing understanding of one's own religion and the religions of others. Two of the reflection questions are particularly helpful as steps toward developing syncretistic critical openness: (1) in the section entitled "Define Your God," each participant is asked "Have their [other members of the faith club] views changed what you believe about God?", which is a firm nudge toward allowing people of other religions to affect one's most explicitly theological assertions; and (2) in the section entitled "Think about Religion on the World Stage," participants are asked to pretend that they are of a religion other than their own while reading the newspaper or hearing the news, which is a way of encountering the world from another religious viewpoint. Both of these strategies encourage people to be open to the world's religious viewpoints while thinking critically about what they see and hear. This is an important aspect of syncretistic critical openness.

ASYMMETRICAL SYNCRETISM:
JOHN COBB'S PROCESS THEOLOGY

Process theology takes a more forthrightly syncretistic approach to religion. Most process theologies owe their origins to Alfred North Whitehead (1861–1947),[13] a mathematician and philosopher who sought to incorporate the insights of twentieth-century science into an account of the nature of God, humanity, and the universe. The roots of process thought are integrative and syncretistic, and so are the impulses that have continued to drive it. One consequence of this is that process thinkers have developed a set of distinctions that makes feasible what I call "syncretistic critical openness," along with an explicit commitment to this kind of thinking. The result can be seen in the universalistic Christology found in the work of John Cobb.

The necessary philosophical distinctions appear in an essay by Jan Van der Veken, with the provocative title, "Can the True God Be the God of One Book?"[14] Van der Veken's answer to his own question is both "Yes" and "No." He answers yes because God is always met in a specific and particular way and the real God is the one whom we meet, and no because God is always more than we encounter in any specific meeting, so that we can also talk about God in a general and abstract way. An encounter with God can result in a real revelation of God, a true meeting in which we understand something real and important about whom God is. Something of God's person really is "disclosed" to seers and prophets.[15] That encounter, however, will not tell us all that there is to know about God, and every experience is affected by all of the usual human limitations including our ability to sense and understand what is being conveyed to us. I've been married for over two decades and I still do not know all that there is to be understood about my wife; I cannot reasonably expect that the complex task of knowing all that there is to be known about God – which is, after all, impossible in principle – can be accomplished by myself or even by the particular religious tradition(s) that I inherit.

Therefore, while we need to be open to the wisdom of holy people, we also need to sustain a distinct kind of conversation about God, about "all-inclusive reality," which is formal and rational.[16] Here, Van der Veken is invoking a critical mindset in the language that we have used about critical openness. His point is that every particular revelation about God says something about who God is and, consequently, every such revelation has universal implications. If God is indeed the Creator of all things, then God's "Creatorness" implies many important characteristics about God. Philosophically trained people can investigate the implications of the statement that God is Creator.

Note that there is a shift in language here. The personal kind of statement that a prophet hears tends to go something like, "Where were you when I laid the foundations of the earth?" (Job 38:4), while the general statement of the formal scholar tends to be in a less poetic mode, and is likely to say, "Creativity looks like this, so if God is Creator, then God is like this." Both kinds of conversation are valid and necessary, but they are different.

This distinction is important because the language of the particular encounter with Ultimate Reality, however named, is the language of a particular religion. In contrast, the language of abstract generalization is the language that can mediate among religions; it facilitates interreligious conversation. It can function as a kind of translation language, a set of symbols in which the particular assertions that are logically consequent upon any meeting with God can be stated in a way that can help other people who have not had the same encounter with God or have not interpreted the encounter in the same way.

Van der Veken distinguishes between "uniqueness" and "onlyness."[17] The word "uniqueness" speaks about a special kind of revelatory experience, a particular something that occurs and causes a person to have a significant insight. Van der Veken uses the example of a piece of art which we call unique. Its uniqueness does not reside in simply being different from every other piece of art, but in what it teaches us about art and about the universe. The point of uniqueness is that it "does not exclude but rather implies generality;" it is a means of access to a larger truth.[18] It "reveals that something universal is present here and now."[19]

By contrast, "'onlyness' excludes other particularity," denying that any elements of the universal can be expressed in any other historical context.[20] In the case of the art example, onlyness implies that the truth found in one piece of art cannot be encountered in any other. No other means of discovering that truth exists. If onlyness is the basic theological position, then the truth expressed in an encounter with Ultimate Reality cannot be generalized, cannot be stated as a larger truth about the universe, precisely because its only state of being is in the one particular example. This means, for example, that Christian assertions are only true for Christians (and even then, only particular Christians who have had a particular sort of encounter with Christ); Christian assertions about reality have neither meaning nor application for anyone who has not had the same religious experience and understood it in precisely the same way. "Onlyness" means that truth is a narrowly individual possession rather than a general statement about what is true for all. Rational religions, amongst which Van der Veken counts Eastern Asiatic religions and those of the Judeo-Christian heritage, want to say something that is both universally true and grounded in their particular revelatory encounters. Therefore, they must choose uniqueness rather than onlyness.

Process thought uses the basic distinctions that Van der Veken makes as grounds for syncretistic theology. John Cobb's Christology (theory of who Christ is and what he does) is built upon the assertion that "Christ is the Way that excludes no Ways"[21] precisely because in his uniqueness, Christ says something – is something – of universal meaning and accessibility. Cobb's major work on Christology is focused upon moving from the particularity of Christian origins in Jesus to a universal, philosophically defensible account of Christ as creative transformation. Moreover, Cobb starts with the challenge of art as representation, just as Van der Veken uses it. Van der Veken has pointed out that a particular piece of art gives rise to a unique insight into the universal. Cobb discovers a very important explanation for the development of Christology in André Malraux's account of the history of the image of Christ in Western art. "In [Malraux's] account Western art triumphs over Christ; for Christ is bound to particularity, whereas Western art finally embraces all art. This struck me as suggestive of the course that Christian thought at its best is now taking."[22] Cobb's argument parallels Malraux's, but argues with it, claiming that Western art does not triumph over Christ but merely follows the same trajectory as Christian theology; moving from the particular, it embraces all religious insights. The disappearance of the figure of Christ from art means that people have found the true Christ, the power of creativity in all nature, including human beings.

Cobb understands Christ as creative transformation, a universal reality, so that the appearance of creative transformation in the Jesus of history and the continual re-expression of the meaning of Christ throughout history are valid and helpful declarations, but not the sole expressions of Christ's identity. In Cobb's words, "Christ is no more bound to any particular system of belief and practice than is the creative power of art to any particular style."[23] This is profoundly important because the power of creative transformation is not just the power of art; it is also the power of all life.[24] It is the power of social transformation seen in movements of human liberation.[25] It is the concern for the creative good that is always new rather than being bound by moral codes devised to suit different historical circumstances.[26] It is the power of growth and transformation in philosophy and science.[27] No aspect of existence is left out of the creative transformation that Christians know as Christ and find in the actual life and teachings of Jesus. In other words, Cobb accomplishes precisely the sort of universalization that Van der Veken calls for, while attempting to remain true to the particular encounter that Christians have had with Jesus.

This assertion about Christ's identity is rooted in Cobb's belief that the essence of divinity is creative transformation. God is the process of creative transformation, the world-spirit that drives growth and renewal. God, therefore, does not have an existence independent of the universe, as Christians have traditionally suggested. Instead, God is part of the universe, the creative force that drives it to give forth new life, to grow and change, and to become something greater. In Cobbs's view, the disappearance of images of Christ from modern art is the all-important move away from Christianity's early mistake: regarding God as immobile, perfectly still and unchanging, existing independently of the universe.

This argument is rooted in an asymmetrical syncretism coming out of Whitehead's attempt to think about God in light of modern science and, especially, in terms of evolutionary theory. For Whitehead, God exists with the universe, growing and developing with it. God's being is dependent on the world's being because God is, initially, the sum total of the universe's potential. In this original form, which Whitehead calls "primordial," God is not conscious because God is merely conceptual. God gains consciousness and actuality as the universe becomes actual, as "creative advance" happens.[28] Thus, God also has a "consequent" nature in which God is conscious and integrated because the temporal universe comes into being and is integrated, and includes in itself conscious beings.[29] The harmony of God's being is the harmony of all the multiplicity of developments of creativity in the universe.[30]

Whitehead's understanding of God helps us to make sense of Cobb's understanding of Christ. Christ is the creative force that makes the universe real and, therefore, makes God actual rather than merely potential. Human creativity, which is what the phrases "living in Christ" and "the Christian life" mean in Cobb's perspective, brings the universe into being and, therefore, brings God into being. Though Cobb expresses these views in Christian language, this is very far away from being traditional Christian thought. Christians have disagreed on many things, but they have always agreed that God has an independent existence. Christians have always insisted that God makes the universe actual; the universe does not give actuality to God. This is a distinctly asymmetric syncretism in which Whitehead's understanding of the universe as being in process determines the meaning of all Christian symbols, every one of which is reinterpreted from the standpoint of God and the universe in process.

As is probably evident, one of the great strengths of Cobb's work is the room that it creates for further syncretism. Process thought is at home wherever creativity is deemed to be paramount, and creativity extends to any form of activity that is undertaken in love and is oriented toward fulfillment of the universe's potential. Although we will not pursue the study here, Cobb's efforts in the area of Buddhist-Christian syncretism are worthy of note. Cobb identifies a real unity between Buddhism and Christianity on the grounds of their common concern for creativity, and he attempts something more like a symmetrical syncretism in his effort to move back and forth between the two traditions.[31] Cobb seeks to employ Mahayana Buddhist insights into the nature of being in an understanding of what Christianity has to say, providing grounds for Christianity to share Christ with Buddhists; he identifies Christ with Amida (a Buddha particularly sacred to the Mahayana) because both are ways of meeting the spirit of creativity that he sees in Christ.[32] Moreover, the idea of process thought is that efforts for unity should not stop there. The emphasis upon universalization is just what it sounds like: an attempt to discover a universal framework for understanding and action, which will enable integration of all the world's thought systems. Process thought is oriented toward a general syncretism.

One of Cobb's central accomplishments which renders his syncretism especially valuable is the relationship that he establishes between his Christological thinking and today's concrete challenges. The strongest defence for Cobb's work is that it makes sense of the contemporary world while providing grounds for moral criticism and action. It answers a broad range of today's questions about the unity of knowledge, including the possibility of bringing together science, art, and religion with politics and ethics. It is creative rather than destructive, and it is creative in ways that allow for the coming-together of many different people from diverse backgrounds in work for social justice. True creativity means being active in caring for the world. Moreover, any oppression, any action that prevents creative living, is unacceptable. That Cobb is central to efforts at Christian social action (he edited a volume of essays for the group, "Progressive Christians Uniting"[33]) and is vigorously active in interfaith work is no accident; instead, these activities testify to the power of his vision, which touches all areas of life. Cobb believes in religion in the strong, inclusive sense that we have spoken of, rather than the weak, closeted kind beloved of the Enlightenment. His syncretism, therefore, is not merely universal in the intellectual sense; it is also universal in that it has practical implications for the lives of everyone and everything, which is the best justification for syncretist critical openness.

Symmetrical Syncretism: Mahatma Gandhi

One of the most influential syncretists of the twentieth century was Mahatma Mohandas K. Gandhi. Studying Gandhi is a notable shift in flavour from discussing process theology. While process thought is primarily oriented toward a theory of the order of the cosmos, with ethical consequences, Gandhi's approach was always toward living the good, with a sense that right understanding would follow. He was officially a Hindu, but the term "Hindu" is even less useful than religious labels ordinarily are. Gandhi was raised in a thoroughly syncretistic household and followed his parents' example by seeking to learn from many religious traditions. Indeed, the commitment to such learning was one of his most basic religious principles. Gandhi formulated an overarching account of being that served his practical concerns, including an understanding of God as Truth and of humans as agents of change on behalf of the weak and oppressed. Gandhi's most significant and influential accomplishments include his explanation of the human problem of violence and his proposed solutions: *satyagraha* (which literally means "firmness in truth," but is translated as "soul-force," which describes how it works); *ahimsa* (non-violence); and fasting. Both Gandhi's explanations of these and his commitment to them are rooted in several religious traditions, most notably Hinduism, Jainism, Buddhism, and Christianity.

Gandhi must always be studied biographically, because his ideas flowed out of his life and were continually tested in action. His roots are fundamentally syncretistic. One of the challenges of understanding Hinduism is recognizing that each person – and often family – tends to participate in one aspect of the religious heritage, paying particular homage to one manifestation of *Brahman* (ultimate reality), while not rejecting other aspects of the heritage or other manifestations of Brahman. His mother was a devout Vaishnava (worshipper of Vishnu), and her life taught Mohandas that religious symbols are a valuable means of finding and expressing truth, even if they must be radically reinterpreted to suit new meanings.[34] Gandhi's father had many Jain friends; Jains tend to be particularly open to syncretism because they commonly believe what one scholar calls "the Jain doctrines of relativity."[35] *Anekantavada*, which translates literally as "non-one-sided," is a claim that reality is "irreducibly complex."[36] *Nayavada* is a doctrine which draws out a consequence of the complexity of reality for human knowing; "anything may be known from a variety of *nayas*, or perspectives, that correspond to its many aspects."[37] *Syadvada*, literally "the maybe doctrine," follows with the assertion that the truth-value of any statement depends upon the perspective from which it is made.[38] The result is that Jains tend to be open to many sources of wisdom. In an important sense, Gandhi's fundamental principles are rooted here, in the specific piety of his mother and the openness of his father. Gandhi became firmly opposed to closed-minded exclusivism which asserts the absolute finality of its own system and the essential falseness of all others; he regarded it as true idolatry, worse than the use of statues and other human-crafted objects in worship because these could be means of attaining truth, but exclu-sive, fundamentalist mindsets make reaching truth impossible.[39]

Gandhi is famous for saying "Truth [*Satya*] is God"; this is a 1926 re-formulation of his earlier declaration that "God is Truth."[40] Gandhi was very hesitant about defining God, taking a common Hindu attitude but also an approach that suited his focus upon practical concerns. The focus upon truth as a statement about God reflects Gandhi's openness; it is an assertion that allows all religions to make a contribution. Gand-hi's priority is a right answer rather than a familiar source. The other advantage of this formulation is that it avoids anthropomorphism. Gandhi was not comfortable speaking of God as a person, regarding that sort of attribution as a human attempt to adjust God to fit human expectations.[41] For Gandhi, the assertion that God is spirit is a state-ment that God is ultimate reality, the final truth of things, rather than a friend with whom we can interact. The danger in the claim that God is Truth is that one might come to understand God as the object of a kind of pure philosophical contemplation, which is precisely contrary to Gandhi's intention. Instead, satya is the principle of order in the uni-verse; it enforces justice in much the way that Stoic (Roman) natural law thinkers understand justice as the right ordering of things so that living against satya will bring practical consequences.

Humans, therefore, are understood in relation to satya as beings who can and ought to live satyagraha. The two translations of satya-graha, "firmness-in-truth" and "soul-force," are both helpful. This is the essential power of satya, or Truth, as Gandhi understands It. In the world, satyagraha is the power to live the good, to live in a manner consistent with ultimate reality. To know Gandhi is to understand that living satyagraha is not merely a matter of self-transformation, though it is always that, but is also a means of changing the world. "Firmness-in-truth" is a reminder of the discipline involved; one must always seek to know the Truth, which requires endless commitment, including whatever formal disciplines one finds helpful for remain-ing in the Truth, such as the year of silence that Gandhi took in 1926, to recharge himself.[42] One must always seek to live in the Truth, which demands a commitment to action against injustice, along with immovability when others try to force one away from the Truth. "Soul-force" is a reminder that living in the Truth changes the world; no matter what satyagraha suggests to the observer, it is never passive or without impact. Living in the Truth transforms the universe in every aspect, human or not.

This is the key to understanding Gandhi's actions and their consequences. This is why Gandhi launched a Non-co-operation Movement against the British colonial masters in India in 1920. The movement lasted only two years and was a failure. However, the failure was not necessarily in the principle, but in the execution. The idea was for all of Indian society to stop participating in colonial life, but many people refused, for various reasons. The most important significant aspect of its failure was the distressing impact that it had on Hindu-Muslim relations, because the Muslims saw non-co-operation as a danger to their hard-won gains in society. On the other hand, the trial gave Gandhi an opportunity to publicize his stance, which had a notable impact on the British judges and served notice to the British that colonialism was failing. Satyagraha was similarly behind his efforts to improve the lots of the poor, women, and untouchables; Gandhi was firmly opposed to untouchability because it denies the equality of all in God. In 1930, Gandhi stepped up his campaign; along with seventy-eight companions, he undertook a twenty-four-day march (about 240 miles long) to the coast in order to protest the British-imposed salt tax. Emphasizing the religious meaning of his actions, Gandhi took a copy of the Bhagavad Gita and a copy of the Bible, reading aloud from both as he went. He picked up a handful of salt at the ocean, encouraging Indian people to harvest salt illegally – a kind of obvious defiance which signalled the end of British rule. This is soul-force changing the world.

Satyagraha is also the explanation of Gandhi's warm response to some aspects of Christianity. In the Sermon on the Mount, Gandhi found a statement of his own attitude toward the poor and needy, a call to sacrifice oneself for the other and, in the process, discover one's real self – an attitude that Gandhi recognized from his own Hinduism.[43] He described these verses as Jesus' "definition of perfect dharma."[44] *Dharma* is that which upholds satya; in other words, dharma is the kind of behaviour that is consistent with the Truth of being, the natural law that structures the universe. In Jesus, Gandhi discovered a teacher in the Indian sense, one who proclaims the Truth by example in addition to stating it in terms that reach both his contemporaries and the whole world, in all times and places. The crucifix (a model cross with Jesus suffering on it) came to have great meaning for Gandhi.[45] The cross is the place where Gandhi sees true love displayed as Jesus demonstrates to all the world that his love does not break down when he is threatened; instead, Jesus perseveres and, in suffering and dying, shows the world how deep love goes. Gandhi called this "the law of suffering," and regarded it as the fullest demonstration of the soul-power upon which he depended. "For satyagraha and its off-shoots, non-co-operation and civil resistance, are nothing but names for the law of suffering. The *rishis* who discovered the law of violence in the midst of violence were greater geniuses than Newton."[46] A rishi is a prophet, which is a key to understanding how Gandhi viewed Jesus; Gandhi understood Jesus as a prophet of universal love, one who "expressed, as no other could, the spirit and will of God."[47]

Thus, Gandhi rejected Christianity's statements about the nature of Jesus, partly because Gandhi did not share the basic Greek and Latin assumptions about nature that gave rise to the Christian belief in the full humanity and full divinity of Jesus. This is one of the reasons that Gandhi was irked by Christian claims to sole possession of the full-ness of truth; we have seen others in Jainism and in the similarity of Gandhi's Hinduism to his Christianity. However, Gandhi accepted Jesus as a full expression of Godness, "the prince of satyagrahis"[48] who shows the world the true meaning of life.

The power of "soul-force" is the root and explanation of Gandhi's commitment to non-violence (ahimsa); indeed, satyagraha is Gandhi's explanation of ahimsa. Non-violence is an ancient principle of most religious traditions native to India. Hinduism, Jainism, and Buddhism all value non-violence, although in varying ways and with different degrees of stringency. Gandhi is probably the most famous exponent of this approach in the contemporary world, however, befitting his position as one who has mediated Indian traditions to the rest of the world and Western traditions to India. Gandhi's argument is that non-violence is not mere inaction, and Gandhi's form of non-violence should not be understood as passive. Instead, it is a deployment of satyagraha against the aggressor.

Fasting is an important means of cultivating and displaying satya-graha. Fasting is a means of self-purification, though Gandhi noted that its appetite-sharpening capacity could cultivate indulgence.[49] More significantly, it shows the commitment that Jesus showed: the willingness to give one's life for love. Consequently, Gandhi employed fasting as a public statement in addition to using it as a personal discipline. In 1924, Gandhi went on a twenty-one-day fast to encourage Hindus and Muslims to improve relations and co-operate. In 1926, Gandhi took a year of silence to strengthen his spirit, to recharge with soul-force, as it were. In 1932, Gandhi forced the British to change their electoral policy for untouchables by fasting in prison. In 1946–47, as India was being torn apart by Hindu-Muslim violence and the call for a separate Muslim state (Pakistan was created in 1947), Gandhi engaged in a series of fasts. He made visits to riot-torn areas and engaged in multi-religious prayer meetings, including readings of the Qur'an, which angered Hindus already embittered by the Muslim desire to separate from India. "In order to shock the 'conscience of all' in both India and Pakistan, he commenced his last fast on 13 January 1948 to create 'real peace' instead of the deadly calm imposed by the troops" and to ensure that India kept its promises to transfer territory to the newly created Pakistan.[50] Gandhi was reviled for his openness to Islam. On 30 January 1948, he was assassinated by a well-educated Hindu. This brought Gandhi's desired conclusion: his death gave everyone pause, destroyed the credibility of Hindu militarism, and brought a measure of calm to the situation. Soul-force, satyagraha, was the decisive meaning of Gandhi's life. Fasting was an important part of this precisely because it put Gandhi's own life on the line; fasting can lead to death and will, almost inevitably, shorten one's life. Ultimately, Gandhi's death by assassination is at one with his fasting, and both served the cause of Truth.

A standard theme that runs through Gandhi's story is his openness to religious wisdom, whatever the source. Gandhi had a whole-hearted commitment to truth and love which he regarded as satya, and a determination to practice his faith in a non-violent way, even if that meant suffering, satyagraha, ahimsa, and fasting. Gandhi's understanding of life is so thoroughly a symmetrical syncretism that any effort to identify one religious identity as the root to which other parts are grafted is simply impossible. Indeed, his way of thinking and being is the purest example of symmetrical syncretism that I can find, and Gandhi would be greatly pleased to hear that said of him. He found the cues for his way in Hinduism, Jainism, Buddhism, Christianity, and Islam. Hinduism gave him a respect for piety and an entry

into the world of his country. Jainism gave him the principle of finding wisdom everywhere. Buddhism, Christianity, and Islam contributed to his understanding of, and firmness in his principles.
Indeed, Christianity gave Gandhi the example of Jesus, who taught
Gandhi's way and reminded him of the necessity for and danger of
obedience unto death. His openness to Islam is what brought about
that death. While the native religions of India claimed him as their
own, Christians wondered why, since Gandhi was so obviously Christian, he did not convert. Gandhi detested the notion of conversion,
preferring syncretism. The accusation that he had become a Muslim
– he was derisively called "Mohamed Gandhi"[51] – led a militant
Hindu to kill him. His death became, in a sense, salvific for Hindus.
He intentionally belonged to all people, to all religions, because he
valued what he could learn from anyone, and what he could teach
everyone.

CONCLUSION:
THE ADVOCACY APPROACH TO SYNCRETISM

The Faith Club, John Cobb and other process theologians, and Mahatma Gandhi are all examples of what I call the "advocacy" approach to
syncretism: not only do they recognize and celebrate the reality of
syncretism, they also encourage others to participate and even establish structures to enable participation. In all of these cases, the syncretists are involved in the life of the world; each syncretism makes
the world a better place or, at least, tries to do so. All are trying to be
creative rather than destructive and see their religious efforts as a
means to prevent unnecessary violence. All are trying to discover
truth, insofar as that is possible. These examples also remind us of the
hard work involved in constructing and living a helpful syncretism,
especially in the effort to be fair to the various religious viewpoints
being included in the conversation. Syncretism is not always easy, but
it is worthwhile.

Although the faith club that Idliby, Oliver, and Warner built was
originally founded upon a need to understand the other religions –
always, the first step in interreligious conversation is an effort to
understand the other as other – the club's purpose shifted. The participants came to realize that the real value in their conversation was

not the fairly straightforward intellectual development that comes with knowing more about other religions. Instead, the most profound transformation came from the discovery that interfaith conversation was really about the participants' own religious journeys. Some of the most valuable insights came from other religions. Idliby discovered religious community and a way to understand death; Warner rethought her relationship to Jesus, in addition to changing both her understanding and actions in relation to Jewish thinking about the Promised Land; Oliver encountered Moses and Abraham as Jews, and rejected an unhealthy view of sin. These changes in their thinking were a result of encounters with the other religions, even though the new ways of thinking often (though not always) fit comfortably into the religious traditions in which the women had been raised.

The result is that Idliby, Oliver, and Warner have become public advocates for interfaith conversation and have created a framework for others to participate. From the perspective of our discussion, the most important fact about the system that the women recommend is that it is not structured in a way that only encourages people to burrow deeper into their own traditions and present those views to others. Instead, the idea of faith clubs is that the insights received from other religious heritages should be transformational. A Muslim may remain a Muslim; a Christian may remain a Christian; a Jew may remain a Jew. However, the process is oriented toward enabling participants to incorporate insights from other traditions into their lives (asymmetric syncretism) and, most especially, drawing from other traditions insights that have a traditional place in participants' own traditions (reflexive syncretism).

The challenge presented by the authors of *The Faith Club* comes out of the strict honesty with which they pursued their conversation, a forthrightness that is evident in the book that they have written. There is a very real difference between a warning that seriously engaging in syncretistic critical openness is a risky endeavour, demanding tremendous levels of clarity, vulnerability, and flexibility, and the hard work of taking risks. The most astonishing characteristic of *The Faith Club*, simply as a book, is that its authors have dared to tell the world, in wrenching emotional terms, how difficult and existential a process this sort of interfaith learning can be. Syncretistic critical openness is not simply an academic exercise for isolated minds in ivory towers, if such things even exist. Rather, it is an immediate, often painful requirement for ordinary people to accept that many of their cherished assumptions will be brought into question. Religious growth in today's world demands that we engage in the syncretistic process, but it is not an easy way of life.

Process thinkers tend to be even more vigorous advocates for syncretism. While the authors of *The Faith Club* provide an example of syncretistic critical openness, process thinkers combine their public commitment to such activity with a philosophical/theological basis for it. The arguments for uniqueness as opposed to onlyness, and universalization rather than narrowness, encourage people to move toward syncretism. The drive is toward transforming all religion into a welcoming force directed toward the true and the good. Cobb's Christology, in which Christ is defined as the power of creativity present throughout the world and evident in every creative act, is as universal as process thought claims it to be. Indeed, it is quite consistent with Gandhi's thinking about soul-force, with a similar sense of power for good in everyone and everything.

There is a challenge at the heart of Cobb's work that must be taken seriously when thinking syncretistically, and it is part of the reason that the process thought we've discussed falls into the category of asymmetric syncretism. Cobb warns us that religious traditions must be studied in terms that make sense within their own contexts; studying Gautama Buddha from a Freudian context, in which Freud is made sacred (the sacralisation process that we have discussed), does not make one a true student of the Buddha, but only a Freudian using Buddhist evidence for Freudian conclusions.[52] This leads us to a very important issue for syncretistic critical openness, the assertion that we need to understand the other as other if we are to garner real wisdom from that other. Simply following our own methods and assumptions into new territory will only leave us convinced of what we already knew.

While this sounds simple enough, listening to another solely on the other's own terms can be a fiendishly difficult, perhaps impossible, trick to manage in practice. Moreover, while Cobb gives us good and important advice, he risks making a very complex challenge of translation seem simpler than it is. For instance, Cobb uses this sort of argument in his criticism of the early Christian church's use of Greek and Latin thought in its understanding of God; Cobb thinks this was what we would call an unhealthy asymmetrical syncretism, in which Greek and Latin meanings were clothed in Christian garments instead of Christianity using the other ways of thinking to express meanings suited to the message of Jesus.[53] Thinkers in the Classical style looked at Jesus and saw Classical meanings, so they emphasized a vision of God as unchangeable and present to all times and places simultaneously ("eternal," in the technical language of Christian theology). The difficulty is that someone accustomed to thinking in a Classical, philosophical mode probably cannot dismiss all of those categories when trying to accomplish a new syncretism, just as Freudians will not be able to forget all they have learned from Freud or maintain two streams of thought on independent, discrete, tracks. Part of the reason that this is important is because this syncretism – the blending of biblical stories with Classical thought – yielded a tremendously powerful and helpful overarching explanation of reality, which answered the questions that society raised.

Cobb has raised an important challenge and one that is completely current. It is not just about what should have happened 1,500 or 2,000 years ago. The issue is still present when Cobb interprets various religious viewpoints, including those of early Christianity, from the standpoint of modern science as explicated by Whitehead, Charles Hartshorne, and others. Cobb's position is not obviously more biblical than Athanasius', and Whitehead's is not evidently more biblical than Plato's. That is the point of a syncretism, two or more, possibly alien, strains of thought meet and are used to create something new. The challenge is to do justice to all contributors, as much as possible, especially because a syncretism is valuable to the degree that it answers existing questions that have arisen in a particular historical context.

There is a balance to be found here. We need to avoid having our prior conclusions determine what we will discover in another text. This is a basic and necessary principle of syncretism; without this rule we will always find what we expect to find in other traditions. Nonetheless, we will always bring our prior formation with us when we try to understand something different. Critical openness is the key.

Cobb's point also displays an important kind of honesty that we need to remember. The process thought that we have discussed, including Cobb's, counts as an asymmetrical syncretism precisely because these people are clear and up-front about their theoretical commitments. Van der Veken is perfectly aware, and wants everyone to be aware, that his vision derives from a particular historical event and heritage. He does not wish to pretend that his history is irrelevant to his viewpoint, which is always the danger of any effort to construct a symmetrical syncretism. We can too easily convince ourselves that we are utterly impartial, treating every position from a kind of Archimedean standpoint outside the entire discussion. This is not what really happens. Instead, we always work from where we are, building upon principles that we have learned from somewhere and of which we are, at least somewhat, convinced. Precisely because of this, truly symmetrical syncretisms of the kind that Gandhi manages are exceedingly rare.

Although Gandhi is not the systematic thinker that Van der Veken and Cobb are – which may be part of the secret of the symmetrical nature of his syncretism – he also develops a philosophical/theological basis for his position. Gandhi's belief that Truth is God is the ground of his commitment to firmness-in-truth, or soul-power. Non-violent forms of action, including non-cooperation, public marches, and fasts, follow reasonably from his notion of soul-power. There is no need to enter into the endless cycle by which violence breeds violence, and people remain trapped in samsara, the cycle of death and rebirth conditioned by the moral quality of one's actions, because soul-power is able to overcome destruction and death. Gandhi's point is precisely the one that we saw earlier: a syncretism is unhelpful when it is destructive of life. Gandhi finds his message of soul-power in numerous religions, enabling him to construct a genuine symmetrical syncretism. He calls all people of good will to learn from this message and to live in love together.

Perhaps more to the point, however, is the reality of Gandhi's strong existential rootedness. His understanding of the world was less defined by the thought that he encountered than by the life that he lived and the consequences that his life brought about. Gandhi sought always to be creative, to live against the forces that would cause destruction. In an important sense, the course of life was his real testing place for religion. Violence did not improve the lives of the people around him; non-violence did not solve every problem, especially because violence continually re-appeared, but non-violence accomplished much more. Soul-power broke the British Raj, improved the standing of untouchables, and made possible real progress in the economic lives of the Indian people. Though it did not resolve challenges between Hindus and Muslims, one can fairly say that it could have if others had been willing to try it. Gandhi proved that the soul-power concentrated in one person can bring about profound change. However, permanent changes in whole societies require the commitment of others to true satyagraha. In his sufferings, Gandhi has given us a powerful warning of the risk that can accompany syncretistic efforts. Syncretism is widely rejected, often at a visceral level, so that publically defined syncretists can look like traitors. Religion is intimately personal, which makes it a matter of intense concern. Religion is also the heart of people's explanations of life and their justifications for actions. Consequently, to have someone declare one's religion inadequate and claim that there is a real need for it to be combined with another can be threatening; it feels like a real loss of "face," of honour. In any culture, this sort of loss is unwelcome; in traditional honour cultures, it is desperately painful. The threat is increased when syncretism will cause a real loss in material wealth or social standing. Partly because of all the history behind the Hindu-Muslim difficulties, including generations of Muslim domination in parts of India, Gandhi's attempts to demonstrate the existence of mutual ground between them were never really acceptable to either group. Moreover, these efforts did make Gandhi look like a traitor: while Hinduism is broadly open to other religious views, Islam has traditionally held itself to be incompatible with the older Indian religious heritages. Social and economic differences contributed to the split and, when the Muslim community began to demand a separate country, political allegiances became distinct. The result was that the Hindu syncretism and the Muslim syncretism became enemies. A syncretism that publically declared itself as such, attempting to embrace both camps, simply looked like it had no allegiance to either, while insulting both. As a result, Gandhi paid the ultimate price, sacrificing his life.

Gandhi, of course, is a rather dramatic example. His life's accomplishments are greater than most of us can even imagine. Similarly, the price that he paid is especially high. We cannot necessarily expect either the same world-changing role or the same consequences. Nonetheless, Gandhi has issued us a warning. The syncretistic critical openness that he displayed in all that he did, always being attentive to the wisdom and the needs of the other, is not likely to win popularity contests. It requires a kind of flexibility when others prefer unchanging solidity, and a kind of firmness when others prefer a willingness to bend. Gandhi's style of syncretistic critical openness is intrinsically counter-cultural. It can be dangerous.

9

The Last Taboo:
Education about Religion

Syncretistic critical openness is impossible without some sort of intellectual preparation. The question is: If religion is an important and inevitable part of human existence, and if we all learn from other religions, then should there be some explicitly religious component to the education of our children? Must it be the last taboo in a world where all other topics are discussed? The simplest answer is that there will be religion in education, public or private, whether we admit it or not. Education completely without values and priorities is simply impossible; even if our children's education is defined solely by economic considerations, then our children are learning that jobs and money are all that matters.

As a matter of fact, many teachers in public and private school systems around the world have some other religious commitments, and completely isolating their life-defining principles and characteristics from the work that they do is not easy. It is also unsustainable. Teachers are, on the whole, a dedicated lot, and they want to share what is best in them. Inevitably, their religious commitments will have a formative impact on the classroom, even if only in subtle ways. A teacher whose religion encourages Earth's exploitation will be noticeably less sympathetic to environmental concerns than a teacher whose religion emphasizes human stewardship of the Earth, for example. Curriculum can never entirely paper over these sorts of differences. Besides, a reflective person would not want them all to vanish; vigorous debate over strongly held opinions is what drives education – the more so as young people grow. Removing all the individuality from teachers would simply leach all colour out of them and, consequently, make them altogether boring to any person unlucky enough to be forced to listen to them. Even if the G-word (God) is never mentioned, religion will be present in the classroom. Thus, we can recognize that religious education occurs and choose to do something intelligent and responsible about it, or we can choose to turn a blind eye and pretend that religious education does not really happen so that we can avoid facing the complicated problems and public discomfort that conversation about religion always brings.

The difficulty with pretending that religious education does not happen and simply ignoring what does occur is that we have no idea what is transpiring. As in the above example about teachers and their attitudes about the environment, the underlying commitments cannot be brought to the surface if religion is banned from classroom investigation. Instead, it lurks in the background for educators and students. Nobody admits to anything and everyone tiptoes around the elephant in the room. This is both dishonest and unhealthy. Besides, in a context like this, young people learn to be embarrassed about religion. Many pick up the exact message that is being taught: we are always wisest to pretend that we do not have any religion and life is really all about money and sex, which cannot possibly be their own religions. Life becomes both shallow and unhealthy; we are stuck with what Milan Kundera astutely calls "the unbearable lightness of being."[1]

Besides, with the "pretend religion is not there" approach, religious education ends up being done largely by people who have, at most, limited training in relation to the questions. A syncretistic world requires that we know something about what religion is, about the nature of our own religious heritages, and about other religious traditions. We need to understand religions as thoroughly as we possibly can because we must live with them and in them. Young people need solid, reliable information in order to make healthy decisions. This is one of those truisms that has become a truism by being both true and obvious; I am continually astounded by how often we forget it.

If we ignore religion in formal education, then the only formal preparation that young people will receive is what parents give them. You may be an actively religious person with solid religious training in the tradition(s) that you follow, in which case you may be quite happy to see such education left in your hands. Fair enough. However, there are two obvious difficulties with this approach: (1) you know your own tradition(s), but you may not know any others well enough to help your children grow up with a solid and fair understanding of other religions – a severe disadvantage (possibly even a danger) in a syncretistic world; and (2) you may not trust everyone else in your community to do an equally good job, meaning that other children may not grow up being prepared to be fair to your heritage.

If you are a Khalsa Sikh, do you want other people to grow up misunderstanding the significance of the great symbols of your faith, including your bracelet and ceremonial dagger? If so, you may find yourself deprived of them. If you are a Muslim, do you want others to be educated in ignorance about and fear of Islam, especially in relation to its views on violence toward innocent strangers? If so, you may find yourself mistreated and even forced to choose between your religion and your country. If you are a Christian, do you want to see Jesus being publically abused because others have not had enough religious education to understand why he's so important to you? Oppose religious education and you may expect this and worse.

The point of communal education is precisely that it goes beyond what parents can do; it trains young people for life in the larger community. In a world as tightly integrated and cosmopolitan as ours, such training is indispensable. Even home-schooling needs to engage curriculum that goes beyond parental background; just as we do not assume that a parent has adequate preparation in mathematics or history to be able to train young people to function in the community, we cannot assume that a majority (or a substantial minority) have the knowledge and capacity to provide a full religious education to their children. In a multi-religious and syncretistic world, we depend upon this training to enable good judgements. I cannot determine whether Sikh symbols should be acceptable in public spaces until I know something about the meaning and use of each item.

I am most certainly not rejecting a role for parents. Indeed, I strongly encourage parents to be involved in the religious education of children. If our children come to understand what our religion means to us, then they're more likely to understand the significance that other people attach to their religious views. In addition, we can introduce some of the complexities of our own heritages to our kids. The varieties of opinion will start to emerge. ("Some people say this about Jesus, while other people say that. Why, Dad?") The family context can provide an element of safety for speaking about some of the less savoury parts of our traditions. ("How have Christian people treated Jewish people, Dad? After all, Jesus was a Jew, wasn't he?") The home is also a great place to celebrate the many accomplishments of our traditions. ("Why do so many hospitals have saints' names on them, Dad?") At home, children can learn both to value and critique our heritages. This is invaluable, perhaps irreplaceable, training.

At least as important a matter is the role that home learning plays in normalizing discussion of religion. If the issues are continually raised in the family context, then they will not seem alien when they are encountered on the street or at school. The home provides a kind of anchorage, a standpoint from which to learn about other religious heritages and begin assessing them. Inheriting everything may mean inheriting nothing if it all lands at once or if it seems like merely another subject in the academic environment. Serious engagement with the family's heritages is part of what makes further growth possible when children start to learn about religion outside the home.

Instead of rejecting a parental role, I am suggesting that relying solely on home education in religion makes no more sense than depending entirely upon families to teach mathematics. If only parents and siblings were to teach mathematics, then only children in mathematical families would get beyond rudimentary arithmetic, and many children would not even receive that. They would be disadvantaged from early life all the way through to the end, unless they were able to focus intensively on the subject at a later age. Mathematics confronts us constantly, and people who lack basic skills in the area are locked out of a whole variety of important jobs. The whole realm of specialized occupations that depend upon advanced mathematics would simply be alien to mathematically challenged school graduates. I am, of course, speaking in absurdities. Nobody can even imagine setting up such a school system in the modern, technological world, except in the contexts of religious extremism that I have criticized.

The reality is that people in modern societies have no idea how one could train anyone to do anything without mathematics. Yet, religion is as omnipresent as mathematics, and we have no hesitation in raising whole generations of religiously ignorant citizens. Many Western young people grow up without the slightest introduction to the field. As a result, they are cut off from a very large portion of themselves. They make the assumption that most of the larger questions about meaning and value cannot be answered, in principle. They may be right, but how would they know? We have deprived them of the tools to make the attempt. Their agnosticism is merely the agnosticism of ignorance rather than a conclusion bolstered by serious investigation. Moreover, we have rendered completely inaccessible the answers that have been suggested in the past. The whole Western intellectual heritage – philosophy, literature, art, music, and even natural science – is all intimately connected with Christianity, so a solid education in that religion and its historical development is an absolute necessity for access to the wisdom and knowledge that is available to us.

In a similar way, the intellectual heritages available to every other culture in the world are shot through with religious viewpoints. Nobody should need to go through life without access to the great traditions of India (or China, or Japan, etc.). However, the whole point of this book is that those traditions are permeated with religious meanings. We cannot remove the religion and expect to find some purified remainder. Connecting these last two points, we need to recognize that rendering our own heritage inaccessible to ourselves dramatically increases the challenge involved when trying to understand other traditions, whether from our own land or from somewhere else. Moreover, if we treat religion as merely irrelevant superstition, a cover story for other motivations that is unworthy of serious investigation, then we will not understand any past insights from any of the world's cultures, small or great. Muslims do not celebrate Ramadan simply because they believe that fasting is good for the body. Indeed, some Muslims may profoundly dislike the act of fasting. Their reasons are religious, having to do with purification, self-restraint, and dedication to Allah's purposes. As we have seen, Buddhism was not adopted in China simply because it responded to political needs. Instead, Buddhism was welcomed because it explained the world's unfolding in terms that people could understand and accept. Religion is real. It is not just a smokescreen.

The consequences of ignoring religion are not solely individual, though, not entirely a matter of deficiencies in the lives of the young people whom we keep from understanding themselves and their history. Our approach also has an impact on the world because our simpleminded incomprehension causes us to behave in some very unhelpful ways in relation to others. These range from a kind of uncultured clumsiness to the perpetration of great injustices. Islam has, once again, entered the awareness of Western countries. Our relations with Islam have been characterized by all these sorts of foolish behaviours. We have no clue about the nature of Islam, its law, theology, history, politics, or economics. Consequently, when cartoonists wanted to ridicule violent Islamic jihadism, as in the case of the *Jyllands-Posten* affair of 2005 – in which a number of cartoonists made contributions to a Danish newspaper at the newspaper's request – Westerners were incredulous or offended at the strong reaction of the Muslim world. Those cartoons sparked an international outcry, partly because they included portrayals of the Prophet Muhammad, some of which were insulting. Some Muslims explicitly reject the visual depiction of the human form,[2] which is one of the reasons why Islam developed the use of calligraphic letters to a high art form. Since the late nineteenth century, rejection of representational art has been on the decline in Islam, largely because of growing Western influence.[3] Nonetheless, even some people who are less strict tend to be uncomfortable with pictures of Muhammad, or may find them explicitly unacceptable. Unflattering portrayals, therefore, are particularly offensive. This was not a helpful form of critique if the cartoonists really wanted to attack the use of Islam as an excuse for foolishly violent behaviour. If the intention was to describe Islam in general as violent and destructive, then commentators missed a whole variety of complex questions that could not easily be reduced to cartoon caricatures: Is there such a thing as Islam in general? Or are there only Islams? If there is an Islam per se, then how does it relate to Muhammad's message and actions? How does contemporary jihadist Islamic terrorism relate to Islamic tradition/s? This sounds like rather a lot of knowledge to expect of a cartoonist, I agree. However, what right do we have to make ourselves harsh commentators on profound issues if we know nothing whatsoever about those issues and their background? A basic religious education would seem to be an obvious pre-requisite for public comment on religion.

The religiously uneducated are culturally deficient. They cannot be competent citizens in their own towns and are utterly at a loss as citizens of the world. Our young people know that; their electronic world is full of religion and they do not necessarily have the commitment to ignorance that characterizes their parents. Consequently, they either blog shared ignorance or obtain what religious education they can get. Many younger people today are very sensitive toward differences, aware of the complexities of life, and interested in different points of view. They do remarkably well at educating themselves. Besides, haphazard education, driven by one's own specific questions, can be the best kind as long as it is being conducted by a capable person who has learned how to learn and is committed to the process. Unfortunately, with young people as with older ones, many do not have the relevant capacities or interest. These sorts of people get short-changed. Some of them end up blogging ignorance; the worst of them become abusive toward others.

However young people choose to respond to the situation, we have been unfair to them if we have not provided even a minimum of education about religion. It cannot be a taboo topic in a world where we are explicit about everything else. Young people deserve to be introduced to religion as religion, and to the religious aspects of various issues. This would be true even if religion were the kind of limited thing that modern Western thought has treated it as: a simple-minded reflection upon life after death, combined with an archaic mindset about problems that science can solve all by itself. Given that this is a wholly inadequate account of the nature of religion, as we have seen, and that religion is a central aspect of everyone's life, we simply cannot excuse ourselves from the task of speaking about it in our educational systems.

STRUCTURING RELIGIOUS EDUCATION

The tough question – the one where the conversation often falls apart – is: "How are we to discuss religion in public, often explicitly non-religious, educational systems?" Educators (and those who care about education) fear creating strong reactions which will undermine the civil atmosphere that makes possible education for large, divergent groups of people. The approach of sticking to safe topics appears to be a necessity, especially when extremists threaten the lives of those with whom they disagree. This is a real and appropriate concern which is not adequately answered by noting that we talk extensively about other risky subjects in schools or that religion becomes more dangerous for being treated as an unacceptable issue for discussion. Nonetheless, there are ways that religion can be discussed, helpfully and safely, at all levels of education, from primary to post-secondary, with proper post-secondary training being the necessary pre-condition for civil conversation in earlier grades.

The reality is that religions of every sort have done themselves few favours on the matter of civil conversation in the public square. Because religious views are, by definition, both profound and all-encompassing, true syncretistic critical openness is rare. Instead, we tend to respond strongly when our religious views are challenged. Unfortunately, there is no shortage of examples of overreaction. While the *Jyllands-Posten* cartoons do seem to have been inappropriate, an indication that the cartoonists did not understand either Islam in general or the particular behaviours that they were critiquing (as well as having a doubtful grasp of the powers and responsibilities of editorial cartoonists), the responses from the Muslim world were not particularly helpful, either. The cause of a deeper understanding of Islam was hardly strengthened by massive (sometimes fatal) riots, the burning of embassies, and the mistreatment of flags. Indeed, this sort of activity merely tended to convince uninformed observers that the cartoonists were right to imply that Islam is intrinsically violent. This is exactly the message that Muslims needed to resist sending under the circumstances.

Traditionally religious people are not the only ones prone to overreaction; we also see it in avid supporters of secular religion. Hence, when there were difficulties with one woman wearing a niqab in a Montreal classroom, suddenly the Canadian province of Quebec was taken up with a battle of "duelling manifestos," as one journalist put it.[4] One of those manifestoes, entitled "For a Secular and Pluralist Quebec," expressed its purpose to eliminate all religious symbols from public space. Such a radical course may seem unlikely, but the mere fact that a significant number of highly educated people could call for it in a public space indicates something about the extreme attitude that some people bring to their anti-religious religion, and the Charter of Values proposed by the Quebec government in 2013 is a deliberate effort to fulfil the same set of goals. This type of anti-religious extremism is also visible in the recent effort to ban minarets in Switzerland, where they can hardly be said to dominate the landscape. These are not violent examples, I realize, but that does not mean that anti-religious people cannot be brutal. Mao's China and Stalin's Soviet Union are better examples of how secular religion can use violence against the more traditional religions; these cases also show how vigorous and deep-seated secularist religious views can be.

Political unwillingness to support religious education is not always based in vigorous anti-religious views. Certainly, those are evident in parts of the world. France has a history of secularist rationalism, preached by Voltaire (1694–1778) and other Enlightenment thinkers, which always makes the public discussion of religion a prickly subject. The United States has an interesting dynamic of opposition between the strongly religious and those who are vigorous champions of secularist religion. In many places, however, such as most of Canada, these complex and intense conversations are barely visible – yet religious education tends to be unpopular.

That is because there are other reasons to oppose public education in religion. Religious education can all too easily end up dominated by one particular religious viewpoint that then drives out or demonizes all other beliefs. In the Canadian province of Ontario, religious education was removed from the public system largely because of the efforts of a Methodist Christian layman, Egerton Ryerson. Ryerson was the first provincial Chief Superintendent of Education and a firm believer in secularization, in the mid-nineteenth century. This combination of being an active Methodist (former editor of a church magazine) and prophet of secular education may seem odd to us, but Ryerson's views were driven primarily by his opposition to The Church of England and its dominant role in the province's politics, economics, and educational system. Both the Church of England's traditional hold on the levers of power, and the somewhat high-handed manner of Upper Canada's leading Anglican Churchman, John Strachan, caused Ryerson to become ever more radical in his views. He came to the conclusion that Upper Canada's educational system needed to become officially non-religious in order to eliminate the animosity that arose among Anglicans, Presbyterians, and Methodists. The problem was not that Ryerson was anti-religious, but that (what seemed to him to be) domination by Anglicanism so irritated him and others that he could see no way to design a fair curriculum and simply opted to oppose religion in public education entirely. He, of course, could hardly foresee the contemporary situation in which his choice to leave religious education to families and churches would contribute to widespread ignorance about religion. That is, however, what has happened.

Of course, formulation of curriculum is not the only place that injustice can appear. Teachers can also be unfair, whether intentionally or inadvertently. This is always a possibility in any discipline. Academic debates are built upon the assumption that other people do not correctly understand a matter of real importance. That is why people set out to encourage others to think and teach differently. I am convinced that my high school history teacher completely failed to recognize the importance of political philosophy. This caused debate, some of which could be rather intense because neither of us was particularly willing to be seen as losing the battle. Then again, one of my first-year university professors was a Sudanese Marxist; though he certainly did not regard political philosophy as unimportant, I firmly believe that he seriously overestimated what governments can accomplish. On the whole, these sorts of debates are not a problem. Disagreements happen, which means that they will happen in the classroom.

Disagreements about how to teach religions, or any topic, become a challenge when there is a sense that underlying them is a real lack of respect. That is one of the reasons that critical openness is so important. Critical openness begins from an assumption of respectful and caring interest rather than swift rejection. This approach gives room for genuine understanding, which is the starting point for serious engagement. Criticizing something that we do not understand is mere foolishness. The larger challenge, though, is that disrespect is what happens when we do not teach people. In other words, the most fundamental condition for creating the respect that will make rational conversation possible is not for religions to change – as necessary as that is in some notable cases – but for education to begin. Educational systems need to take the risk of starting the conversation, even if this happens in a charged environment, because the public square will deteriorate further if ignorance increases.

My own personal stake in this comes in the form of dismay and exhaustion over the contemporary Western reaction to Islam; I am tired of listening to people getting all pumped-up about how destructive of human rights Islam (in every form) is, and about how it is taking over the world. This sort of demonization merely polarizes debate instead of fostering understanding and respect or even appropriate disagreement and criticism. As far as I can tell, most of the people who are panicking, including those who post on news websites, simply have no idea what Islam is all about. Since reporters have received no education about Islam and related issues, the media cannot be much help. Instead, they become clearinghouses for collective insanity.

How then are we to undertake public religious education in a manner that will not create unnecessary tensions and will be as fair as possible to all concerned? The first priority must be communicating basic information about religions. On the face of it, this sounds like a mammoth task, given contemporary ignorance and strong feelings. A good visit to a public library should erase that impression. I am routinely astounded at the fine quality of books of all kinds that are available for young people today. Religion is no exception. There are numerous excellent resources for the study of religions. These can serve as basic sources for children, especially if such books are stocked in school libraries. Solid research can be undertaken so that social studies classes can include investigations of religious priorities, principles, and practices. Plus, numerous curricula exist to help classes discuss religious issues.

The most powerful encounters with other religions often occur when we come face-to-face with people with different viewpoints. This is especially true when those people are our friends and colleagues. Consequently, the strategy of inviting students to make classroom presentations about aspects of their own religions can be tremendously helpful. Most children are naturally curious. Often, their priority is to find out about things that are different rather than to destroy them. Giving Sikh children the opportunity to explain their head-coverings is much more helpful than simply ignoring the difference or pretending that it is insignificant. Children want to know why Jewish people celebrate Sabbath from Friday sundown through Saturday, and they find special meals interesting, so having a class member make a presentation about such rituals and why they are observed can be the beginning of deeper understanding.

If children in a school are given these opportunities, then we need not fear controversy in the classroom. Misbehaviour around these issues can be handled in much the same fashion as any other sort of inappropriate activity in school. Plus, students are given a chance to explain themselves and earn marks at the same time. Groundwork is laid for deeper mutual understanding. In short, everyone wins.

The work of having children share their heritages is good work and the basis for deeper reflection. This, however, is the easy part and one which goes on, to a greater or lesser degree, in many schools already. It is commonly treated as "culture," by which we tend to mean one of two things. The first is that culture is treated as something that is bound by walls. ("That is how they do things. This is how we do things. They're different from us and that is the way it is.") This is what some people regard as conservatism. The alternative approach is to think of cultures as interchangeable and, while occasionally beautiful, essentially meaningless. ("That is the way that they do things. Isn't that charming?") This is what some people understand as liberalism.

Neither approach is particularly accurate. The walls do not really exist, though we sometimes try to create them, and differences are not simply matters of indifference. Moreover, neither way of thinking helps us all that much. That is because we are interested in doing the hard work of developing real understanding. We need to be prepared to admit the existence of differences and similarities, and the possibility that they may be important. We are trying to reach beyond most standard discussions of religion and its place in life, to recognize that we are all religious and our religions have a history of informing one another. In short, we want to point to the reality of syncretism and to foster healthy syncretism. We want the very best education for our children, not merely to help them succeed financially (a means whereby capitalism defines education), but also to enable them to grow in religion, and to understand themselves and their world in as profound and accurate a way as possible.

Students need to move beyond a basic social studies introduction to a solid encounter with religious education. At the high school level, this means learning something about the history of religions and the degree to which they have influenced each other. History, when I was in high school and undergraduate university, meant political and social history. We talked about rulers, how they came to rule, and how successful they were. We talked about social arrangements, styles of housing, and various kinds of implements, especially when we discussed indigenous peoples. Religion was, at most, peripheral to the conversation. We recognized that the French and Spanish who came to what is now North America were largely Catholic while the British were not, but this was little more than an additional detail in a picture that was largely defined by political, military, and economic considerations.

The situation may have improved somewhat, but I am inclined to doubt it. Religious studies departments in universities appear to be in decline, and courses in the history of religions are not that easy to find. As I write this, my local university campus – a small-to-medium sized campus of one of Canada's largest universities – has neither. The main campus has a handful of professors of religion (perhaps five, depending upon how you count), mixed into the Department of Classical, Near Eastern, and Religious Studies. Courses in religion are not particularly evident elsewhere, either; even the First Nations Studies Programme is largely oriented toward politics and literature. The most religious portion of the university is probably the Department of Asian Studies, which boasts half-a-dozen or so faculty teaching the breadth of Asian religions. By way of contrast, the same university has fifteen faculty teaching mathematics at the smaller campus and sixty-six at the main campus, for a total of eighty-one! Religion evidently cannot compare in importance. When Martha Nussbaum laments the cuts to education in the humanities at universities, she points out that only programmes labeled "core" tend to survive. In her example, philosophy is core, while religious studies is not.[5] Universities simply do not believe that they need to talk about religion. If people are not learning the material at university, then I rather doubt that they're teaching it in elementary and high schools. Teachers simply lack the expertise.

This means that a two-pronged approach is necessary. Religion must become a visible and required part of high-school education because it is a universal and significant part of life. Religious education ought to be regarded as basic, just as mathematics and English are treated as basic. I suspect the majority of people spend more time dealing with religious questions than writing essays, once they graduate. Religion is a part of everyday life. We need to know what it is, what it does, and what it seeks to do. The prejudices of those who want freedom from religion are no more meaningful than the prejudices of those who want freedom from algebra or the modern novel.

Religious education at the secondary level, therefore, must begin with information about religious viewpoints. Students should be given fundamental data, both historical and contemporary, about religions of the world. Such a process needs to start with what might be regarded as basic literacy skills in the field. "What are religions? What are the religions in our world today? How large are they? Where do they come from? How prevalent or significant are they in our parts of the world? What are their major holidays? What are their central activities? What things do they tend to be sensitive about?" These are the sorts of things that everyone needs to know, simply in order to be a well-informed citizen of planet Earth. Consequently, a course structured around this information ought to be required for every student as a graduation expectation.

More-advanced education about religions ought to be an option for those who find the subject fascinating and wish to investigate it more deeply, though still within the realm of high school capabilities. A course of this kind might ask: "What are religions all about? What are the questions that religions attempt to answer?" Without necessarily getting into the complexities of theological and philosophical thought that such questions involve, students can become aware of some of the deeper aspects of religions. Religions come to be seen as having a point. In the process, students will discover the pervasiveness of religions and religious life. The falseness of the assumption about our ability to wall ourselves off from religion will be recognized. This will likely spark an interest on the part of students, who will begin to understand why people choose religion as a field of study. The reasons are not merely antiquarian; religions are not merely quaint remnants of a superstitious past. Instead, they ask and answer important questions about life in the present and future. The world simply cannot function without religions; without them, humans become no more thoughtful than the household pets that we keep.

These basic forms of education provide the grounding for university study in religion, and all students ought to be required to take an introductory course that builds on their secondary school work. At this level, students ought to be engaging in in-depth study of the history and sociology of religions. These are necessary pieces of data that help to construct pictures of religions as they really are. This is the sort of material that everyone really needs to know. Average members of any religion ought to have a richer knowledge of the way in which their religion has come to be, and what it has become. The process of investigating the history and sociology of a religion reveals all sorts of things. Among the most obvious, partly because they make for great publications, are the warts, the black marks on the history of any religion. For our purposes, though, the more important revelation is about syncretism. In these branches of study, syncretism becomes visible as a real force in the world as constructed by religious viewpoints.

With the basic data drawn from high school study and from courses in history and sociology of religions, students can undertake comparative studies in religion. Students have been prepared to recognize aspects of major religions and have an understanding of some basic characteristics of religions. Comparisons become possible and similarities and differences can be identified and understood. Precisely because students have already discovered the reality of syncretism, simplistic categories of religions can be overcome. Students can begin to see the degrees of variation that exist within religions as well as among them. The comparative study of Buddhisms alone is quite a substantial branch of religious investigation because there is not simply one form of Buddhism. Overlaps can be identified so that the apparently solid walls around religions begin to dissolve; the soft boundaries and immense complexities of religions become evident. African Christianity influenced by Islam is different from African Christianity influenced by animism, and both are different from American Christianity influenced by capitalism.

The various sorts of syncretistic developments make comparative religions into a very challenging field. Scholars are forced to engage in the "What is it now?" game that we described earlier, an exercise that can only be engaged in historically. We are forced to work genetically, addressing lines of historical development rather than simple and seemingly evident groupings. The intuitively obvious – such as, "All those who consider themselves to be Christians may be treated as one class, consisting of members of the Christian Church," turns out to be rather less than obvious, even if it is, in important ways, true.

The point of all this is that the study of religion always has to recognize the complexity of religions. Indeed, the discipline of religious studies is the place where that should happen, and ought to be the source of that insight for the whole academy. As students come to understand the syncretistic nature of religions, those students are prepared to become teachers of religion for younger people in elementary and high schools (or equivalents) around the world.

Religious studies cannot stop at this point, however. The purpose of the discipline cannot simply be to gather data, to know about religion. What would be the use of students of mathematics who can tell us all about the history of mathematics and compare the various branches, but are utterly incapable of doing any math of any kind, whatsoever? Similarly, there is no value to producing scholars of religion who cannot address the questions that religions answer.

Ultimately, university students should engage the more profound questions that bring religions into being. Timidity does not gain anything for people who pursue the study of religion; it certainly has not strengthened the field in the organized academy. We need to be willing to do something more than describe religions by outlining their principles, histories, and prospects. The study of religion must entail a serious encounter with the questions that religions ask and answer – the questions that make religions relevant today rather than merely historical realities or archaic remnants.

What, then, are those more profound questions? They are the awkward ones about the true and the good. We can describe the God or gods of a religion, the Jewish YHWH, the Christian Trinity, the Muslim Allah, the Hindu Brahman, the capitalist dollar, the Marxist History, etc. Similarly, we can more or less clearly define the understanding of human challenges, such as maintaining the covenant in Judaism, living in unity with God in Christianity, professing the oneness of Allah in Islam, honouring the kami in Shinto, accumulating material wealth in capitalism, and being freed from economic oppression in Marxism, etc. Identifying one as superior to the other, however, is a more difficult and dangerous task. This is the sort of risk taken in other disciplines where people will identify superior and inferior playwrights, or more accurate and less accurate theories of climate change. However, scholars in religion tend to shy away from such judgements. The point of syncretism is that we need to learn from one another. If there is evidence in favour of particular ways of seeing the world, then everyone needs to know that. We need to know how these religions can work together; we also need to know how they are fated to collide. We need to know which answers to these questions are more accurate and helpful and which are less accurate and helpful.

Living in a world of soft boundaries and syncretism means that these sorts of judgements can be genuinely useful. Too often, religious traditions are protected by the mindset which emphasizes the integrity of traditions. The poor excuse that goes "But that principle is alien to our tradition" gets regarded as a valid defence against criticism. However, that defence is not borne out by history. There are no pure traditions. Practices and principles have criss-crossed religious boundaries forever.. We all live syncretistic variants of traditions, variations that exist because no religious heritage is able to provide valid answers to every question. Consequently, we can embrace syncretistic critical openness.

The sheer practicality of religious questions means that we all need better answers from one another. We are not just asking about another life beginning after death. Instead, we are talking about the meaning of this one, and about the best ways to act in the here and now. If Tibetan Buddhism can offer more helpful ways of thinking about economics, then capitalist Christianity needs to hear them. Together, we bear the responsibility of being challenged by other religious viewpoints, and of challenging them, in turn. We truly need critical openness on all sides of these conversations.

The fact of syncretism makes comparative judgements difficult but more necessary. They are challenging because most generalizations about religions will fail to account for the complex reality. There are simply too many ways for Jews to understand fidelity to the covenant, or Christians to think about oneness with God, for easy typecasting and simple statements about rightness or wrongness, goodness or badness. Furthermore, the deepest challenge in any such conversation is finding grounds upon which to make any such judgements. The difficulty of these tasks, however, does not free us from the necessity of undertaking them. We have decisions to make, decisions that affect our lives and the life of the world, every day. Those choices will be made upon religious bases, whether intentionally or not. People carry with them an overarching account of life, even if it is not deeply thought through. We all have some sort of justification for our choices; we need to live on the basis of the best available answers, making the best possible decisions.

Unfortunately, controversy in religious studies is rarely about the deep, complex questions. Instead, it tends to arise from the wilder forms of historical speculation – for example, that Jesus had a mistress, and suchlike headline-makers that add nothing to the larger discussions – which hide the fact that real issues are being ignored. This is all fun, I am sure, but the world needs to move beyond it. Justice demands that scholars, elementary and secondary school teachers, and journalists (who accomplish most of the popularizing, after all) do better.

At first glance, movements of thought and action that have not usually been regarded as religious may not appear to have the same questions as those we immediately recognize as "religions" and, therefore, may not be analyzed in the same way. After all, the idea of transcendence which gives meaning to the asking and defines the answers to these questions in Judaism, Christianity, and Islam (the three traditional religions by which all others are commonly measured), is absent from some religions and is present only in attenuated form in others. However, religions other than those three tend to promise variants on what the three offer. Given our knowledge about syncretism, we should not be surprised to find parallels and commonalities between what is generally termed "religion" and what is not. The difference is not as significant as we think – or as secular thinkers hope and pretend. The god of capitalism is no less a god simply because we do not usually name it as such. People still worship it and measure their world and their lives by its standards.

This brings us back to the question that we tackled earlier, in the chapter entitled "What is Religion?" What makes a religion into a religion if the decisive issue is not belief in a God or gods, on the Abrahamic model or some other traditional model? From the perspective of theory (rather than structure, for example), a worldview becomes a religion when it offers a vision of the whole, an overarching explanation of reality, and an understanding of the place and purpose of humanity in relation to the larger order (or disorder, for those whose theories tend toward the chaotic). This overall explanation of the meaning of being must include an account of human predicaments, both identifying those which are significant and clarifying the means by which they may be resolved. Religions call for substantial responses from practitioners, including solid faith commitment and willingness to let their values be formed by the religion. When a theory reaches into these realms, no matter whether it started out as astrophysics or zoology or anything in between, it is addressing religious questions. If a theory reaches a point at which it fulfils all of these requirements, then it becomes a full-fledged religious account of being (what theists call a theology). Marxism has accomplished this, so has capitalism, and so has evolution. Marxism is explicitly atheistic (denying the identity of even its own god), while the others tend toward atheism but need not reach that point, especially as they commonly exist in syncretisms with theistic religious viewpoints. Evolutionary theory is especially notable for its explanatory reach, it is the "go-to" explanation for every sort of happening or action in our world. Indeed, our discussion of syncretism is based on evolutionary assumptions, as you have probably noticed.

We are on religious ground whenever we address questions about these issues. In the largest of senses, this means that every question has a religious aspect. All questions are related to religion, which is why the discovery that everything in the universe evolves has transformed all aspects of Christianity. Every part of Christian thinking, from accounts of how creation happened/happens, to understandings of how doctrine comes to be, has been rethought in light of the fact of evolution. Scientific and historical investigations have religious implications. By the same token, religious insights affect all aspects of life because an overarching account of life touches on every issue. Thus, religious thinkers are involved with reflecting on the appropriateness of a variety of medical procedures and the research practices that lead to them; that is one of the reasons that many hospitals have ethics committees to discuss these matters. This is merely one more reminder that the effort to banish religion and morality from public discussion is simply foolish. All public decisions are made on religious and moral grounds, and the argument that religion is not an acceptable basis for public discussion is, itself, based upon religious assumptions.

The interlocked character of all knowledge is one of the greatest challenges faced by Western approaches to learning. We split up every topic to be discussed and investigate it in pieces owned by various specialized disciplines. There is always a danger that the bits will never be joined again. Even worse, someone may employ an aspect of the knowledge in a new technology before other disciplines have assessed its implications. That is how DDT came to be used as a pesticide for controlling malaria; it is highly effective in this application, but its implications for the larger ecology were not sufficiently understood before it entered widespread use.

There is a benefit to the division of specialties developed in Western society and sustained in our educational institutions; this is the most efficient way that we have discovered to maintain growth in knowledge. There are limits to the amount of information that one person can uncover and carry; these limits, combined with personal talents and preferences, especially in relation to methods of inquiry, can be transcended by the whole community if we work together. In short, we can learn more and do so more quickly if we break up topics and consider them in various ways in the context of different disciplines.

The task of studies in religion is to consider all worldviews that address religious questions and to try to answer them insofar as these questions are at issue. In other words, a student of religion need not understand all of the complexities of economics (which is the task of economists – I cannot comment on their degree of success) in order to address capitalism as a religion. The subtleties of supply-and-demand curves are beyond the realm of the religion scholar. The use of supply-and-demand curves as a way of establishing the world's priorities, however, is a religious issue. These are what define a hockey player as being worthy of earning millions of dollars every year while many farmers (especially in nations that cannot afford heavy agricultural subsidies) earn relatively little. The religion scholar can point out that defining value by a supply-and-demand curve makes capitalism religiously decisive, even when the official religion is supposed to be Christianity or Islam or Buddhism or Shinto. Fundamental values emerge. Syncretism becomes evident rather than being disguised.

In short, scholars need to take religion seriously, do the hard work, and face the tough questions. Scholars need to address issues of fact and value, and the many ways that religions strive to respond. Scholarly work must be shared with university students, who must be prepared to bring it to primary, elementary, and high school classrooms. Parents cannot do it all, especially if they do not have an education that recognizes the fact and value of syncretism. Religious education is necessary if we are to understand that we do not exist in walled cities defined by the names on the signs outside. The potential for conflict in the classroom should not drive us to ignorance, especially because ignorance causes conflict. We need to know about the complex world in which we live. We need the information that will make possible the basic decisions of our lives. Religious education is a necessity, not merely an option.

10

An Intellectual Transformation

This book is built around three insights: (1) religion is everywhere; (2) everyone's religion is a syncretism; and (3) on the whole, though not inevitably, that is a good thing. I have discovered that these insights, once fully digested, are inescapable. They have transformed the way that I think, the way that I solve problems, and the way that I approach the world. Syncretism really is ubiquitous. It is at the heart of the way that I think about politics, economics, and even literature. Syncretism is that important because questions that seem small are often about major principles. Our attitudes to seemingly minor things reflect and form our overarching theories about the world. Our religious outlooks are made visible in all of our decisions, small or large, carefully analyzed or nearly thoughtless.

Central to this outlook is the recognition that we are not all the same. The common bromide which states that all religions are the same is wrong in significantly unhelpful ways. If every time that we look at the other we see only ourselves, then we will miss out on some of the great insights of human history. Plus, we will inevitably misunderstand and perhaps even destroy the other. Canada faces this challenge in relation to First Nations people. Routinely, we propose that, since all they really want (or ought to want) is to be like modern white people, they should simply start acting like white people and use their land and resources for real profit. The idea that First Nations people might genuinely be different, and have a different religious relationship to the land and the world as a whole, seems impossible for many people to grasp.

Indeed, if syncretism is necessary to religious development and we are all fundamentally religious, then difference attains a basic and decisive value for human life. Jacques Derrida said as much in an essay that he entitled "Différance," a spelling that gives my computer fits because Derrida intentionally produced a word with an erroneous spelling. It looks like French, but the correct French would be "différence." The purpose of the misspelling is to emphasize the two arguments that he makes in the essay: (1) difference is central to the way that the world is and efforts to suppress or eliminate differences will create both misunderstanding and destruction, and (2) leaping to conclusions is a terrible mistake, but one to which the contemporary world is particularly susceptible, and so, an intentional spelling error forces us to slow down and defer the moment of closure that occurs when we are certain that we understand. A différance, then, is both a difference and a deferral; it causes us to recognize otherness and to give both time and effort to the process involved in understanding the other.[1] Derrida pushes his point further than I would go, making the theological argument that différance is at the root of everything, apparently including existence;[2] the latter has puzzled theologians and started more than one argument. Derrida's position would seem to defer the moment of closure forever, which, as we have seen, is impossible and undesirable.

Derrida's basic advice, however, is both important and helpful. Too often, we try to make everyone look exactly like ourselves. Though certainly not alone in the world, Christians are legendary for doing this, even using missionary activity to impose our own denominational distinctions on bewildered peoples worldwide, who had neither need nor use for all of the differences between Lutheran and Catholic, or whatever. Even as we struggle to overcome these demands for hard boundaries and carbon copies of ourselves, we still fall into the trap. The most popular contemporary Christian model for human community, designed explicitly to strengthen equality among all people, fails to escape the problem. This model argues that human community (not just Christian community, so this model applies to the church and the whole world) ought to look like the Trinity – God as Christians understand God. Too little consideration has been given to the basic assumption of theology about the Christian God, which is that the Three Persons never disagree, willing all things in common.

A dangerous, surely unintentional, side-effect of this idea is to rein-force the permanent institutional bias toward requiring everyone to agree before unity is possible. This is not a good model for a world in which multiple viewpoints are important contributors to finding the true and the good. It does not encourage healthy syncretism.

Indeed, in our syncretistic world, one of the things that we most need is a model for human community that fosters the sharing of insights and sees the principle of progress at work in the syncretistic process. The principle of preservation of insights too easily turns into a "my way" attitude which, at its worst, turns into outright suppres-sion (even violent oppression) of ways of life that do not deserve to be destroyed. The electronic world may be enabling the emergence of just such a human community. The speed and extent of inter-religious sharing and debate is unprecedented. Moreover, it occurs at all levels of society in a way never before seen. Syncretism is possible, and, as a matter of fact, happens without formal discussion amongst trained theologians or identified leaders in an extraordinary number of ways and on a daily basis. Online, we can easily encounter people of all reli-gious persuasions at any time of the day or night and can learn from them, even comparing their views to others who lay claim to the same label, without leaving our chairs.

This is not to say that all is wine and roses; after all, some religions refuse wine and every rosebush has more thorns than blossoms. Der-rida's celebration of difference is extended by his call to defer judge-ment. Judgement cannot be deferred forever. Conclusions must be reached and decisions made, and they will be. Even if I pretend not to have religious views, I will make choices based upon some kind of religious position, though I may obscure it from myself. Humans cannot live between positions, with no real landing place. Indeed, any in-between position is its own landing place. If you doubt it, treat the common phrase "sitting on the fence" as literal, and perch on the closest one that you can find. You may be between two fields, but your lower parts will remind you very decisively that you are still somewhere. "The fence" is also a place in the metaphorical sense, not only the literal. As the rock music group, Rush, says, "If you choose not to decide, you still have made a choice."[3] We cannot live without making intellectual commitments, without affirming some truths.

However, a rush to judgement is no more helpful than an unconscionable delay. The great challenge of the wired world is precisely that it encourages us to rush. The 24/7 news cycle and constant connection push us to think at high speed. We send e-mails instantly and expect nearly instant replies; not for us is the approach of sending a query across the ocean by sailing ship, anticipating an answer nine months or a year later. This presses us to assume that answers to big questions, as well as small, can be generated without lapse of time. Plus, we know that our competitors are trying to move faster than we are; that niggling fear that "the other guy" will get ahead of us if we do not move instantly haunts our every thought and action. Our world is always in a hurry.

Worse yet, we are too prone to assume that we understand what the other is saying, especially when we are sure that we disagree, or, even more problematic, when we anticipate disagreeing and are unwilling to give real effort to understanding. I can speak about this with real feeling, because one of my besetting sins is swift judgement. This characteristic can help in those moments when time is of the essence and speed is necessary, but it means that I always stand in danger of giving too little attention to the wisdom of others when judgement can be deferred. I know that the other person is wrong; why should I give the presentation more attention? Instead, the inclination is to sail in with all guns blazing, using my most powerful arguments to overcome what I think is being said. Of course, the speed and competitiveness of our world tends to exacerbate this inclination, also. Paying real attention to the other, based in a true desire to understand, has always been challenging; the need to win, and win quickly, increases the challenge.

Derrida's emphasis upon difference must also be balanced by a sense of commonality. The possibility of syncretistic critical openness hinges upon the existence of both common questions and common answers. This is true within any religious identity sustained by an agreed-upon label; Buddhists, in spite of all the differences among them, share a tradition which defines both questions and answers. When one ceases to find either the questions or answers helpful, one is likely to seek a religious identity that bears another label, even if that label is only "non-believer." Commonality also extends to all humanity. The value of syncretism is precisely that Gandhi, officially

a Hindu, may have a question about the meaning of human self-sac-
rifice and may find the answer in Christianity, in Jesus' acceptance of
death on the cross. Similarly, a Christian may face challenges in finding unity in herself and may discover the answer in Taoism and the
practices of t'ai chi. Difference is a central, too easily overlooked, reality of human life, but it is only half of the story, which is one of the
reasons why I balk at Derrida's assertion that différance is at the root
of life. At the heart of human existence we find both difference and
commonality.

Both the importance of judgement and the balance between difference and commonality serve as reminders of the need for religious
education, as was discussed in the previous chapter. We need to cultivate the possibility of true understanding and to develop enough of a
knowledge base about religions to hear what is being said rather than
respond to what a limited background prepares us to expect will
be said. One of today's major scholarly discussions is the problem
of hermeneutics. "Hermeneutics" is academic jargon for "theories of
interpretation." A syncretistic world requires of us two kinds of hermeneutics: a hermeneutic of trust and a hermeneutic of suspicion. A
hermeneutic of trust allows me to place myself in the hands of the
other, ready to learn from and with the other. This establishes the
availability and readiness to learn that syncretistic critical openness
demands. A hermeneutic of suspicion requires that I ask hard questions and not take statements at face value, whether the statements are
made by me or by another. The "critical" aspect of critical openness
makes me a question to myself, just as much as it makes others into
questions for me.

Approaching the world in a spirit of critical openness, attempting
to maintain both a hermeneutic of trust and a hermeneutic of suspicion, reveals to me the constant presence of syncretism. I genuinely do
find it everywhere. I have begun to realize that it is even a helpful
insight for understanding literature and music. The notion of syncretism resolves for me the question of the relationship between the
Roman heritage and medieval Christianity in Dante Alighieri's *Divine
Comedy*, explaining the presence of the Emperor Trajan in Paradise,
where a non-Christian is ineligible to appear, by the rules that Dante
himself creates. Similarly, syncretism helps to explain the dark and
foreboding mood of J.R.R. Tolkien's *The Lord of the Rings*, which

incorporates the bleak fatalism of Norse religion with the more optimistic Catholicism that came out of the Mediterranean world. Listen to David Fanshawe's "African Sanctus," a magnificent example of asymmetrical syncretism in which a Christian mass setting has material from various African traditions woven into it. Syncretism is everywhere.

Once we begin to recognize the fact and importance of syncretism, we are in possession of a tremendously powerful tool for understanding the world. It works in the realms of art and literature. It also helps us to understand the contemporary issues of world conflict. The Balkan states have been a flash-point for the last one hundred years. The First World War began there, with the assassination of Archduke Franz Ferdinand of Austria by a Serbian. Important parts of World War II occurred in that region. Some of the differences went underground in the post-war period under Josip Broz Tito's Communist government, but, by 1990, war was the reality in the Balkans again. This time, NATO decided to intervene. The difficulty in finding peace, order, and justice in the Balkans is that complicated syncretisms are at work. Nationalism and imperialism have been mixed with Nazism and Communism in odd combinations with Catholic and Orthodox Christianity, and with Islam.

The most obvious evidence that syncretism is at work appears just where we might expect it, in the question of highest priorities and ruling values. After all, what is one to make of the news that Catholic churches in Zagreb and Split held memorial services for Ante Pavelic, the brutal World-War-II-era Croatian Nazi leader, in December of 2011?[4] The Serbian Orthodox nationalism that sparked the shooting of Franz Ferdinand also played a role in the "ethnic cleansing" of Bosnia; ranking clerics in the Serbian Orthodox Church showed great respect for such war criminals as Radovan Karadzic.[5] Muslim Bosnians, themselves at least partly a legacy of Ottoman imperialism, have appropriated the name "Bosniak," previously used for all inhabitants of the region, to create a new identity for themselves that links Islam with ethnicity, and, in the process, caused fears of extinction among peoples of other identities in Bosnia.[6]

These complicated viewpoints are evidently religious; our difficulty in understanding them comes partly from our assumption that they are a mixture of a politics (nationalism, imperialism, Nazism, Commu-

nism) with religion (Catholicism, Orthodoxy, Islam), in which a fairly
neat line can be drawn between politics and religion. In fact, the participants, the Balkan people, do not see the distinction that we assume
because it is not really there. In real life, each is a syncretistic religion
with highest values established by more than one of the included elements. A Catholic mass, conducted by Croatian nationalists, commem-
orating a Croatian Nazi, is a symbolic activity with its own religious
identity, an unhealthy syncretism. It is a ritual that is simply unimaginable in the context of St Ignatius Church, the Catholic parish next door
to Boston College where I occasionally worshipped when I was a student. The common label, "Catholic," certainly identifies a similarity –
undoubtedly, the mass in Croatia will share decisive symbols with the
one in Boston, including the elements of bread and wine – but tends to
obscure the profound difference in religious identity.

The key to employing the syncretism tool, therefore, is in the recognition that religion is not as simple and narrowly focused as Western
liberalism would have us believe. We all have some sort of religion
which will differ from the religions of others who bear the same label,
and everyone's religion is astoundingly complex. Ultimately, that complexity is a good thing because the world is astoundingly complex. One
religion is not enough. The world would not be improved either by
eliminating all religions – the contexts of discussion for many important questions – or by reducing the diversity of religions. Unanswered
questions would accumulate swiftly. We would have neither the equipment for solving them nor a context in which to discuss them. We need
our religions, and the existence of destructive syncretisms does not
eliminate the need for healthy and beneficial ones.

Consequently, the notion of syncretism is not merely a tool for
interpreting the world. Instead, it is a call to action. I have adopted an
"advocacy" view of syncretism because it is a call to change the world.
I am asking us to recognize the complex syncretisms that we compose, in addition to those that others create and follow. This way of
thinking about the world means that the "other" is less other and
more of a conversation partner. We can begin to think in terms of
what others have to offer us and what we have to offer them. This
removes some of the win/lose-us/them dynamic from religious conversation. The recognition that incorporating wisdom from other
sources simply offers the possibility of improving an existing syn-

cretism rather than compromising religious purity, and allows dialogue to become mutually beneficial. The fear factor dissipates.

We can see this in places like Claremont Lincoln University (CLU), which has come into existence in response to the syncretism insight, the need for religions to learn from other religions. It was founded as an amalgam of three schools: Claremont School of Theology, which is Christian; The Academy for Jewish Religion, California; and Bayan Claremont, an Islamic graduate school. In addition, CLU is developing collaborative enterprises with Hindu, Jain, and Buddhist institutions. A traditional religious studies department tends to have an ethos built around academic distance and "objectivity" so that its work is largely focused upon describing various religions. This is not CLU's approach. Instead, CLU explicitly brings "partners together in conversation, collaboration, and the shared mission to teach, learn, and serve."[7] The school's purpose is to recognize similarities where they exist, as in the commitment to the Golden Rule ("Treat other people as you would have them treat you"), and to discuss differences in ways that are mutually enlightening. The intention is that these conversations will be educational for all involved, and will give rise to helpful work in areas such as "domestic social policy, international development, conflict resolution, global peace building, ecology, sustainability, law, medicine; all areas where multi-religious perspectives can improve life of many kinds."[8] Claremont Lincoln will suit the inclinations of some, while its theology and politics will be unacceptable to others. My purpose is not to advertise for the school (with which I have no association), but to point out that they have the right idea: the value of syncretism is that it means that we no longer need to pretend that we live in our own little boxes. Now, we can publically and intentionally work together on the needs of our world. The time has come for us to take up the challenge!

Religions differ, partly because they are composed from different constituent elements. This is good because we have questions to bring and answers to offer each other. All human knowing is partial; this is a basic insight common to most religions. Indeed, many people who consider themselves "non-religious" take that position because they are suspicious of anybody who claims to have all the answers. All of us need to recognize our own limitations and be willing to consider other ways of thinking. We need to understand the other more accurately, and, in the process, discover ways in which the other may help us. Our task as religious people is to learn and grow together, to remain open to other viewpoints and be prepared to attend to them flexibly and thoughtfully.

Consequently, the kind of soft boundaries that I find around religions can be strengths. Soft boundaries are a condition of growth and learning. Soft boundaries allow us to modify our existing understanding of the world as we encounter new information, new questions, and new possibilities. Absolutely closed minds are frozen in time and place; they can answer only those questions which fit strictly within the existing theological and religious structure. But such closed minds do not really exist. There are only approximations, people striving to convince themselves that their views are utterly timeless and without change. These people also develop and create syncretisms, but their self-deception drives efforts to construct hard boundaries.

Soft boundaries allow for the possibility of mutual commitment to a common project of knowing and doing. They link us in complicated, often surprising, ways. Being aware of those attachments changes our values. The priority ceases to be "ours" and "yours" or "us" and "them." Instead, we can think in terms of "true" and "false," "better" and "worse." Moreover, we can do this without trying to sustain the Western Enlightenment assumption that somehow we are without viewpoints, religious or otherwise. We can bring our own beliefs to the conversation, recognizing that our positions have originated in interreligious discussion and will develop in that sort of dialogue.

This changes the identity of the people who are on my "team." No longer are they only those who share the religious label in which I rejoice who may, indeed, be more distant from me spiritually and intellectually than others who wear a radically different label. My team expands to include everyone who genuinely wants to attend to the data, understand correctly, judge well, and act appropriately. I can participate in the human conversation rather than hiding in my own colony. Working together, we can be more creative and less destructive, as we have proven in the past. That, ultimately, is why I think that syncretism is a solution and that the universal mixing of religions is a good thing.

Notes

CHAPTER ONE

1 Marguerite Del Giudice, "Ancient Soul of Iran: The Glories of Persia Inspire the Modern Nation," *National Geographic,* August, 2008, 63.

2 I follow the contemporary academic standard for dating, which replaces BC ("Before Christ") with BCE ("Before Common Era") and AD ("Anno Domini" – "The Year of Our Lord") with CE ("Common Era"). I am somewhat uncomfortable with this system, which follows Christian dating but tries to disguise it by changing the name. Truly, there is nothing common about it. If there is such a thing as a common era, it probably began about five hundred years earlier, or perhaps two thousand years earlier. That said, I recognize that the traditional language is not viable because it requires non-Christians to express allegiances which are not theirs (The Year of "Our" Lord). Thinking of CE as "Christian Era" seems to be more honest and helpful.

3 Mary Boyce, *Zoroastrianism: Its Antiquity And Constant Vigour*, Columbia Lectures on Iranian Studies, no. 7 (Costa Mesa, CA: Mazda Publishers, 1992), 104–6. See also Alessandro Bausani, *Religion in Iran, From Zoroaster to Baha'ullah*, trans. J.M. Marchesi (New York: Bibliotheca Persica Press, 2000), 61.

4 Boyce, 180.

5 Paul Kriwaczek, *In Search of Zarathustra* (London: Weidenfield and Nicolson, 2002).

6 Rashna Writer, *Contemporary Zoroastrians: An Unstructured Nation* (Lanham, MD: University Press of America, 1994), 4.

7 Nader Ahmadi, "Individuality and Politics," *Iranian Islam: The Concept of the Individual* (London: Macmillan, 1998), 124–79.

8 Kathryn Babayan, *Mystics, Monarchs, and Messiahs: Cultural Landscapes of Early Modern Iran* (Cambridge, MA: Center for Middle Eastern Studies of Harvard University/Harvard University Press, 2002), 483–96. Comments on the survival of ancient Zoroastrian/Persian practice in contemporary times appear in the epilogue.

9 John Breen and Mark Teeuwen, *A New History of Shinto* (Chichester: Wiley-Blackwell, 2010), 1.

10 Stephen Turnbull, *The Samurai and the Sacred* (Oxford: Osprey, 2009), 7–10, 52–60. Buddhism already had a significant history of being connected to war. See Michael Jerryson and Mark Juergensmeyer, eds., *Buddhist Warfare* (New York: Oxford University Press, 2010).

11 Mark Teeuwen and Fabio Rambelli, "Combinatory Religion and the *Honji Suijaku* Paradigm in Pre-modern Japan," *Buddhas and Kami in Japan:* Honji Suijaku *as a Combinatory Paradigm*, ed. Mark Teeuwen and Fabio Rambelli (London and New York: Routledge and Curzon, 2003), 1. The complexities of this development and the varying status of kami are discussed in Breen and Teeuwen, esp. 87–90.

12 Turnbull, 30–2.

13 Teeuwen and Rambelli, 21–3. Turnbull, 173. See also Joseph M. Kitagawa, *On Understanding Japanese Religion* (Princeton: Princeton University, 1987), 156–66.

14 Turnbull, 52. Italics in original. Turnbull quotes Thomas D. Conlan, *State of War: The Violent Order of Fourteenth-Century Japan* (Ann Arbor, MI: Centre for Japanese Studies/University of Michigan, 2003), 173.

15 Kitagawa, 164.

16 Turnbull, 174–6.

17 "All My Relations," http://www.vst.edu/main/native-ministries/nmc/all-my-relations.

18 André Droogers, "Syncretism: The Problem of Definition, the Definition of the Problem," *Dialogue and Syncretism: An Interdisciplinary Approach*, ed. Jerald D. Gort et al (Grand Rapids: Eerdmans, 1989), 7–25.

19 This account of Celtic religious observance is drawn from Barry Cunliffe, *The Celtic World* (London: Constable and Co., 1992), 88–91.

20 "Mixing Sexes in Saudi Arabia: Not So Terrible after All?," *The Economist*, 9 January 2010, 48.

21 "Polygamy in South Africa: A President Who Promotes Tradition," *The Economist*, 9 January 2010, 49.

22 "Gus Dur: Abdurrahman Wahid (Gus Dur), Intellectual and President of Indonesia, Died on December 30th, Aged 69," *The Economist*, 9 January 2010, 85.

23 Ibid.

24 Church of England, "The Form of Solemnization of Matrimony," *The Book of Common Prayer, 1662*. http://www.churchofengland.org/prayer-worship/worship/book-of-common-prayer.aspx.

25 Meyer Fortes, "Some Reflections on Ancestor Worship in Africa," *African Systems of Thought: Studies Presented and Discussed at the Third International African Seminar in Salisbury, December 1960*, ed. M. Fortes and G. Dieterlen (London and New York: Oxford University Press, 1965, 122–42. http://www.afrikaworld.net/afrel/fortes2.html.

26 "Solution," *Webster's Third New International Dictionary* (Springfield, MA: Merriam-Webster, 2002).

27 Hendrik Kraemer, *The Christian Message in a Non-Christian World* (New York/London: Harper and Brothers, 1938), 142.

28 Ibid., 156.

29 Ibid., 210.

30 Ibid., 152.

31 Ibid., 102.

32 Ibid., 113–14.

33 Ibid., 77.

34 Ibid., 115.

35 Ibid., 114–16.

36 James M. Gray, "The Inspiration of the Word of God: Definition, Extent and Proof," *The Fundamentals*, vol. 2, ed. R.A. Torrey, A.C. Dixon, et al (Rio, WI: Ages Software, 2000), 8. http://www.ntslibrary.com/PDF%20Books%20II/Torrey%20-%20The%20Fundamentals%202.pdf.

37 Ibid., 9.

38 F. Bettex, "The Bible and Modern Criticism," *The Fundamentals*, vol. 1, 67. http://www.ntslibrary.com/PDF%20Books%20II/Torrey%20-%20The%20Fundamentals%201.pdf..

39 Ibid., 64.

40 David James Burrell, "The Knowledge of God," *The Fundamentals*, vol. 4, 26. http://www.ntslibrary.com/PDF%20Books%20II/Torrey%20-%20The%20Fundamentals%204.pdf.

41 Ibid., 25–6.

42 Natana J. DeLong-Bas, *Wahhabi Islam: From Revival and Reform to Global Jihad* (Oxford: Oxford University Press, 2004), 56–91.

43 Ibid., 56.

44 Ibid., 57.

45 Ibid.

46 Ibid., 63. The included quotation is from Ibn Abd al-Wahhab, "Kitab al-Tawhid," 43.

47 David Commins, *The Wahhabi Mission and Saudi Arabia* (London: I.B. Tauris, 2006), 16.

48 Ibid., 14.

49 Ibid., 105.

50 Ibid., 108.

51 Ibid., 110.

52 Ibid., 108–9.

53 Ibid., 155–204.

54 This discussion is based upon the following accounts: Douglas Todd, "UBC Stands by Sikh Professor's Right to Publish," *Vancouver Sun*, 20 June 1994, B2; Douglas Todd, "Local Sikhs Seeking Removal of 'Heretical' UBC Professor," *Vancouver Sun* 16 June 1994, B1; Darsha Singh Tatla, *Diaspora: The Search for Statehood* (London: Taylor and Francis, 2005), 65; Cynthia Keppley Mahmood, "Sikhs in Canada: Identity and Commitment," *Religion and Ethnicity in Canada*, ed. Paul Bramadat and David Seljak (Toronto: University of Toronto Press, 2009), 60.

55 Mahmood's article is especially helpful on this issue. See esp. 56–61.

56 I.J. Singh and Hakam Singh, "Chairs in Sikh Studies in America: Problems and Solutions," *Sikh Review*, May 1996, http://www.sikhreview.org/pdf/may 1996/pdf-files/perspective.pdf.

57 Stanley Hauerwas and William Willimon, *Resident Aliens: Life in the Christian Colony* (Nashville, TN: Abingdon Press, 1989). Stanley Hauerwas and William Willimon have argued that Christians should form a Christian colony visibly different from the world around it. They do not explain how this can be done in a way that is not entirely and profoundly dependent upon the rest of the world. For example, they recommend that Christians support other Christians in hospital, but fail to say anything about the extent to which health care possibilities in the US (home of their example) are a product of efforts by Christians and people of many other religious viewpoints. The colony simply cannot be.

CHAPTER TWO

1 Sarah Pulliam Bailey, "Q and A: Billy Graham on Aging, Regrets, and Evangelical," *Christianity Today*, January 24, 2011. http://www.christianitytoday .com/ct/2011/januaryweb-only/qabillygraham.html?start=2.

2 For the standard discussion of Jewish views on the afterlife, see Simcha Paull Raphael, *Jewish Views of the Afterlife*, second edition (Lanham, MD: Rowman and Littlefield, 2009).

3 Raphael, 43–57.

4 Raphael notes that the reasons for the decline in Jewish attention to the afterlife are complex. They include an exclusive reliance on Moses Maimonides' rationalism (20–2) and the cultural shift from pre-modern Europe to modern North America and Europe (15), along with biblical ambivalence (16–18). Raphael's book is partly a response to contemporary Jewish assertions that Judaism has little to say about the afterlife (13).

5 This argument reflects the influence of Paul Tillich, who named "ultimate concern" as the heart of religious meaning. While Tillich finally makes the argument that God, the Unconditional (in Christian understanding), is the only right focus of religious attention, Tillich begins by noting that ultimate concern of any kind is what causes religion. See Paul Tillich, *Theology of Culture*, ed. Robert C. Kimball (Oxford: Oxford University Press, 1959) and Tillich, *What Is Religion?*, ed. and intro. by James Luther Adams (New York: Harper and Row, 1969). The Introduction by Adams is especially helpful.

6 Ernst Feil, "From the Classical *Religio* to the Modern *Religion*: Elements of a Transformation between 1550 and 1650," *Religion in History: The Word, the Idea, the Reality/La religion dans l'histoire: Le mot, l'idée, la réalité*, ed. Michel Despland and Gérard Vallée (Waterloo, ON: Wilfrid Laurier University Press, for Canadian Corporation for Studies in Religion, 1992), 32.

7 Hugh B. Urban, *The Church of Scientology: A History of a New Religion* (Princeton: Princeton University Press, 2011).

8 Noble Ross Reat, *Buddhism: A History* (Berkeley, CA: Asian Humanities Press, 1994), 76.

9 Max Weber, "Politics as a Vocation," *From Max Weber: Essays in Sociology*, ed. H.H. Gerth and C. Wright Mills (New York: Oxford University Press, 1946), 77–128.

10 Augustine, *Confessions*, trans. with intro. and notes Henry Chadwick (Oxford: Oxford University Press, 1998), 3.

242 Notes to pages 45–66

11 Tillich, *Systematic Theology*, vol. 1 (Chicago: University of Chicago Press, 1951), 47–8.
12 O. Henry, "The Gift of the Magi," Project Gutenberg. http://www.auburn.edu/~vestmon/Gift_of_the_Magi.html.
13 Sergio Sismondo and Mathieu Doucet, "Publication Ethics and the Ghost Management of Medical Publication," *Bioethics* (2009), 1–11, http://www.law-lib.utoronto.ca/ghostwriter/Sismondo%20and%20Doucet%20Publication%20Ethics.pdf.
14 Ibid., 3.
15 Ibid., 4.
16 Jody Bart, "Feminist Theories of Knowledge: The Good, the Bad, and the Ugly," *Women Succeeding in the Sciences: Theories and Practices Across Disciplines*, ed. Jody Bart (West Lafayette, IN: Purdue University Press, 2000), 205–20; Amy Bug, "Gender and Physical Science: A Hard Look at a Hard Science," *Theories and Practices*, 221–44; Colleen M. Belk, "Gender Bias in Biological Theory Formation," *Theories and Practices*, 169–75.
17 Thomas Kuhn, *The Structure of Scientific Revolutions*, second edition., enlarged, *International Encyclopedia of Unified Science*, II:2 (Chicago: University of Chicago Press, 1970).
18 Kuhn, 152.
19 Steven Johnson, *The Ghost Map: The Story of London's Most Terrifying Epidemic – and How It Changed Science, Cities, and the Modern World* (New York: Riverhead, 2006).
20 See, for example, Elizabeth Schüssler Fiorenza, *In Memory of Her: A Feminist Theological Account of Christian Origins* (New York: Crossroads, 1983).
21 Maria Hsia Chang, *Falun Gong: The End of Days* (New Haven: Yale University Press, 2004), 96–123.
22 John F. Kennedy, "Transcript: JFK's Speech on His Religion," http://www.npr.org/templates/story/story.php?storyId=16920600.
23 Leonard Swidler and Paul Mojzes, *The Study of Religion in an Age of Global Dialogue* (Philadelphia: Temple University Press, 2000), 7–8.
24 John E. Smith, *Quasi-Religions: Humanism, Marxism and Nationalism* (New York: St. Martin's Press, 1994), 45–81.
25 John Locke, *The Reasonableness of Christianity As delivered in the Scriptures*, ed. John C. Higgins-Biddle (Oxford: Clarendon Press, 1999). See also Steven Forde, "John Locke's Natural Religion." Paper presented at the American Political Science Association, Chicago, 2004. http://www.allacademic

.com//meta/p_mla_apa_research_citation/o/6/1/8/4/pages61841/p61841-
1.php.

26 Francis Fukuyama, *The End of History and the Last Man* (New York: Free
    Press/Macmillan, 1992).

27 Smith, 2–5.

28 Margaret Drabble, *The Witch of Exmoor* (Toronto: McClelland and Stewart,
    1996), 18–19.

29 Jill Vardy and Chris Wattie, "Shopping is Patriotic, Leaders Say," *National
    Post*, September 28, 2001. http://www.commondreams.org/headlines01/
    0929-04.htm.

30 Rudolph Giuliani, "America's New War: Giuliani on Local Radio Show,"
    aired September 21, 2001. http://transcripts.cnn.com/TRANSCRIPTS
    /0109/21/se.20.html.

CHAPTER THREE

1 Harjot Oberoi, *The Construction of Religious Boundaries: Culture, Identity,
   and Diversity in the Sikh Tradition* (Oxford: Oxford University Press, 1994),
   1.

2 John Locke, "A Letter Concerning Toleration," *A Letter Concerning Toleration
   in Focus*, ed. John Horton and Susan Mendus (London/New York: Routledge, 1991), 22. The edition I use is by William Popple, published in
   Oxford in 1690.

3 Oberoi, 4–8.

4 N.K. Das, ed., *Culture, Religion, and Philosophy: Critical Studies in Syncretism
   and Inter-Faith Harmony* (Jaipur: Rawat Publications, 2003).

5 W.H. McLeod, *Guru Nanak and the Sikh Religion* (Oxford: Oxford University
   Press, 1968), 151–7.

6 McLeod, 150–1.

7 For the seminal discussion of the development of the *Adi Granth*, see
   Pashaura Singh, *The Guru Granth Sahib: Canon, Meaning and Authority* (New
   Delhi: Oxford University Press, 2000). Singh investigates the complicated
   development of the text, including sixteenth-century and later efforts to
   remove selections that have been found to be insufficiently Sikh, and the
   variants of the text that existed until a standard version emerged in the
   twentieth century.

8 Mahmood, 54.

9   Victoria Clark, *Why Angels Fall: A Journey Through Orthodox Europe from Byzantium to Kosovo* (New York: St. Martin's Press, 2000), 172.

10 W.H. McLeod, "Khalsa," *Historical Dictionary of Sikhism* (Oxford: Oxford University, 1995), 121–2.

11 Steven W. Ramey, *Hindu, Sufi, or Sikh: Contested Practices and Identifications of Sindhi Hindus in India and Beyond* (New York: Palgrave Macmillan, 2008), 1.

12 Ibid.

13 Ibid., 2.

14 Ibid., 76–81.

15 Ibid., 80.

16 Robert Gordis, *The Dynamics of Judaism: A Study in Jewish Law* (Bloomington and Indianapolis, Indiana: Indiana University Press, 1990), 4.

17 Steven M. Wasserstrom, *Between Muslim and Jew: The Problem of Symbiosis Under Early Islam* (Princeton: Princeton University Press, 1995).

18 Wasserstrom, 71–89.

19 A.J. Jacobs, *The Year of Living Biblically* (New York: Simon and Schuster, 2007).

20 Mordechai Breuer, *Modernity Within Tradition: The Social History of Orthodox Jewry in Imperial Germany*, trans. Elizabeth Petuchowski (New York: Columbia University Press, 1992), viii.

21 David Golovensky, "The Judaism of Tomorrow: The Orthodox Tradition," *Dialogues in Judaism: Jewish Dilemmas Defined, Debated, and Explored*, ed. William Berkowitz (Northvale, NJ: Jason Aronson, 1991), 9–10.

22 Breuer, 5.

23 Ibid., 260–3.

24 Efraim Schmueli, *Seven Jewish Cultures: A Reinterpretation of Jewish History and Thought*, trans. Gila Shmueli (Cambridge: Cambridge University Press, 1990), 12.

25 Edward Klein, "The Judaism of Tomorrow: The Reform Tradition," Berkowitz, 12–13.

26 Klein, 13.

27 Ibid., 17.

28 Berkowitz, 17.

CHAPTER FOUR

1   Jacques Derrida, *Specters of Marx: The State of the Debt, the Work of Mourning and the New International*, trans. Peggy Kamuf (New York and London:

Routledge, 1994), 61–95. On Derrida's messianic expectation, see 110–13.

2 Kraemer, 41. 7

3 Mu Soeng Sunim, *Thousand Peaks: Korean Zen –Tradition and Teachers* (Cumberland, RI: Primary Point Press, 1991), 12.

4 This account of the origins of Buddhism follows Peter Harvey, *An Introduction to Buddhism: Teachings, History and Practices* (Cambridge: Cambridge University Press, 1990) and Reat, *Buddhism: A History.*

5 Harvey, 21.

6 See Kenneth K.S. Ch'en, *Buddhism in China: A Historical Survey* (Princeton, New Jersey: Princeton University Press, 1964); Zenryu Tsukamoto, *A History of Early Chinese Buddhism: From Its Introduction to the Death of Hui-yüan, Volumes 1 and 2*, trans. Leon Hurvitz (Tokyo: Kodansha International Ltd., 1985); and Arthur F. Wright, *Buddhism in Chinese History* (Stanford, CA: Stanford University Press, 1959).

7 Theravada Buddhism has a closed canon now. Mahayana Buddhism, the kind that most influenced Chinese Buddhism, possesses several sets of sutras in different manuscript traditions, which function as something of a canon.

8 Wright, 33.

9 This account of the meeting between Buddhism and Taoism is based upon Christine Mollier, *Buddhism and Taoism, Face to Face: Scripture, Ritual and Iconographic Exchange in Medieval China* (Honolulu: University of Hawai'i Press, 2008).

10 Mollier, 177.

11 Daisetz T. Suzuki, "History of Zen Buddhism From Bodhidharma to Eno (Hui-Neng) (A.D. 520–A.D. 713)," *The Essentials of Zen Buddhism* (Westport, CN: Greenwood Press, 1962), 95.

12 Ibid., 104.

13 Ibid., 106.

14 Nancy Wilson Ross, "What Is Zen?: Introduction," *The World of Zen: An East-West Anthology* (New York: Random House, 1960), 6–7.

15 Ibid.

16 Joel L. Kraemer, "Humanism in the Renaissance of Islam: A Preliminary Study," *Journal of the American Oriental Society* 104, no. 1 (Jan-Mar 1984), 135.

17 Fred M. Donner, "Muhammad and the Caliphate: Political History of the Islamic Empire Up To the Mongol Conquest," *The Oxford History of Islam*, ed. John L. Esposito (Oxford: Oxford University Press, 1999), 1–61.

18 This story is neatly and simply told in Colin Wells, *Sailing From Byzantium: How a Lost Empire Shaped the World* (New York: Delacorte/Bantam Dell/ Random House, 2006), 117–74.

19 Wells, 131. Italics in original.

20 Majid Fakhry, "Philosophy and Theology: From the Eighth Century CE to the Present," *The Oxford History of Islam*, ed. John L. Esposito (Oxford: Oxford University Press, 1999), 269.

21 Erica C.D. Hunter, "The Transmission of Greek Philosophy Via the 'School of Edessa', in *Literacy, Education and Manuscript Education in Byzantium and Beyond*, ed. Catherine Holmes and Judith Waring (Leiden: Brill, 2002), 238–39. Wells suggests that the "house of wisdom" may not really have existed and may be a later invention (Wells, 146–47)

22 Ibid.

23 Wells, *Sailing from Byzantium*, 145–71.

24 F.E. Peters, "The Origins of Islamic Platonism: The School Tradition," *Islamic Philosophical Theology*, ed. Parviz Morewedge (Albany: State University of New York Press, 1979), 14–45.

25 Richard C. Martin and Mark R. Woodward with Dwi S. Atmaja, *Defenders of Reason in Islam: Mu'tazilism from Medieval School to Modern Symbol* (Oxford: Oneworld Publications, 1997). See also F.E. Peters, *Aristotle and the Arabs: The Aristotelian Tradition in Islam* (New York: New York University Press, 1968).

26 Ibrahim Madkour, "La logique d'Aristote chez les Mutakallimun," Morewedge, 59–62.

27 Cafer S. Yaran, *Understanding Islam* (Edinburgh: Dunedin Academic Press, 2007), 25–7.

28 Dominic J. O'Meara, "Platonopolis in Islam: Al-Farabi's Perfect State," *Platonic Political Philosophy in Late Antiquity* (Oxford: Oxford Scholarship Online, 2007), http://www.oxfordscholarship.com.ezproxy.library.ubc .ca/view/10.1093/acprof:oso/9780199285532.001.0001/acprof-9780199285532.

29 Syed Nomanul Haq, "Science in Islam," *Science and Islam* 7 no. 2 (Winter 2009), 152.

30 A helpful outline of the challenges surrounding Celtic tales appears in Miranda Jane Green, *Celtic Myths In The Legendary Past* (Austin, TX: British Museum Press/University of Texas Press, 1993.)

31 Ibid., 10.

32 Ibid., 12.

33 Ibid.

34 Ibid., 15–28.

35 Ibid., 21.

36 Miranda Green, *Celtic Goddesses: Warriors, Virgins and Mothers* (London: British Museum Press, 1995), 188.

37 Ibid., passim, esp. 196–202.

38 Liam De Paor, *Saint Patrick's World: The Christian Culture of Ireland's Apostolic Age* (Dublin: Four Courts Press, 1993), 227.

39 John R. Walsh and Thomas Bradley, *A History of the Irish Church, 400–700 AD* (Dublin: Columba Press, 2003), 167–79.

40 Miranda Green, *The World of the Druids* (London: Thames and Hudson, 1997), 76–7.

41 Edward Culleton, *Celtic and Early Christian Wexford, AD 400 to 1166* (Dublin: Four Courts Press, 1999), 37.

42 For an overview of the relevant literature and various theories of the Sheela-na-gig, see Barbara Freitag, *Sheela-na-gigs: Unravelling an Enigma* (London and New York: Routledge/Taylor and Francis, 2004). Freitag provides a thorough account of the discussion and evidence, with a helpful focus on the Celtic examples. Her own view is that Sheela-na-gigs are associated with childbirth, as a charm and aid.

43 Caitlin Corning, *The Celtic and Roman Church: Conflict and Consensus in the Early Medieval Church* (New York/Basingstoke, Hampshire: Palgrave Macmillan, 2006), esp. 1–3.

CHAPTER FIVE

1 Ayn Rand, *The Virtue of Selfishness: A New Concept of Egoism, with Additional Articles by Nathaniel Branden* (New York: Penguin/Signet, 1964).

2 Kenneth Copeland, *The Laws of Prosperity* (Fort Worth, TX: Kenneth Copeland Publications, 1974), http://www.scribd.com/doc/4633292/The-Laws-of-Prosperity.

3 Keith Cameron Smith, *The Spiritual Millionaire: The Spirit of Wisdom Will Make You Rich* (Ormond Beach, FL: WKU Publishing, 2004), 27.

4 Copeland, 19–20.

5 Friedrich Nietzsche, *The Genealogy of Morals*, trans. Horace B. Samuel (New York: Boni and Liveright). Originally published in 1887.

6 Hanna Rosin, "Did Christianity Cause the Crash? How Preachers Are Spreading A Gospel of Debt," *The Atlantic,* December, 2009, 38–49.

7 James William Coleman, *The New Buddhism: The Western Transformation of an Ancient Tradition* (Oxford: Oxford University, 2001).

8 For a discussion of the meaning of *sunya*, see David Snellgrove, *Indo-Tibetan Buddhism: Indian Buddhists and Their Tibetan Successors* (Boston: Shambhala, 2002), 37–38.

9 Michael Roach, *The Diamond Cutter: The Buddha on Managing Your Business and Your Life* (New York: Doubleday, 2000), 33.

10 Ibid., 191.

11 Ibid., 204.

12 Snellgrove, 19. Tashi Tsering, *Relative Truth, Absolute Truth: The Foundation of Buddhist Thought*, vol. 2, intro. Zopa Rinpoche, ed. Gordon McDougall (Somerville, MA: Wisdom Publications, 2008), 17–33.

13 Richard Gombrich, *What the Buddha Thought* (London: Equinox, 2009), 103–4.

14 Gautama Buddha, "The First Sermon of the Buddha," trans. John Knoblock, http://www.as.miami.edu/phi/bio/Buddha/firstsermon.html. See also Gautama Buddha, "The Foundation of the Kingdom of the Norm," *The Book of the Kindred Sayings (Sanyutta-Nikaya) or Grouped Sutras*, trans. F.L. Woodward, intro. Rhys Davids (Oxford: Pali Text Society, 1990), LVI, XII, II, I; 356–60.

15 Tertullian, "The Prescription Against Heretics," *The Ante-Nicene Fathers:* Vol. 3, ed. Alexander Roberts and James Donaldson (Peabody, MA: Hendrickson, 1994), 246. Originally published by Christian Literature Publishing in 1885.

16 Jean Daniélou, "The Origins to the End of the Third Century," *The Christian Centuries*, Vol. 1, trans. Vincent Cronin (London: Darton, Longman, and Todd, 1964), 156.

17 Daniélou, 156–7.

18 The vexed question of numbers of Christians is discussed in T.G. Elliott, *The Christianity of Constantine the Great* (Scranton, PA: University of Scranton Press, 1996), 13–16. Elliott accepts Adolph Harnack's suggestion that Christians were more numerous in the east than in the west and that they totalled approximately ten percent of the population.

19 Elliott, passim.

20 H.A. Drake, "The Impact of Constantine on Christianity," *The Cambridge Companion to the Age of Constantine*, ed. Noel Lenski (Cambridge: Cambridge University Press, 2006), 111–36. A helpful, accessible account of these developments can be found in John McManners, ed., *The Oxford Illustrated History of Christianity* (Oxford: Oxford University Press, 1990).

21 Michele Renee Salzman, *The Making of a Christian Aristocracy: Social and*

Religious Change in the Western Roman Empire (Cambridge, Massachusetts: Harvard University Press, 2002), passim, esp. 200–19.

22 Neil Christie, *From Constantine to Charlemagne: An Archeology of Italy, AD 300–800* (Aldershot: Ashgate Publishing, 2006), 37.

23 G.R. Evans, "The Church in the Early Middle Ages," *The I.B. Taurus History of the Christian Church*, Vol. 2 (London: I.B. Taurus, 2007), 43–4.

24 McManners, 86–7.

25 Ibid.

26 Details of these developments may be found in Evans, *The Church in the Early Middle Ages*.

27 Christopher Dawson, *Religion and the Rise of Western Culture* (New York: Sheed and Ward, 1950), 52.

28 Dawson, 47–72.

29 Jonathan Phillips, *The Crusades: 1095–1197* (Harlow: Pearson Education/ Longman, 2002), 16–17.

30 Phillips, 70.

31 W.B. Bartlett, *An Ungodly War: The Sack of Constantinople and the Fourth Crusade* (Thrupp: Sutton, 2000).

32 Ibid., 195.

33 Ibid., 192–205.

34 Alfred J. Andrea, "Fourth Crusade," *Encyclopedia of the Crusades* (Westport, CN: Greenwood Press, 2003), 128.

35 Ibid., 120–1.

36 Phillips, 25.

37 Andrea, "Adrianople," *Encyclopedia*, 4.

CHAPTER SIX

1 Stephen Fry, *Making History* (London: Arrow, 1997).

2 Isaiah Berlin, "Soviet Self-Insulation," *The Soviet Mind: The Russian Culture Under Communism*, ed. Henry Hardy (Washington: Brookings Institution Press, 2004), 97. Originally published in 1946.

3 "Sovnarkom Decree 'On Freedom of Conscience, Church and Religious Associations,'" *The Rise and Fall of the Soviet Union: 1917–1991*, ed. Richard Sakwa (London and New York: Routledge, 1999), 78.

4 Paul Froese, *The Plot to Kill God: Findings from the Soviet Experiment in Secularization* (Berkeley: University of California Press, 2008), 79, 109–12.

5 See, for example, R.F. Atkinson, "Historical Materialism," *Marx and Marxisms* (Cambridge: Cambridge University Press, 1982), 64.

6 Roy Medvedev, *Let History Judge: The Origins and Consequences of Stalinism*, ed. and trans. George Shriver (New York: Columbia University Press, 1989).

7 This process is described in Froese and is the subject of his book.

8 Froese, 59.

9 Ibid.

10 For an account of these debates, see Sheila Fitzpatrick, *The Cultural Front: Power and Culture in Revolutionary Russia* (Ithaca, NY: Cornell University Press, 1992).

11 Anatoli Vishnevsky and Zhanna Zayonchkovskya, "Emigration from the Former Soviet Union: The Fourth Wave," *European Migration in the Late Twentieth Century: Historical Patterns, Actual Trends, and Social Implications*, ed. Heinz Fassmann and Rainer Münz (Aldershot: Edward Elgar Publishing, 1994), 239–43.

CHAPTER SEVEN

1 Carol Kaesuk Yoon, *Naming Nature: The Clash Between Instinct and Science* (New York: W.W. Norton, 2009).

2 Elizabeth Breuilly, Joanne O'Brien, and Martin Palmer, *Religions of the World: The Illustrated Guide to Origins, Beliefs, Traditions and Festivals* (New York: Transedition Ltd. and Fernleigh Books Ltd., 2005), 50–1.

3 Michael Ruse, *Darwinism and its Discontents* (Cambridge: Cambridge University Press, 2006), 96–7.

4 Yoon, 100–2.

5 C.S. Lewis, *Mere Christianity* (New York: Macmillan, 1960). The phrase "always, everywhere, and by all" is usually traced to Vincent of Lérins, a fifth-century thinker (in Latin: "quod semper, quod ubique, quod ab omnibus").

6 See, for example, Omid Safi, ed., *Progressive Muslims: On Justice, Gender and Pluralism* (Oxford: Oneworld Press, 2003).

7 Michael Finkel, "Facing Down the Fanatics: A More Tolerant Islam Is Confronting Extremism in the World's Most Populous Muslim Country," *National Geographic*, October 2009, 93.

8 Clifford Geertz, *Islam Observed: Religious Development in Morocco and Indonesia* (New Haven and London: Yale University Press, 1968).

CHAPTER EIGHT

1 Blaise Pascal, *Pensées*, trans. A.J. Krailsheimer (London: Penguin Books, 1966), ii, 23, 154. Krailsheimer uses an ordering of the Pensées which differs from some other texts, claiming to follow Pascal more exactly. Other texts list this quotation at iv, 277.

2 Idliby et al., 55. Italics in original.

3 Ibid., 4.

4 Ibid., 54.

5 Ibid., 55.

6 Ibid., 73.

7 Ibid., 84.

8 Ibid., 85.

9 Ibid., 232–3.

10 Ibid., 120–2.

11 Ibid., 134–8.

12 Ibid., 157.

13 The Whiteheadian tradition has mostly taken in root in Protestant and Anglican Christian circles. An alternative tradition draws on the work of Pierre Teilhard de Chardin, a Catholic.

14 Jan Van der Veken, "Can the True God Be the God of One Book?" *Religious Experience and Process Theology: The Pastoral Implications of a Major Modern Movement*, ed. Harry James Cargas and Bernard Lee (New York: Paulist Press, 1976), 263–79.

15 Ibid., 269.

16 Ibid., 271.

17 Ibid., 273.

18 Ibid.

19 Ibid., 274.

20 Ibid., 273.

21 John Cobb, *Christ in a Pluralistic Age*, http://www.thefishersofmenministries .com/Christ%20in%20a%20Pluralistic%20Age%20by%20John%20B.pdf., 5.

22 Ibid., 6.

23 Ibid., 9.

24 Ibid., 18.

25 Ibid., 29–30.

26 Ibid., 31.

27 Ibid., 34.

28 Alfred North Whitehead, *Process and Reality: An Essay in Cosmology* (New York: Macmillan, 1978), 343–5.

29 Ibid., 344–6.

30 Ibid., 349–51.

31 John Cobb, *Beyond Dialogue: Toward a Mutual Transformation of Christianity and Buddhism* (Philadelphia: Fortress Press, 1982).

32 Ibid., 123–8.

33 John Cobb, ed., *Progressive Christians Speak: A Different Voice on Faith and Politics – Progressive Christians Uniting* (Louisville, KY: Westminster John Knox Press, 2003). Originally published by Pinch Publications in 2000.

34 Margaret Chatterjee, *Gandhi's Religious Thought* (London/Basingstoke: Macmillan Press, 1983), 23.

35 Jeffrey D. Long, *Jainism: An Introduction* (London/New York: I.B. Tauris, 2009), 117.

36 Ibid., 117.

37 Ibid.

38 Ibid.

39 Chatterjee, 23.

40 Bhiku Parekh, *Gandhi: A Very Short Introduction* (Oxford: Oxford University Press, 1997), 35.

41 Ibid.

42 This account follows Parekh's useful abbreviated biography in Parekh, 1–35. The biographical literature on Gandhi is vast. Gandhi's own autobiography is a helpful starting place: Mohandas K. Gandhi, *An Autobiography, or, The Story of My Experiments with Truth* (Ahmenabad: Navajivan Publishing House, 1927).

43 Chatterjee, 50–2.

44 Ibid., 51.

45 Ibid., 52–3.

46 Mohandas K. Gandhi, *Gandhi: In My Own Words* (London: Hodder and Stoughton, 2002), 44. Italics in original.

47 Mohandas K. Gandhi, *The Modern Review*, 1941, 406. Quoted in Chatterjee, 55.

48 Mohandas K. Gandhi, *Gandhi Marg*, April, 1959. Quoted in Chatterjee, 56. Italics in original.

49 Gandhi, *Autobiography*, 267–8.

50 Parekh, 31.

51 Ibid., 32.

52 Cobb, *Christ*, 30.
53 Ibid., 28.

CHAPTER NINE

1 Milan Kundera, *The Unbearable Lightness of Being*, trans. Michael Henry
   Heim (New York: Harper and Row, 1984).
2 The representation of human beings is not forbidden by the Qur'an, but
   developed in sharia out of custom. Representational art is not really necessary to Islam because the Qur'an contains much less narrative than the
   Bible and, therefore, requires less illustration. Sheila S. Blair and Jonathan
   M. Bloom, "Art and Architecture," *The Oxford History of Islam*, 230–6.
3 These developments are discussed in Nada M. Shabout, *Modern Arab Art*
   (Gainesville, FL: University Press of Florida, 2007), 16, 62–3.
4 Lysiane Gagnon, "Quebec's Duelling Manifestos," *The Globe and Mail*, 22
   March 2010, A13, http://www.theglobeandmail.com/news/opinions/
   quebecs-duelling-manifestos/article1506486/.
5 Martha C. Nussbaum, *Not for Profit: Why Democracy Needs the Humanities*
   (Princeton: Princeton University Press, 2010), 123–4.

CHAPTER TEN

1 Jacques Derrida, "Différance," *Margins of Philosophy*, trans. Alan Bass (Chicago: University of Chicago Press, 1982), 7–9.
2 Derrida, "Différance," 25–7.
3 Alex Lifeson, Geddy Lee, and Neil Peart, "Freewill," *Exit, Stage Left* (Toronto:
   Anthem Records, 1981).
4 Simon Wiesenthal Center, "Nazi Memorial in Croatia a Disgrace to
   Europe," January 2012, http://www.wiesenthal.com/site/apps/nlnet/content2
   .aspx?c=lsKWLbPJLnF&db=7929811&ct=11577565.
5 Clark, *Angels*, 55–66.
6 Robert J. Donia, "The New Bosniak History," *Nationalities Papers* 28 no. 2
   (2000), 351–2.
7 Claremont Lincoln University, "The Right Vision," http://www.claremont
   lincoln.org/about/from-vision-to-history/the-right-vision.
8 Claremont Lincoln University, "A Model for Solutions," http://www
   .claremontlincoln.org/about/a-new-university/a-model-for-solutions.

Index

Adi Granth, 31, 78, 82, 83, 244n7
African Sanctus, 232
ahimsa, 194, 197, 198
Ailbe of Emly, 121
Allah, 25–6, 56, 111–13, 115, 210,
    221; as one, 25–6, 109, 111–13,
    128, 221; to be worshipped and
    obeyed, 25–6
Amaterasu, 5, 47
Amida, 192
anekantavada, 194
Anglicanism. *See* Christianity, Angli-
    can
Anglo-Saxon religion, 165–6
animism, 38, 220
Aquinas, Thomas, 21, 111, 169
Arabs, 35, 52, 108–12, 128, 148
Aristotelian, 52, 109–12, 141
Aristotle, 52, 89, 111–12, 160
atheism, 38, 63–5, 156, 224
Augustine of Hippo, 111, 117, 119,
    129; and the body, 126, 141; and
    just war, 145; and restless heart,
    44; and syncretism, 52, 169

Baha'i, 41
Baha'u'llah, 41
Balkans, 232
Beltane, 121
Berkowitz, William, 90
Bible, 6, 16, 37; as a closed canon,
    99; and fundamentalism, 21–4,
    31–2, 57–8; and Gandhi, 196; and
    Hendrik Kraemer, 21–4; as
    unchanging, 81, 160
bodhisattva, 4–5, 47, 101
Bolsheviks, 152–3
boundaries, 32–3, 167, 171, 183, 187;
    and Celtic religion, 124; and first-
    century Christianity, 140; hard,
    33, 76, 79–84, 156–9, 163, 174–5,
    178, 228, 235; soft, 43, 73, 74–90,
    96, 112, 179, 186, 220, 222, 235
Brahman, 194, 221
Brigit of Kildare, 121, 124, 126, 129
Buddha, 4–5, 47, 98, 102; and
    Christ, 192
Buddha, Gautama, 5, 18, 41, 63, 103;
    biography, 98–9; and Freud, 201;

and Michael Roach, 137–9; sayings, 5, 100–3; and Taliban, 172
Buddhism, 5, 9, 10, 17, 45–6, 220;
Ch'an (Zen), 38, 46, 101–3, 106,
128; in China, 95–106, 128,
210–11, 245n7; and Christianity,
192; and Gandhi, 193–4, 197–9;
and god, 38, 47–8; in India, 77–8,
98, 103; as indigenous in China,
100, 105; Mahayana, 4, 46, 100–2,
192, 245n7; and the middle way,
52; Nath (*see also* Buddhism,
tantric), 77; organization of, 39;
origins of, 98; and prosperity theology, 136–9, 148; and Pure Land,
46; as religion, 56, 62–4; and
Shinto, 5–6; tantric, 77, 137;
Theravada, 46, 245n7; Tibetan, 35,
61, 137–8, 222

Cailleach, 123
capitalism, 131–2, 148, 163, 217,
220; and Buddhism, 136–9, 148;
and Christianity 132–6, 148; and
Marxism, 92, 151–9, 221–2; and
Protestantism, 32; as religion, 47,
62–72, 223–5
Celtic religion, 11, 165; and Christianity, 12, 95, 97, 115–27, 129,
140, 148, 149, 165
Christianity: ancient, 52, 117–18,
140–3; Anglican, 7, 14, 162, 164,
168, 214–5; and Buddhism,
192–3; Catholic, 7, 15, 21, 34, 35,
39, 60, 61, 65, 153–4, 161, 162,
164, 218, 231–2, 232–3; and capitalism, 70, 131, 132–6, 148; and
Celtic religion, 95, 97, 115–27,

129, 140, 148, 149, 165; evangelical, 16, 161–2, 163; fundamentalist, 22–4, 28, 31–2, 34, 81, 161,
168, 179, 194–5; and Gandhi,
193–4, 196–9; and Greek
thought, 109–12; history of,
140–4; and hybrid vigour, 9; and
Islam, 109–12; and Hendrik Kraemer, 20–2, 31–2; and Latin
thought, 130–1, 141; and Indigenous people, 6–8; and Judaism,
140; and Marxism, 153–4;
Methodist, 7, 164, 214–5; Orthodox, 15, 21, 80 151, 153, 154–6,
232–3; Presbyterian 7, 164–5, 215;
and prosperity theology, 132–6,
148; Protestant, 20–2, 24, 31–2,
35, 39, 45, 60–1, 65, 161–5, 179; as
prototype of religion, 37–8; as
religion, 37, 38, 41–2, 44, 45,
51–2, 75; and Rome, 117–18,
140–2; and Taoism, 10; and soft
boundaries, 90; and South
African traditional religion,
13–14, 15; as syncretism, 140–7,
148–9; and United Church, 7;
and war, 130–1, 145–7; and yoga,
10
cladism, 161
Claremont Lincoln University, 234
Cobb, John, 188–93, 199, 201–3
Cohen, Leonard, 103, 137
Coleman, James William, 136–7
Communism, 66, 92, 105, 232; as a
religion, 10, 62, 152. *See also*
Marxism
Communist Party, 61, 153–7. *See
also* Marxism

Confucianism, 60, 99, 103–6; and Buddhism, 5, 95, 103–6, 128
Constantine the Great, Emperor, 117–8, 141–2
Copeland, Kenneth, 132–3
Corning, Caitlin, 126
creative transformation, 190–1
critical openness, 174–205; and education, 206, 213, 215, 222, 230–2
Crusades, 144–7

Dalai Lama, 60–1, 170
Deloria, Vine, 6
Derrida, Jacques, 93, 228–9, 230–1
Desert Fathers, 125–6
dharma, 196
dialectical materialism, 153
différance, 228, 231
Divine Comedy, The, 231
Dream of the Rood, 125
Dyophisitism, 109

Education, 206–26, 231; affecting particular syncretisms, 27, 107–9, 152, 156; and group identity, 168; as interpretation, 58
emotion, 75–6, 81, 180–2, 200. See also feeling
Engels, Friedrich, 152–4. See also Marxism
Enlightenment, the, 8, 32, 35–7, 76, 214; and objectivity, 24, 180–1, 235 and Plato's cave, 75–6
eschatology, 4, 66, 154
Evangelicalism, 161–2, 163

faith club, 184–6, 187, 199–200

Faith Club, The, 61, 183–7, 199–201
faith commitment, 39, 43, 47–59, 70, 224 definition of, 23, 48; and reason, 23–4, 48, 50
Falun Gong, 60
Farabi, Muhammad ibn Muhammad ibn Tarkhan ibn Awzalagh al-, 112
fear of the other, principle of, 81, 151–2
feeling, in processes of knowing, 24, 64. See also emotion
filidh, 121
Fionn Cycle, 119–20
Four Noble Truths, 138–9
Freud, Sigmund, 201–2
Fry, Stephen, 151
Fundamentals, The, 22–3

Gandhi, Mahatma Mohandas K., 184, 193–9, 201, 203–5, 231–2
Garay, Fernando, 135, 148
Germanic religion, 11
Ghazali, Abu Hamid Muhammad ibn Muhammad al-, 112
Giuliani, Rudolph, 68–9
Glasnost, 152
Graham, Billy, 34
Gray, James M., 22
Greek thought, 12–3, 75; and Christianity, 21, 52, 106–12, 148–51, 197, 201–2; and Islam, 17, 95–7, 106–15, 128–9, 148, 151
Green, Miranda, 121
Gregory the Great, Pope, 143–4
gurdwara, 83

Hadith, 26, 28, 114

Hallowe'en, 12, 121
Harmandir (*also* Hari Om Mandir),
  83, 85
Harper, Stephen, 34, 65
Hauerwas, Stanley, 33, 240n57
Hebrew religion, 36–7
Henry, O. (William Sydney Porter),
  49
hermeneutics, 22–3, 231
heuristic, 96
Hinduism: and animism and Islam,
  13, 14; Brahman, 221; and Buddhism, 98; and complexity, 176;
  and death and rebirth, 98; and
  education, 231, 234; and Gandhi,
  193–9, 204, 231; and Islam, 30,
  35, 173; as religion, 38, 39, 42, 65,
  74, 178; and Santism, 77; and
  Sikhism, 29, 77–85; and syncretism, 76–7; and texts, 41; and
  yoga, 10
history: discipline of, 218, 220; of
  ideas, 166–7; as supernatural, 64,
  153–5;
honji sujaku, 5
house of wisdom, 110 ʌ vmaniʃ mʒ 63
Hunayn, ibn Ishaq, 109–10
hybrid vigour, 9, 10

ibn-Rushd, Abu l-Walid Muhammad bin Ahmad (also known as
  Averroes), 111, 112
Idliby, Ranya, 61, 184–7, 199–201
Indian language, 99–100
Indigenous economics, 70–1
indigenous people: and Europe,
  151; North American, xiv, 218,
  227; and religion, 6–8, 42, 94, 151

insight, definition of, 55
intuition, 23, 55–6
Irenaeus of Lyon, 8, 125
Islam, x, xii, xiv, 221; and Allah, 220;
  and ancient Arabs, 52; Balkan,
  232–3; and capitalism, 15, 131,
  226; and education, 167, 208,
  210–11, 213, 234; and Empire,
  107; in Faith Club, 61, 183–7,
  200; and Gandhi, 196, 198–9, 204;
  and Greek thought, 17, 52, 95, 96,
  106–15, 128–9, 150–1, 160; Indian, 77; Indonesian, 13, 14; and
  Judaism, 87; and labels, 172–3,
  175; and openness, 183; opposed
  to syncretism, 24–8; and prejudice, 176; progressive, 172; as religion, 38, 43, 74, 77, 90, 223; rooted in Prophet Muhammad and
  Qur'an, 41, 42, 43; as religion of
  revelation, 20, 21; and Sikhism,
  29, 77–9, 82, 83, 84; Salafi, 43,
  171; Shia, 3–4, 26, 43, 160, 167; in
  Soviet Union, 153; Sufi, 43, 61,
  77, 83, 86, 176; Sunni, 43, 77, 160,
  167; and syncretism, 3–4, 9,
  13–14, 93–4, 160, 169, 178, 220;
  and unity, 92, 107; and violence,
  35, 39, 98, 114, 145–7, 216; Wahhabi, 20, 25–8, 61, 160

Jacobs, A. J., 87
Jainism, 10, 77, 98, 194–5, 199
Japan, 210; and Ch'an (Zen), 103;
  and Shinto and Buddhism, 4–6,
  17, 47, 160
Jesus Christ, 12, 15, 41, 144; beliefs
  about, 142, 185, 186, 200; and

capitalism, 70; in Christian theology of salvation, 45; as creative transformation, 190–1; as divine and human, 42, 125; and Dyophisitism, 109; and Eucharist, 125; and education, 208, 209, 223; and Gandhi, 196–9; interpreted in light of Classical thought, 202; as self-giving, 135, 146–7; in syncretism, 230–1

jihadism, 27–8, 131, 211

Johnson, Steven, 54

Judaism, x, xii, xiv; and afterlife, 36–7; and capitalism, 132; as centering on Tanakh, 41; Conservative, 89, 90; and covenant, 221, 222; and Faith Club, 183–7; and education, 167, 217, 234; and *Haredim*, 87, 130; Hasidic, 89; and Jesus, 209; and labels, 38, 175, 176–7; Orthodox, 61, 87–8, 89; as part of syncretisms, 9, 13, 93, 106, 112, 160, 161; and prejudice, 176–7; Reform, 61, 87, 88–9, 90; as religion, 37, 61, 223; as religion of revelation, 20, 21; as religion of the book, 77; and Roman Empire, 117, 140, 170; and soft boundaries, 86–90; as syncretistic, 9, 77; and transvaluation of values, 134; and violence, 35, 146, 147; and YHWH, 221. *See also* Hebrew religion

just war theory, 131, 145, 146

Jyllands-Posten, 211, 213

Kraemer,

League of Militant Atheists, 155

Lenin, Vladimir Ilyich, 152–3, 155

Liberalism, 185, 217, 233; and worship, 15, 16; and founding texts, 42; as a religion, 64–6; in syncretism, 161, 163

Locke, John, 42, 65, 75, 84

Lord of the Rings, The, 231–2

love, xii; and critical investigation, 59; priority in Christianity, 135; and Gandhi, 197–8, 203; and knowing, 49–50, 55, 177, 181; in process thought, 192

Manichaeism, 9, 126

Marxism-Leninism, 39, 151–9, 160, 169

Marxism, 64, 93, 222, 224

Middle Way (Buddhism), 52, 137

Minerva, 117

Mondo, 102–3

Mormon, Book of, 57

Mu'tazilism, 110

Muhammad, Prophet: cartoons of, 211; as heart of Islam, 43; and religious change, 52; revelation to, 56, 114; and *ummah*, 107; in Wahhabism, 26, 27

Muslim Brotherhood, 27

Mythological Cycle (Celtic), 119, 121

Nanak, Guru, 30, 77–84

Nayavada, 194

Neo-Platonism, 52, 110, 112, 113, 140–1

Nestorian, 109

Nietzsche, Friedrich, 131, 134

nirvana, 45–7, 98, 100, 139

Nowruz, 3–4

Obama, Barack, 74
Oberoi, Harjot, 20, 28–31, 74, 76
Oliver, Suzanne, 184–7, 199–200
oneness, in Islam, 111, 115, 221
onlyness, in process thought, 189–90, 201
Origen, 141

paganism, 17, 38, 118–19, 127, 141. *See also* Anglo-Saxon religion, Celtic religion, Germanic religion
Pelagius I, Pope, 143
Perestroika, 151–2
philosophy. *See also* Greek thought, Roman thought
Plato, 52, 65–6, 75–6, 112, 202
Platonism, 21, 110, 125–6, 144
prejudice, 175–7
preservation of insights, principle of, 32, 79–84; in Buddhism, Taoism, Ch'an Buddhism, 102–3, 128; and destructive syncretism, 130, 149–50; in Greek thought and Islam, 115, 129; in Judaism, 86, 88–90; and shared wisdom, 168, 229; and in relation to Sikhism, 79–84; part of syncretistic critical openness, 183
process theology, 184, 188–93, 199, 201–3
progress, principle of, 32, 78–84, 91–3; in Buddhism, Taoism, and Ch'an Buddhism, 102–3, 106, 128; in Christianity and Celtic religion, 115, 129; and destructive syncretism, 130, 148–50; in Greek thought and Islam, 114–15, 129;

in Judaism, 86, 88–90; and shared wisdom, 168, 229; in relation to Sikhism, 79–84; as part of syncretistic critical openness, 183
prosperity theology: in Buddhism, 136–9, 148; in Christianity, 70, 132–6, 148

qadi, 108
quasi-religion, 63
Qur'an: in Wahhabism, 26, 28; as characteristic of Islamic religion, 43; as divine revelation, 57, 114; and permanence, 81; as closed canon, 99, 114; as root principle of Islam, 109, 111; and syncretism, 160; Gandhi's use of, 198

Rand, Ayn, 131
religion: definition of, 17–19, 20–1, 34–73; five characteristics of, 39–61; as naturalistic, 20–1; of revelation, 20–1, 31, 32; theory of, ix–x (rebirth; reincarnation) 98
religious studies, 30, 218, 221, 223, 234
revelation: religions of, 20–1, 31, 32; as evidence, 52; texts as presenting, 56–7; and criticism, 57–9; and syncretism, 141; in divine encounter, 188–9; and education about syncretism, 220
rishi, 197
Roach, Michael, 137–9
Roman Empire: and Celts, 117–18, 123–4; and Christianity, 52, 130, 140–4, 231; Eastern, 107, 108; and multiple religions, 170

Roman thought: and Christianity, 9, 52, 144–7; and Islam, 106, 108, 112; and natural law, 195; and survival, 11–13. *See also* Stoicism

Rosin, Hanna, 134

Ryerson, Egerton, 214–15

Sa'ud, House of, 27–8

Samhain, 12, 121,

Samsara: and Buddhism, 45, 62, 98, 104, 106; and Gandhi, 203; and Sikhism, 77, 79

Santism, 77–8, 79, 82, 83

satori, 102,

Satya, 192, 195

satyagraha, 194–8, 204

Schmueli, Efraim, 88

science: in Bible, 24; as source of knowledge, 35–6; as method, 48–56

scientific materialism. *See* dialectical materialism

Scientology, 38

Scripture of the Five Kitchens, 101

secularism, 93–4, 214–15

separation of church and state, 61, 75–6

sharia, 13, 108

sheela-na-gig, 123–4, 126, 127, 165

Shia. *See* Islam

shinbutsu bunri, 6

Shinto: and Buddhism, 5–6, 17, 47, 160; and capitalism, 226; and focus upon action, 60; and fundamental problem of life, 44–5, 221; and purpose in life, 72

Shirk, 25–6,

Shiv Shanti Ashram, 84–5

Shostakovich, Dmitri, 156

Sikhism, xiv; and education, 167, 208, 216; and Harjot Oberoi, 20, 28–31, 32–3, 89; as religion, 38, 74; origin of, 42; as syncretism, 78–85; and soft boundaries, 86, 90, 179

Smith, Joseph, 57–8

Smith, Keith Cameron, 133

Snow, John, 54–6,

solution, definition of, 17–19

Stoicism, 21, 141

Summer Days of Youth, 155

sunya, 137–8

Sutra of the Three Interrupted Kitchens, 101

sutra, 100–1

Suzuki, Daisetz, 101–2

Syadvada, 195

Syncretism: advocacy view of, x, 8–14, 19, 33, 183, 199–205, 233–5; as asymmetrical, 95, 96, 106–15, 116, 128–9, 139, 188–93; definition of, ix–x, xiv–xv, 8–14; objective view of, 9; as reflexive, 95, 96–7, 115–27, 183–7, 200; subjective view of, 8–9; as symmetrical, 95, 96, 97–106, 114, 128, 129, 137, 145, 184, 193–9, 203

t'ai chi, 10, 95, 231

Taliban, 172

Tanakh, 36, 41,

Taoism: and Buddhism, x, 95, 96, 97–106, 114; and t'ai chi, 10, 231; and texts, 56

tawhid, 25–8

taxonomy, 161, 170

Tertullian, 141, 148
theoria, 114
Tillich, Paul, 46, 241n5
Torah, 41, 57, 87–90, 160
totalitarianism, 20–1, 156–7, 177
tradition: and authority, 79; as evidence, 76; and fear, 171; and hard boundaries, 82–4; and language, 99–100; and principle of preservation of insights, 167–9; as revisable, 79; and syncretism, 82, 84–5, 97, 115
transcendence: in definition of religion, 63–4; and God, 48, 56, 77; and value, 49
Tusi, Nasir al-Din al-, 113

Ulster Cycle, 118, 119–20, 123
ultimate value, 17, 62, 65–6
ummah, 107–8. *See also* oneness, in Islam
uniqueness, 26; in process theology, 189–90, 201
Upanishads, 41

Vaisnava, 77, 194
values, x, xiii, 28; in Buddhism, Taoism, and Confucianism, 106, 128; Christian, Roman, and Western European, 145–7; as criteria for a religion, 39, 43, 59–61, 62–76, 224, 226; in critical openness, 192; and education, 206; and evidence of syncretism, 232–3; in Islam and Greek thought, 107, 114, 123; and prosperity theology,

148; and soft boundaries, 235; and Soviet Marxism, 154; and transvaluation, 134
Van der Veken, Jan, 188–90, 191, 203
Vancouver School of Theology, 7–8
Vedas, 42–3, 76–7, 82
Violence: and education, 208; as human problem, 194, 197, 203–4; and imposition reinforcing boundaries, 86; and maintaining purity, 171, 178; and religion as source, xii, 35, 198; and secular religion as source, 214; and syncretism, 9, 91–2, 130–1, 144–7, 199. *See also ahimsa*

Wahhab, Muhammad ibn Abd al-, 25–8
Wall Street, 131, 139
Wallis, Jim, 161
Warner, Priscilla, 184–7, 199–200
Weber, Max, 40, 67
Whitehead, Alfred North, 188, 191–2, 202
Whitehead, Henry, 55–6
Willimon, William, 33, 240n57
worship, definition of, 14–16

Yom Kippur, 186
Yoon, Carol Kaesuk, 161, 165

Zen. *See* Ch'an
Zoroastrianism, x, 3–4, 110, 141, 160,
Zulu, 13